Chairing Academic Departments

Chairing Academic Departments

Traditional and Emerging Expectations

N. Douglas Lees
Indiana University–Purdue University Indianapolis

ANKER PUBLISHING COMPANY, INC.
Bolton, Massachusetts

Chairing Academic Departments
Traditional and Emerging Expectations

ISBN 1-933371-03-X

Composition by Julie Phinney
Cover design by Dutton and Sherman Design

Anker Publishing Company, Inc.
563 Main Street
P.O. Box 249
Bolton, MA 01740-0249 USA

www.ankerpub.com

Library of Congress Cataloging-in-Publication Data

Lees, N. Doug.
Chairing academic departments : traditional and emerging
    expectations / N. Douglas Lees.
        p. cm.
Includes bibliographical references and index.
    ISBN 1-933371-03-X
    1. Departmental chairmen (Universities)—United States.
    2. Universities and colleges—United States—Administration.
    I. Title.

LB2341.L28 2006
378.1'110973—dc22   2006007472

Table of Contents

Part V • Next Steps

About the Author

N. *Douglas Lees* is professor and chair of biology at Indiana University–Purdue University Indianapolis (IUPUI). He received his undergraduate degree in biology from Providence College and his Ph.D. in biological sciences from Northwestern University. Upon arriving at IUPUI in the early 1970s, he began a journey of simultaneous career and institution building. He has witnessed and participated in the conversion of a pair of two-year feeder campuses into an urban research university that will serve as a model for the future.

His personal research has focused on sterol biosynthesis in fungi with an interest in identifying new targets for the development of antifungal drugs. Since being named chair in 1992, he has developed interests in chair leadership and several other difficult issues facing higher education in this current era of change. Away from the office, Doug and his wife Stephanie are occupied with raising and educating their four children, who range in age from 13 to 24.

PREFACE

After completing the first draft of this manuscript, I began to write this preface and realized that I had arrived at a place never imagined upon entering the academy. Like many academics, I took my first position with the intention of working hard to clear the essential hurdle—tenure—to a productive life dominated by teaching and research. Administration was the furthest thing from my mind, and writing about it was not even a consideration.

I have spent more than a decade as chair (after accepting a temporary appointment during a difficult period pending the availability of resources for a full, external search), and have seen the position grow far more demanding than it was in the early 1990s. I considered the possibility that age and wear and tear accounted for the feeling that it was more of a challenge, but colleagues from both my own and other institutions confirmed that, indeed, more was expected and the challenges were growing. Others on my faculty recognized some of the new pressures, and I have heard, more than once, statements indicating a lack of interest in taking on the job. It is not a healthy situation for higher education when bright, thoughtful individuals express an aversion to assuming leadership posts. We need this talent more than ever.

The position of academic department chair is now regarded as a critical element in implementing the changes necessary for the higher education enterprise of the future. I think we all realize that much of what we have been doing must change for most institutions to succeed and, for some, even just to survive. Chairs will be pivotal in this process, not only for carrying out the decisions of others, but for guiding decision-making to ensure that there is basic support for change and for identifying pathways in the transformation that preserve what we value from educational and scholarly perspectives while adapting to the new world order.

Over the years I have read many excellent books describing and informing the work of chairs. I decided to contribute to this area because the pace of change in higher education and the increasing responsibilities of chairs have been so profound in recent years as to warrant another look at this evolving administrative post. Related to this is the notion that perhaps the impact of change on the chair position might be viewed and presented by someone who is currently doing this work. Other books have been contributed by former chairs, some of whom have moved to higher administrative positions. While there is value in these perspectives, such views become influenced by what used to be or by what one would like to be. There is nothing like wearing the shoes to assess their fit and feel.

The view that a sitting chair brings to the conversation also contributes to the element of the faculty perspective. Much has been said and written about the faculty in higher education, and much of it is not complimentary. I won't go into detail here except to say that chairs at most institutions are members of the faculty and actually do faculty work. Thus they can bring this perspective to the table when discussing elements of the change agenda.

In this book, there are times when I depart from the "accepted" or "organizational policy" assignment of both chair and faculty responsibilities. I fully realize that this is shooting from the hip, but the positions taken are my opinions on these subjects. These sections are not supported by references, such that I take sole and full responsibility for them. Some of these areas revolve around faculty work, an area about which I have had considerable concern for some time. New responsibilities seem to be added without identifying what will be omitted to allow for the addition. Those adding new expectations are not apt to give up anything and wonder why faculty members resist the new assignments.

My position is that most institutions get exactly the faculty behaviors they ask for in their searches and in their institutional guidelines for promotion and tenure. On the other hand, there are times when faculty personalities and expectations present obstacles to positive change. Chairs need to work effectively in both directions to facilitate understanding and to define routes to improvement.

In sections of this book, I will also take the position that the department chair must be more than an instrument for administratively mandated change and more than just an advocate for the department. Rather, the department chair needs to be part of the team that shapes change. Knowing what will work and what will not, determining the timing of change, identifying champions for positive alterations, and finding ways to accommodate those for whom change will be particularly difficult are among the areas where chair input is critical. Upper administrators will not have this level of knowledge and experience with the individuals whose contributions will bring about new approaches to institutional work. On the other side, chairs need to present faculty members with justification for change in some areas along with innovative ways for the department to maintain its traditional forms of excellence while improving in other areas.

When I became chair, I decided at the outset that chairing would be the primary focus of my work. While I maintained a modest research agenda and continued to teach (doing faculty work is critical to chairing and to personal credibility), I defined my success by the performance of my department. I also realized that I was just a faculty member with no experience in doing this work and with only a few models—some good and some poor—to guide me. Thus I did my best to read and learn about chairing academic departments. Along the way I had the good fortune to work with several talented individuals who had been, were, or later became chairs, as well as those who held other administrative posts but were attuned to the importance of chair work. Through conversations and collaborative work with these individuals, many of the ideas presented in the book were developed. Of course, those that are controversial and get me into trouble with readers are to be attributed only to me.

Several years ago I became involved in the implementation of post-tenure review at Indiana University–Purdue University Indianapolis (IUPUI) and became part of an American Association for Higher Education (AAHE)-sponsored project to facilitate that work. That work led me to the related areas of faculty evaluation and opened many opportunities for me on and beyond my campus. I am thankful to our AAHE liaison, Christine Licata, associate vice president for academic affairs at Rochester Institute of Technology/National Technical Institute for the Deaf, and partnering institutional leaders Betsy Brown, then of Winthrop University and now associate vice president for academic affairs in the Office of the President at the University of North Carolina, and Susan Barr, dean of student support and cadet services at Virginia Military Institute, for their guidance and help in formulating ways to make this controversial initiative a positive developmental process for higher education.

In my activities directed more globally to the work of chairs, I am thankful for the input and collaboration of Laura Jenski, who served several years as my associate chair before moving on to a position as head of the Division of Biological Sciences at Marshall University. She is now vice president for research at South Dakota University. Upon her departure from IUPUI, we worked together on several subjects related to department chairing, the results of which are presented in several places in this book.

Finally, I would like to acknowledge David Malik, chancellor's professor and former chair of the Department of Chemistry at IUPUI. We worked together for more than a decade, through presentations and publications, on many topics that appear in this book. Many of the ideas expressed have been sharpened and refined through the numerous ad hoc conversations we have had over the years while we were both chairing our related academic departments. These exchanges continue, even though David has moved on to other activities at the university.

N. Douglas Lees
December 2005

1

THE DEPARTMENT CHAIR: THEN, NOW, AND SOON TO BE

If you are currently a department chair, much of what is about to be presented will already be woven into the fabric of your regular cycle of activities and considerations. If you are a new chair or a potential chair (a faculty member thinking about a move to department administration), some of this material will be either new or a synthesis of items that formerly were not brought together in a coherent description of the position. On the other hand, if you are a dean or a provost, some of the discussion will elicit memories of the past (if being a department chair was a stop in the career path) while other subjects will present more current challenges facing chairs at your institution.

The way faculty members who move into chair positions view the work of the chair is shaped largely by watching how others have performed the duties of the position. The greatest input about chairing is derived from those who have already served as chair in your own department. Secondary information is gathered from colleagues from other departments who may share chair policies, attitudes, and characteristics. Potential chairs document behaviors both to emulate and to avoid during this period of observation. Think back to all the issues that have been confronted by the department chairs under whom you have served, and you may identify some evenhanded solutions to difficult problems, some sensitive ways of handing delicate personal issues, some policy changes that have benefited students, and some curricula changes that have enhanced the image and success of the department. You may also recall episodes of lost opportunity due to inaction or inappropriate choices, ill-conceived or poorly implemented strategies that have alienated faculty, administration, or other academic units, and instances of perceived inequity. While you must understand that faculty members rarely have all the relevant data for such judgments, the potential chair should recognize that steps resulting in positive outcomes may be useful for future applications and that those resulting in problems, whether real or perceived, may produce better results with an alternative or modified approach.

Traditional Chair Roles

During the period of undeclared apprenticeship, one can gain a sense of what the chair does and thus what the position entails. As in the situations described earlier, this picture is not complete. After well over a decade as a department chair, I suspect that any list of my activities prepared by individual faculty would represent less than half of what I do. They recognize that I occupy the main office, that I am a source of answers for their many questions, and that I manage the budget, schedule classes, and conduct annual reviews. Beyond those duties and my faculty work in teaching and research, they assume I go to meetings with other administrators where I receive information that constitutes a set of announcements made during faculty meetings. This is all correct, but there is so much more. What has been listed here are primarily management tasks. The exception is the annual review process where the individual nature of these encounters sometimes results in discussion that goes far beyond management.

What roles, then, do department chairs actually fill in higher education? A book of this sort is mandated to provide such a listing, as similar volumes of the past have done. The original work of Tucker (1992) lists close to 30 roles for academic department chairs. Broad interpretation of each possible role results in areas of overlap among some and in other cases establishes a hierarchical relationship. The vast majority of the roles can also be placed into categories that may represent *management functions* and what I will call *dynamic functions*. The latter include activities associated with innovation and leadership, two roles listed by Tucker. A third category that only indirectly fits these two categories includes what I call *things you will bring with you when you become chair*. The term *baggage functions* may be used to describe these roles. The department chair at many institutions will be expected to perform the work of faculty in teaching, research, or both. Doing the work of faculty will be discussed in Chapter 2, where the characteristic of chair credibility is considered.

The category of management functions includes representation, coordination, planning (to some degree), advocating, delegating, recruiting (to some degree), recommending, and supervising. The more dynamic functions include entrepreneurial work, evaluation and motivation, problem solving, and various roles associated with interpersonal interactions such as advising, mediating, negotiating, and mentoring. Clearly, there are elements of planning that are largely management. For example, planning the scheduling of courses over the next three years is a management function. However, planning staffing for a department with eight vacancies and a dire need to update the curriculum and the research agenda requires a different approach that goes far beyond the management function.

A later version of Tucker's list of chair roles subdivides the roles along other lines (Hecht, Higgerson, Gmelch, & Tucker, 1999). Tucker's list can be divided into roles that deal with faculty, students, and program or curriculum development. Other roles are typical office management functions and department organization (policies, procedures, committee structure) to allow a framework for conducting the unit's work. Another group of roles deals with resource management, including budgetary decisions and the allocation of department resources.

This book also recognizes some emerging new roles and extensions of traditional roles that chairs must now assume as the pace of change in higher education accelerates. One of these extends the concept of chair as a communication agent to external audiences. This role will be fully explored in Chapter 8. Another role, though certainly not new, is the role of the chair in fiscal management. Chairs have always managed budgets, but in recent years many of the restrictions on expenditures have been lifted so that chairs now have greater discretion in how department resources are expended. Personally, I recall the time when our department was allotted $100 per faculty member per year for travel. That type of restriction would allow one faculty per year to attend a conference, assuming a bicycle rental and a stay at a nearby campground! Budgeting flexibility has migrated away from such restricted expenditure categories all the way to fully flexible systems at the department level and responsibility-centered budgeting at the institutional level. While such a system allows great discretionary authority for the chair, it also creates equally great responsibility and accountability expectations. In the past, the chair would be able to say "We could not purchase a new (fill in the instrument of your choice) because there were insufficient funds in this year's capital budget line." Under more recent budget models, resources can be moved from other categories to make such a purchase. In this situation, the chair may have to justify that the instrument is more or less important than travel, office supplies, or student support in a given budget year. Finally, the impact of technology on how we deliver instruction presents a new challenge for department chairs, and is even more prevalent in the discussion seven years after the publication of Hecht et al. (1999).

More Recent Additions to the Roles of Chairs

The new issues raised by Hecht et al. (1999) are real and continue today in an even more urgent way. In addition, other points of focus have emerged, and chairs have new responsibilities that add to the list or extend the dimensions of the items on the list. The major one is what I will term the *accountability movement*. Some would think of this as the assessment movement in higher education, and although assessment is a major element of this concept, there are many manifestations of accountability, and each adds to the list of roles that a chair must fulfill.

Assessment

The assessment of student learning is a department issue and the call for such evidence is delivered to the chair. Because this type of assessment is ideally suited to come from the faculty who teach the courses and design the curricula, much of this work can be delegated to a faculty committee where data may be collected and analyzed and plans for improvement can be developed. The role of the chair can be one of setting the expectation and keeping the faculty groups on task by creating timelines for each phase of the process. Volumes have been written about this type of assessment, and I won't belabor the point here. Assessment will be discussed again in Chapter 5, where the chair's role in monitoring and assuring quality in the department is addressed.

Faculty Workload

A major objective of accountability requires that faculty time be accounted for, especially as it relates to time spent in the classroom. Criticisms that faculty do not work hard enough or do not spend enough of their time on the "important aspects" of their jobs have led to workload analyses and new expectations of faculty time spent on instruction, sometimes undergraduate instruction specifically. In cases where faculty workloads are mandated by external groups (legislatures or trustees), there are inevitable problems that emerge from a one-size-fits-all approach. For example, one can provide a relative effort value to a section of English composition that meets for three hours per week or a chemistry class that meets for three hours of lecture and four hours of lab per week. But how does one set an equivalency for a clinical section in physical therapy that meets all day or a fine arts section where three drawing classes are meeting simultaneously? In institutions where research and graduate education exist, how does one consider the individualized instruction registrations of research students into a faculty member's workload? These equivalency issues are not easy to anticipate or to resolve by upper administrators who come from a single discipline or for outside agents who have no firsthand notion of faculty work, thus leaving department chairs to make their cases for the unique aspects of the department's instructional contributions in order to achieve an equitable equation for faculty work in the discipline. In addition, the chair would also need to collect data on faculty effort in all areas of department responsibility, make any necessary adjustments in assignments, and ensure that every aspect is addressed in a quality manner.

External Program Review

External program review is not a new concept but one that has been resurrected at some institutions as a way to assess program or department quality and to foster improvement. There are times when program reviews are initiated to address a special circumstance. Examples might include a situation where there is a poorly performing department unable to right its course, or when the institution is considering splitting a unit into two, consolidating units, or eliminating units.

Opinions differ on the effectiveness of external program reviews in assessing department quality. Wergin (2003) casts doubt on this exercise because of the prevailing faculty culture that favors individual, disciplinary achievement over unit achievement. While this may be true in some cases, even some that I know of, departments can approach the process in ways that represent ownership of the entire academic entity.

Program reviews typically occur at regular intervals and require that a department prepare a self-study outlining all of its activities, including degree programs, student data, faculty assignments, budgets, staff functions, and a myriad of other datasets. The roles of the chair in this process include overseeing the writing of the self-study, perhaps even writing significant components of it because the chair has the closest access to the relevant information. It must be anticipated that most faculty will consider this process to be an unnecessary exercise, a waste of their valuable time, and one that will not lead to improvements in areas important to them.

The chair plays a critical role in the external review process by selecting the appropriate data and eliciting, directly or indirectly, recommendations from the committee that are helpful to the department in making progress, reinforcing department needs, validating department plans, and addressing department weaknesses. The institution has an agenda for the external review, and the department should be able to generate information and advice that will foster progress and improvement. The chair will also be the point person in meeting with the external review committee, providing additional information in response to queries. This is another opportunity to ensure that the department's requests for help are at the forefront of the committee's deliberations. Finally, the chair will lead the department's long-term response to the recommendations of the committee. This includes selecting which are appropriate, which can be done quickly and easily, and which require long-term planning. The steps and strategies for planning and hosting a program review will be discussed further in Chapter 5.

Faculty Evaluation and Post-Tenure Review

The roles of the department chair in faculty evaluation and the related issue of post-tenure review have become more significant due to external criticism of the tenured life of professors. The old argument is that no other profession guarantees employment, so why should taxpayers continue to employ professors who can "retire on the job." The implication, again, is that we do not work very hard, but I think we all realize that the vast majority put in hard hours beyond the standard workweek. The "story" that we hear locally is the one where someone complains that a professor is seen cutting his lawn every Tuesday afternoon.

If one examines the written institutional policies of some colleges and universities, one may discover language stating that tenured and tenure-track faculty will be reviewed annually with the exception of full professors. This places senior faculty outside of the review process, sometimes for 20 years. In an era of accountability, that is not easily defensible. In response to new policies, professors are now undergoing the review process for the first time in years. For the chair, it may be the first time that he or she must review senior members of the faculty. This can be a major point of tension, especially if the faculty member under review has higher disciplinary status or seniority than the chair.

The changes in the evaluation process may be linked to or accompanied by new policies in post-tenure review. What one must remember is that, as threatening as such a change may seem, it can also be regarded as a way of protecting tenure. The promise to review tenured faculty and set criteria for improved performance when it has been deemed unsatisfactory has been successful in some states in silencing calls for eliminating tenure altogether. Thus higher education can continue with tenure and the autonomy benefits it includes, if it takes the responsibility for monitoring and dealing with cases where faculty fall far below performance expectations.

The post-tenure review component of the faculty evaluation process takes on special meaning to the department chair at institutions where there is an initiated or triggered form of post-tenure review. In this form, the annual review conducted by the chair is the key event that can place a tenured professor under formal post-tenure review. If the annual review is deemed by the chair to result in an unsatisfactory performance rating (sometimes two such ratings in a row or so many over a specified period of time), the case moves to a faculty committee for review. If the rating is upheld, the committee constructs a development plan with the faculty member. The plan has a timeline for improvement with the possibility of dismissal if expectations are not met. Because the chair plays the key initiating role, this task can be a difficult one for the obvious reasons, especially when dealing with senior faculty at a higher rank than the chair.

Civic Engagement

Beyond the many forms of accountability, another aspect of university life receiving increased attention are activities that fall under the banner of civic engagement. I recall a conference where developing more prominent programs of civic engagement was the major agenda item of the attending institutions. At that time, it was a new concept for me, so I did not know exactly what it meant. In fact, I have yet to formulate a concrete definition for civic engagement and have come to learn that it means different things to different people. Civic engagement is an outgrowth of the "service" promise of colleges and universities that is directed specifically at community-based service. The term *civic engagement* has achieved such an elevated status that it is now an integral part of the mission statements of many institutions.

Department chairs actively document activities that seem to fit the general concept of civic engagement and look for ways to enhance their interactions with their communities in order to meet the expectations of their campuses. Service-learning is a formal classroom-related example of civic engagement that has been noted across the country. While some disciplines such as education, social work, and nursing have natural ways of interacting with their communities, the challenges are greater in disciplines in the arts and sciences. Chairs in such units must be creative in designing and encouraging productive ways for their departments to be seen as active participants in serving or interacting with their communities. This must be done in ways that are meaningful to the community, that benefit students and faculty, and that balance the other expectations of the department and its faculty.

Compliance Issues

The dramatic increase in compliance requirements presents a series of new challenges for department chairs. Some that are common to all disciplines include policies on family leave, sexual harassment, employment, disruptive students, workplace violence, criminal background checks, and other universal campus-level policies. The chair plays a critical role in ensuring that the department's practices are in compliance on these policies and that faculty are aware of them. This becomes very important in units where faculty members employ part-time and full-time employees to help with their professional work. The legal ramifications resulting from lack of attention to these policies can be both embarrassing and expensive.

There are additional compliance issues that vary in the way they affect academic departments and in their financial impact. Examples include safety issues, access and accommodation, and compliance issues brought on by scientific and technological advances. Some believe that this battery of rules and policies is responsible for much of the spiraling cost of higher education. The fiscal cost as well as the time and energy required at the department level to enforce them are not equally distributed across all disciplines. The issue of accommodating students with disabilities in the liberal arts may be as simple as a modified seating arrangement in a classroom. In the sciences, this demand can mean significant changes in laboratory construction and equipment that is repeated in several locations as a student moves through the curriculum. Likewise, safety issues are more prominent in laboratory settings and include storage of various substances, eye protection, gloves and other protective clothing, training for equipment use, and even where faculty and staff store and eat their lunches. Such issues are raised here not because they are new—we have had safety regulations for decades—but because the standards continue to rise. What was acceptable during one inspection may be a violation six months later. Because safety regulations impact both the research and instructional settings, the expense associated with compliance can be substantial. It is not uncommon that the department is expected to use its own budget to achieve a suitable solution.

Other compliance issues involve protection of personal privacy and use of human subjects, animal use rules that are ever tightening and expensive, the use of recombinant DNA protocols, which underpin the explosion of research in molecular biology and medicine, and conflict of interest reporting. More recent are restrictions on the use of certain cell lines and microbial agents in teaching and research. Some of these rules have resulted from terrorist threats since the 9/11 tragedy. They all require the employment of compliance officers and their staff and the time of faculty committees who are held responsible for meeting the requirements of the institution and governmental agencies. While chairs do not directly enforce rules, except as they apply to their own work, they are nonetheless responsible for making certain their faculty are aware of the policies and are in compliance with them. Lack of attention can result in grant proposals kicked back to the investigators for the lack of a reviewed and certified usage protocol or in the banning of exercises used to train students in the laboratory. The oversight of a vigilant chair is needed to alert and remind faculty and staff of these obligations.

What the Future Holds for Chair Work

You may be wondering how the addition of new chair responsibilities could continue. How will the roles and responsibilities of chairs change in the future? One can easily recognize that the recent changes in the higher education environment just discussed will continue in some form in the future. With the traditional roles and these recent additions as a backdrop, the following are what I see as challenges that will loom larger in the next decade.

Student Recruitment and Retention

With the exception of graduate programs, academic departments have depended upon the Office of Admissions or some similar administrative unit to recruit new undergraduate students. Such offices send representatives to meetings for high school counselors, arrange for campus tours, host special campus events, and set up elaborate booths at recruiting fairs. They make hundreds of contacts, follow up with mailings and calls, and report their annual "yield." Several factors drive the competition for students, especially those with strong credentials and the family resources to afford the ever-rising costs of higher education. These factors include the need to raise or preserve the institution's income by admitting more students, elevating the institutional ranking by enhancing the statistical profile of the typical student, achieving diversity goals, and ensuring higher retention and graduation rates.

Today, students and potential students have other access to sources of academic information via the Internet and many are intrigued by elements of academic programs that cannot be articulated with the required depth and understanding by professional staff. For example, if the availability of undergraduate research across the disciplines is a hallmark attraction, a staff member from the admissions office most likely cannot provide examples of the types of projects that might be available for a would-be physics major. Having the requisite expertise to address situations like this can be a difference maker in terms of student recruitment. The need is to find ways to make this type of information available. Faculty members at most institutions are not going to do a great deal of personal recruiting, so chairs have to lead the development of paper, digital, or web-based recruiting materials and the organization of discipline-specific events to bring potential students into contact with the faculty and the opportunities offered by the department.

Student retention is a prominent topic on some campuses, and this emphasis will continue to expand. Retention is a complex topic in that it has several dimensions, and published rates must be closely examined to determine just what is being measured. The two parameters used in *U.S. News & World Report* ratings of U.S. colleges and universities are the first- to second-year retention rate of fall, first-time, full-time freshmen and six-year graduation rates for the same cohorts. The retention picture for a residential, private liberal arts college is quite different from that of a comprehensive, urban, public institution. The latter typically attracts much higher percentages of transfer students, first-generation students, and students from lower socioeconomic groups. National data indicate that the single most effective predictor of students' persistence is the economic status of their families (Muraskin, Lee, Wilner, & Swail, 2004). The less selective nature of admissions standards at public institutions means that more at-risk students are admitted, resulting in increased challenges regarding student success and retention.

There are several compelling reasons to be concerned about and to attempt to address the serious issue of retention. The expanding knowledge-based economy has created a situation where a college degree is now the entry-level credential for a career. The options for those without a degree are shrinking, and those who do not make it will be severely restricted in their ability to enjoy a middle-class life. State legislatures are questioning the public's investment in institutions where students are not successful. This climate invites state intervention, both fiscally and in other operational ways, that could damage elements of the academic enterprise. Finally, the students most likely to drop out are at-risk, first-generation students from groups that are traditionally underrepresented in many of our disciplines. This thwarts the attempts of higher education to achieve diversity among its graduates and create a culture of justice and equity for those seeking to improve themselves and lead productive lives.

Taking into account the work of admissions offices, schools, and departments in recruiting new students each year, the loss of a student after the first year means that another has to be identified and recruited as a replacement. Perhaps with some interventions in the first year, the already enrolled student might be more successful and more inclined to stay. Although I have no data to support this, I suspect that most academic programs at institutions with low retention rates have high introductory course enrollments and untapped "capacity" at the upper level. From an efficiency perspective, increasing the first-year rate of retention would allow departments to fill that capacity and turn out more graduates. Finally, at the risk of being too business-minded, losing students early has a huge impact on tuition flow. The institution and its departments will not receive tuition income from subsequent registrations. One must only do the calculations to see that this is a significant loss.

There are a multitude of elements to the retention problem, many of which are not amenable to institutional or departmental intervention. Some, however, are, and these are the areas in which department chairs will have to be innovative in designing, supporting, and encouraging faculty to develop strategies and programs that will improve student success and retention. Examples might include instituting tutoring, upper-class student mentoring, or supplemental instruction in those beginning classes which are so problematic. While programs such as these may have some costs, the benefits to institutional and department budgets may exceed the costs, and chairs will have to make persuasive arguments that their strategies are worth the risk of experimental funding to supplement the department's investment. Chairs will also have to be sure that the department is at the table when campus-level initiatives to attack this problem are announced. Such programs may involve internal funding opportunities for faculty members and also provide a forum for the sharing of best practices in retention across the campus. Selecting strategies from a larger menu of possibilities can result in faster implementation and the avoidance of ineffective ideas. Chapter 11 will further expand the discussion of student recruitment and retention.

Chair Work Beyond the Department

Chairs of the future will become more involved in work outside the comfortable surroundings of the department's physical domain. Several factors mandate that department chairs become involved with on- and off-campus constituents in ways that improve the unit's image and productivity. Everyone can identify department chairs whose work is directed solely to personal accomplishment and the day-to-day responsibilities of managing the unit. While each of these areas will remain important, the forces of the present and future indicate that increased efforts beyond the department will be required for establishing a competitive and recognized academic unit.

It has been noted that a department should have a visible presence in all discussions and activities concerning student retention. The department will not only be seen as interested, concerned, and active (political capital gained) but also as willing to learn about effective strategies to improve its own performance. A similar advantage can be obtained by participation in other campus initiatives linked to institutional mission. There has been increased emphasis in developing and fine-tuning institutional mission statements, and this has carried through to school and sometimes department-level mission statements. As one would predict, the statements become more specific and focused as they proceed to the unit level. They should, however, be aligned in that what a department proposes can find a place under the umbrella of the school and institutional versions. Chairs or their designees will need to participate in these conversations and craft language describing the department's aspirations that is consistent with statements made at higher levels. New initiatives from the department can then be developed with the language and within the framework of the wider definitions of higher-level mission statements.

The explosion of new interdisciplinary fields has changed and will continue to change some very fundamental ways of doing business. Many of these fields are in the technical and scientific areas, but one can project that the humanities and social sciences will become increasingly involved. Interdisciplinary programs raise the issue of ownership. That is, whose graduates are these? Who sets the requirements? Who approves the new courses? If the program has research dimensions, questions of how the external grant overhead is shared, to whom it is attributed, and who provides the space for the work become paramount. There are also cultural issues concerning team teaching where contributors come from schools with different teaching load expectations (schools of liberal arts and medicine, for example). These and their related aspects, as well as the actual development of such programs, involve the work, input, approval, and insight of department chairs either directly or through designated department faculty members. This topic will be taken up in greater detail in Chapter 19.

Interdisciplinary work in program and research innovation will also take place with external constituents as partners. Such enterprises will raise some of the same issues as cross-school collaborations as well as some new ones related to organizational cultures, cost-sharing, ownership, and shared authority. Some of these external partnerships have begun to surface and can involve industry, local and state governments, civic organizations, business, and the not-for-profit sector. These partnerships are truly exciting in their potential, but much negotiation, sharing of traditional practices, and resource integration must take place for their success. This concept will be further developed in Chapter 20.

Summary

Current department chairs who have been serving for more than a year will recognize that the position is taking on new responsibilities on an almost routine basis. For the subset who have done this work for a decade or more, the change has been considerable. Faculty members considering seeking positions as department chairs will encounter a position with the hallmarks of department leadership rooted in the distant past. Traditional chair roles such as scheduling classes, managing the budget, department advocacy, representing the department at a variety of functions, paperwork, assigning teaching, and handling ad hoc problems remain for current chairs. A review of these and other historical roles reveals that they remain essential to department functioning and thus must endure in the chair portfolio.

The past decade has been a time of significant change in higher education and the work of department chairs. Much of this change has been the result of increased accountability requirements in the academy. Departments now must demonstrate what students know and can do and how the department assesses these outcomes and makes changes to improve student learning. There are also new requirements in setting and reporting on faculty work, reviewing the overall quality of all department-level work, and evaluating individual faculty performance. All of these initiatives place new responsibilities on the department chair. Chairs must oversee and assure that assessment requirements are met, prepare for and participate in major department program reviews, and conduct more regular and extensive reviews of faculty performance. The latter has increased stakes due to the emergence of post-tenure review polices at many colleges and universities. Departments are now asked to become more meaningfully engaged with the community while at the same time managing the increased monitoring and costs related to regulatory mandates.

In looking to the horizon, chairs can expect to be more active in increasing department revenue sources. Beyond fundraising, this will take the form of chairs becoming increasingly active on campus and in the external community in developing innovative programs and partnerships that increase unit value and lead to new revenue streams through increased tuition, external funding from public and private granting agencies, and from local industry, businesses, and other organizations. Departments will be expected to play more active roles in recruiting students and in programs designed to retain those students through graduation. While chairs will not bear the entire burden of these responsibilities, they will have to ensure appropriate department participation, motivate faculty members to do their part, and provide an environment that creates real opportunities for faculty growth and productivity in the 21st-century world of higher education.

2

CHARACTERISTICS OF EFFECTIVE CHAIRS

What is it that makes some department chairs effective over long periods of time while others struggle from the begin-ning of their appointments? While there are many nonpersonal, environmental factors (faculty culture, the personality and style of the dean, available resources, etc.) that can impact a chair's success, there still seem to be some universal factors which, coupled with an appropriate match between the expectations of the position and the skill set of the appointment, predict success or failure. Perhaps considering the traditional and more recent expectations of the chair position discussed in Chapter 1 along with the personal characteristics and skills desired by those who select chairs, department faculty members, and deans, one can identify those features that are predictive of a successful chair appointment.

A few years ago, some colleagues and I participated in a limited, nonscientific survey of department chairs and deans designed to help institutions and chair applicants match expectations so that appropriate appointments could be made. Among the questions posed by the survey, department chairs representing several institutions were asked what their administration and department faculty expected of them as chairs. Deans from a variety of disciplines at several institutions were asked to list the characteristics they sought in department chairs. The findings, although not derived from a professionally designed survey, are instructive and, I expect, predictive of the outcome that would be achieved in larger surveys.

Department chairs perceived that what was expected from administration was improvement in the department through developing programs, increasing faculty accomplishment, and uniting the faculty in working toward common goals. Relatively few chairs identified routine management tasks such as reports and paperwork as primary expectations. The expectations of faculty members (most of the chairs were internal appointments so the expectations of their faculty colleagues were well known) were quite varied and included the development of programs and new resources, advocacy for the department, success in resolving conflict, managing paperwork effectively, and personal traits such as honesty, fairness, and leadership ability.

When deans asked whether they expected newly appointed chairs to be change agents or simply to manage the department, the surprising outcome was that these choices finished in a virtual tie. While this can be interpreted to mean that some departments were regarded as doing just fine and thus were not in need of any major changes, it can also mean that some deans were not eager to confront the discontent, anguish, and cost that change can sometimes evoke. This is not a criticism of the resolve or commitment to improvement by deans but rather a realization that deans have many units to oversee and that attention, focus, and resources can be directed only to so many at a time. Those in the greatest need or those most critical to the institution will and should have priority. Those that seem to be functioning well are not likely to be selected for major change.

Personal characteristics that deans sought in candidates for chair positions were many and varied. In fact, this limited survey generated such a long list that prospective chairs might be advised not to read it for fear of concluding that they are inadequate for the position! The list can be viewed as a set of overlapping characteristics compatible with the abilities of an experienced faculty member who feels equipped and prepared to take on a leadership position. With no intended priority, deans sought chairs who are intelligent and experienced. These expectations are in keeping with a successful professor in higher education. Deans were also interested in chairs with good management skills—they want paperwork done correctly and on time. Deans also wanted chairs who were honest, fair, and trustworthy. Several comments were made that speak to people skills. Included in the responses from the deans were diplomatic characteristics such as maintains good relations with administration, positive attitude, sense of humor, tactful, instills confidence, and treats others with respect even when disagreeing. This is sometimes a place where experienced, intelligent faculty members may come up short as chairs. There were also some characteristics that might be combined into a category labeled "tough-mindedness." Some of the specific terms that deans used to describe this were thick-skinned, driven, persevering, and having stamina. Everyone knows faculty colleagues who do not display one or more of these traits at least some of the time.

Beyond personal characteristics for chairs, deans also identified some other factors that would influence their selection of a new chair. The ability to be an effective communicator was of particular importance. In line with people skills is the ability to work well with others. This is the era of collaboration, not because it sounds trendy, but because it is essential to our survival. Deans are looking for cooperative chairs who have vision and are able to look beyond their own interests. A common mantra in athletics is that there is no "I" in "team." The same is true regarding the department—chairs can have no personal ego and must measure themselves based on the performance of the department. The conversion that is required here is to move from "I, me, and my" to "we, us, and our."

Essential Chair Traits: Credibility

While this information is useful and insightful in terms of defining chair characteristics from the perspectives of those served by chairs, a few traits did not emerge explicitly in the survey and need to be mentioned. When I became chair in 1992, I set as my primary goal making my department "credible." While this may seem unusual, at that time it was an important step for the department to make together. We had just suffered major embarrassment when the previous chair garnered national attention for misappropriation of funds. The department was also being outperformed by other units in the school while clearly having the potential to do much better. Therefore, at the time it seemed that establishing credibility was an appropriate first step. I did not realize that my personal credibility was also an important component to my ability to help achieve credibility for the department and lead it over the coming years.

When I was appointed as chair, a former colleague who had retired years earlier called to congratulate me and advise me to make an initial high-impact decision marking the change in leadership. He suggested firing a secretary or technician. I never considered following that advice, the firing part at least, but did decide to use my "honeymoon influence" to engage a significant component of the department in writing an external proposal for the purchase of a major piece of instrumentation. Looking back on this, I am pleased we were not successful with that proposal; it was not an instrument that was vital to our teaching or research and the space it needed would have limited our ability to grow in the future. The process, however, had enormous value. The department, including some staff, worked toward a common goal that was seen as a team effort and a step forward. Previously, there was no focus, so the project was an exercise in putting our troubles and the malaise of the past behind us. At the same time, we were moving toward a new budget model called responsibility-centered management (RCM). This has since become a more common budgeting system, but in 1992 it was relatively new. Because I had been doing class scheduling for several years, I was privy to information on enrollment patterns as well as on structural limitations about what we could deliver in terms of course sections. I was able to take advan-

tage of the RCM model by strategic investments to dramatically increase enrollments, thus leading to increased department revenues. These two factors provided me with renewed or extended credibility with faculty and administration.

Personal credibility is important when a chair interacts with the dean or other individuals across campus. In dealings with the dean, the chair must provide accurate, honest information when explaining problems and when requesting assistance. The tendency of some chairs to try extracting whatever possible from administration by any means will ultimately lead to the point where future requests, no matter how justified, will fall on deaf ears because of past behavior. Interactions with the dean will be the focus of discussion in Chapter 10.

Working effectively across campus as a new chair also requires personal credibility. Again, there is the bonus period when the new chair is granted personal credibility based solely on his or her appointment. This is assumed credibility, and the way the chair interacts across campus will determine whether it will be permanent. This is much like interviewing for a job: your credentials, vitae, and academic record get you the interview but your performance at the interview gets you the job. Again, honesty is important in intra-campus dealings. If there are problems with a class being taught for students in another unit, they should be investigated and rectified, and information shared with administrators and faculty in the other unit. If the campus interaction is designed to establish a new interdisciplinary program, the chair should come prepared, make firm commitments, and follow through in a timely fashion.

The personal credibility of the chair often has an influence on the credibility of the department. This is why personal credibility is so important for a chair. A visible, dependable, hardworking chair can instill confidence in others that a department can solve its problems, meet its challenges, and achieve its goals. It also means that the chair can easily gain audiences with others on campus to make certain these successes happen. If others have confidence in the ability of the chair, they will have confidence that the department can deliver as well.

Essential Chair Traits: Equity

In the survey cited earlier in this chapter, both faculty and deans identified fairness as an important characteristic of a chair. Before discussing this concept, it should be made clear that, like beauty and a few other things, fairness is in the eyes of the beholder. There will always be differences of opinion as to whether one individual is being treated fairly relative to another. Everyone has seen cases where fair treatment is obvious yet someone is adamant that the opposite is true, and reverse cases where it seems that someone has been singled out for poor treatment.

It should be understood that equitable or fair does not always mean equal. This is where problems sometimes come into play. In fact, there are probably some readers who will not agree. Equity does not mean that everyone is treated in the same way. Rather, it means that everyone will be evaluated according to the same public guidelines and that reward or special consideration will be granted to those who best meet expectations inherent in the guidelines. Merit pay is an example. For those in merit systems, the task of evaluating and making distinctions among the contributions of unit personnel leads to differential salary increments. If this is done correctly, it is equitable but may not be equal.

There are a number of areas where chairs must act equitably in dealing with faculty so that they are stimulated to maintain excellence or to make improvements and increase productivity and so that institutional resources are used wisely. A few examples illustrate this concept. A limiting resource in scientific and technological disciplines at research universities is space. The type of space needed is extremely expensive, requiring built-in instrumentation, extensive utilities, costly safety devices, and expensive bench work and cabinetry. The initial assignment of space is usually made both equitably and equally to all beginning faculty members unless the nature of the scholarly work differs (e.g., theoretical versus experimental). The allocation of this resource is based on the premise that the faculty member will use the space productively. In practical terms, this means that the faculty member will conduct and publish original research and win external funding to help defray the costs associated with operating the research facility. The chair of the department recognizes this outcome as part of the unit's mission and must act in ways that ensure productivity from the resources in his or her domain. Consider a lab that has not received any funding for four years and has not published any results for three, and a lab next door that has been extremely productive in publishing and has just landed its third major external grant that will fund two full-time technical positions and support a Ph.D. student. The question is whether it is fair (equitable) for the chair to give some of the dormant lab space to the productive investigator and reduce the space of the underperforming faculty member.

The scenario has more complexity than can be considered here. But what is important in terms of equity is whether the department has expressed its mission and expectations in ways that state that research is a primary expectation of faculty. If this is the case, then a policy should be developed that prescribes how space is allocated, maintained, and reallocated. If such a policy has been established within the department, then the chair is being equitable in terms of utilizing department resources most effectively toward that end by making the move. The other issue in this scenario is the department culture regarding faculty who are stuck in their research or whose areas of research have fallen out of favor with funding agencies. One must look at the case of the dormant faculty member to see why research has stopped, what efforts the chair has made to restart the work in the lab, the prospects for rekindling the lab, and other factors before pulling the plug. Such factors may lead to deciding not to turn over the space for a period of time during which specific efforts and activities may take place.

Another example may be in the area of faculty access to department resources for the purposes of conference attendance, an item usually in department budgets across most disciplines. It can be a very contentious item in disciplines where external funding with line items for travel is uncommon and where department budgets are small. A department may set priorities for travel based on invited versus open conferences, prestige of the conference, rotation among faculty for travel, or travel allowance based on meeting department objectives. One can imagine that many of these prioritizations could elicit contention as budgets shrink. For example, one faculty member may receive invitations annually, while another never does. There may be endless arguments regarding conference prestige in two distinct areas of the discipline. If allocation of travel funds is tied to department goals, in this scenario visibility and presentations that lead to publications and external funding, then the decision is linked to department advancement and not to individual requests. There will always be cases where a chair wishes to help a faculty member restart a scholarly program or change to a different area of scholarship or provide a new faculty member with an early opportunity. These special development and revitalization activities must be an element of chair discretion in goal-oriented resource investments. It is evident that this type of distribution is not equal, but it may be considered equitable because it matches investments with valued outcomes related to unit objectives.

Essential Chair Traits: Honesty

A final characteristic for effective chairing is honesty. This, too, can be subject to alternative interpretation. Aside from different memories of what was said, there are cases when the overall bottom line of long, difficult conversation can be interpreted differently by the two parties. One way to help clarify such situations is to take notes during or right after the encounter. While these may be challenged for accuracy by the other party, at least the chair has a personal record of what was discussed at the time.

In other cases it is a challenge to be fully honest or revealing in situations where some information made available to the chair cannot be divulged to faculty members. Sometimes chairs may choose not to reveal important information if it is incomplete or tentative. An example is necessary here lest the reader think that being something less than forthcoming is acceptable. In a recent and particularly dismal budget year, administration was considering cash bonuses made to only the highest performing faculty in lieu of the traditional incremental increases in base salary. Understanding that this proposal was just in the discussion stage, the chair chose not to share it with faculty because it was under consideration. When queried about salary increments the chair stated that there was no final decision at that time. This was true, but information was withheld because there was no reason to fuel speculation and possibly generate anxiety until the final decision was made.

The dean also needs to be confident that the chair is dealing honestly when information is requested and when the chair makes a special appeal. Those who have witnessed interactions between chairs and deans are aware of situations where need has been exaggerated and resources have been directed such that more pressing matters have gone unattended. Many faculty and chairs believe that a primary chair role is to garner resources for the department. Since budgets are frequently made by what is called the *begging system,* the chair with the best argument or the one who is more persuasive is sometimes the winner. If this is the game routinely played, the dean would have to sort through the rhetoric and ask the right questions. Thus a chair has to decide whether to be frank and honest about department needs or to overstate (or expand or even fabricate) them to be more competitive. Careful documentation of department needs from budget items to new faculty lines should be recorded and the outcomes or results of the resources granted should be reported in subsequent years in order to establish trust between the chair and the dean.

Summary

Anyone who has spent a good number of years in higher education will remember department chairs who served long and well and others whose appointments were marked by brevity, controversy, and a lack of department progress. The spectrum here can be the result of many variables beyond the characteristics of the individual chair. Faculty culture and its tolerance for and commitment to change, the management style of the dean, and the sense of cohesion and support from higher administration are all important predictors of chair and department success. To place this complexity into a context where one can make a reasonable prediction on what attributes a successful chair might possess, a brief look at what chairs expect of themselves and what deans and faculty members expect of chairs might be instructive.

Chairs assume their appointment expecting to improve the department and to gain the support and cooperation of the faculty in that venture. They hope to convince the faculty to work with them in improving programs, student learning, research, and other aspects of department operation. Faculty members expect chairs to be advocates, garner new resources, develop new programs, accept managerial tasks, and deal with problems. The last has several meanings from dealing with student complaints to shielding faculty from administrative intrusions and requests. Faculty also expect honesty and fairness from the chair: The former is relative easy to define, but the latter is subject to alternative interpretations. Deans expect chairs to be savvy and to have people, communication, and management skills. They also expect honesty and fairness. These expectations have areas of overlap and none seem to be unrealistic. One can also see the perspectives unique to each group.

A chair characteristic that sometimes makes lists like these is credibility. This deserves a much higher profile on the list. The credibility of the chair and the department are linked, and the work of the chair is greatly facilitated when there is personal credibility in department leadership. That individual lends credibility to the department when he or she speaks on behalf of its programs, students, and faculty. A second trait, and one that has already been cited more than once, is fairness or equity. This does not mean that everyone is treated the same. What this means is that everyone knows what the expectations are and has the opportunity and support to be competitive. Merit decisions, whether pay, promotion and tenure, award nominations, or resource allocations, will result in differential evaluations based on meeting those standards.

3

REMAINING PROFESSIONALLY
VIABLE WHILE CHAIR

Although this chapter could be placed in other spots for the purpose of addressing would-be chairs, it probably best belongs at the beginning. Discussing the topic here is appropriate for those contemplating seeking positions as department chairs in the future. As directly stated or strongly implied in other sections of this book, a faculty member usually gives up a good deal to take the helm as chair. As a member of a large complex institution, I can observe several different department environments that change the work of those taking chair positions in very different ways. I can, and will, only guess how the move to chair may impact career transition at a small liberal arts college or at a community college.

Chairs at Major Research Institutions

Faculty members who successfully compete for chair positions in professional schools or in traditional departments at major research universities typically are able to negotiate significant support packages that allow them to continue their professional work. Individuals landing positions like these are recognized as productive scholars who have reached full rank and who are at or near their apex of productivity. By definition, many of these departments expect that the chair will be a true peer among the other scholars in the unit and is, therefore, expected to maintain strong and productive programs in research/scholarship. With all of the usual and emerging responsibilities of chairs, how can a chair be expected to continue running at the front of the pack in scholarship? Watching this happen locally and in other area institutions,

I have seen several factors that provide the support to allow such models. First, the individuals recruited to lead professional school departments or long-standing research-focused departments have built large research infrastructures based primarily on external funding that is mobile. As these programs enlarge, they accumulate senior personnel fully capable of running the day-to-day operations of the research enterprise. While some senior personnel remain only a few years before moving to establish their own independent operations, others become career postdoctoral associates. Coupled with experienced technical employees and graduate students, there are many, sometimes dozens, of people in the group. In nonscience and nontechnical areas, graduate students and other types of assistants would fulfill the support roles. When a faculty member moves to a chair position at another institution, many of these personnel will move along with the appointee. Experienced team members will move the operation, reconstruct it at the new site, and continue the work, losing only a brief period of time to shut-down.

A second factor that facilitates continuing chair scholarship is that the offer made to the new chair likely includes significant new resources to enhance the research operation. They may include more space for research, dollars for equipment, supplies, travel, and other resources, and new positions to replace and expand the research operation. In professional schools, a newly recruited chair can sometimes leverage new faculty positions as part of the recruitment package. In these environments, chairs can have almost unilateral discretion in hiring faculty, and some will use that authority to hire assistant professors whose work is closely aligned with their own. These new "collaborators" thus expand the research scope of the chair. Because the chair must continue a level of productivity that sets a high standard, the institution will provide the tools to make that possible.

Finally, professional schools will not have the added and special responsibilities of dealing with undergraduate students, instead dealing only with selected graduate and professional students. Top-echelon research universities will have undergraduate programs to administer, but their departments routinely have staff and faculty members who serve as directors of various programs. These individuals are responsible for the day-to-day work of administering, monitoring, and assessing the programs while dealing with problems that arise. Teaching is typically not part of the expectation of chairs of units such as these unless they wish to participate. Chairs of such units can then focus on larger issues such as garnering resources, developing new programs, reviewing and setting faculty salaries, and maintaining their disciplinary status. While all institutions and their departments are suffering from fiscal restrictions, the reality is that institutions and departments of the sort described here have significantly more resources (base funds, infrastructure positions that can be morphed, private funds) than most. Suffering is a relative term, and here the lifestyles are very different and pain is measured relative to what you are accustomed to and not to the way the entire higher education world lives. Most readers will not recognize this type of arrangement in their work as chairs or the work of chairs they have observed.

Chairs at Liberal Arts Colleges

In taking a stab at how the work life of a new chair at a liberal arts college might change, there would probably be a reduction in the teaching expectation but not its elimination. Because liberal arts colleges are placing increasingly more emphasis on scholarship, this aspect of chair work may suffer somewhat due to the new administrative responsibilities. If the chair has come from a research institution or a comprehensive institution where disciplinary research or scholarship was expected, he or she will probably find an environment where it will be difficult to maintain this work at the same level because of increased teaching expectations and less infrastructure to support competitive scholarship. Paramount would be the absence of graduate students in most disciplines. This type of career move is rare but does happen. For these individuals, there is much to surrender for the opportunity to work with undergraduate students in ways not possible in large research-oriented institutions. Again, this would be a guess, but the situation in the community college would move one out of the classroom to some degree and into work related to managing and monitoring entry-level teaching and in interacting with external entities to build and modify academic programs to meet constituent needs.

Chairs at Comprehensive Institutions

The setting where taking the position of chair seems to have the greatest impact on professional work is in comprehensive institutions, especially those in urban settings. There are a convergence of factors that make life in such institutions challenging, interesting, and potentially quite rewarding while at the same time threatening to traditional forms of scholarly productivity. Institutions of this type are typically not funded at the same levels as the large public flagships. Urban comprehensives have fewer doctoral programs and lower student FTE. The former are usually controlled and restricted by the flagship or state boards and the latter is due to the prevalence of part-time students. The urban institution also will have greater pressures for access, creating more heterogeneity in the student body, more adult students, more first-generation students, and more students from underrepresented groups. Each of these subpopulations bring special challenges to higher education. To provide funding based on FTE and not the number of students served leaves these institutions in a difficult position for providing the necessary services to promote success among these at-risk groups. All of these factors impact department chairs who must deal with issues of retention and the provision of appropriate advising and academic support services for these students.

Along with facing the challenges of a diverse student body and limited funding, urban universities have increasingly emphasized research as part of their mission. In the eyes of some, this is an example of mission creep. Others feel that this is the normal process of institutional growth and evolution. Most public, urban comprehensives are relatively new institutions, and few of them have reached a status nearing that of the flagships. Most, however, are still trying to balance access and standards, deal with high student-to-faculty ratios, and provide support for a special needs student population while simultaneously trying to provide a research-friendly environment, gain respect for the work faculty do, compete in external funding arenas, and raise scholarship expectations. Chairs in this environment will have a difficult time keeping pace with the increasing research expectations while addressing the many unique issues of their institutional setting and clientele.

Impacts of Becoming Chair

The potential impacts of a faculty member assuming the post of department chair vary greatly in the models listed above. The new chair in the research powerhouse department or well-established professional school overcomes the deficit of the time spent on administration by acquiring access to new resources that can be used to expand the research breadth through new hires of various types. The teaching factor drops out of the equation because this individual usually carries no expectation in this area. Such an individual may very well see an increase in research productivity after such a move. Returning to the faculty would leave re-acclimation to the classroom as the only hurdle to be cleared. Assuming the same environment persists, high-profile research departments or professional school departments, teaching loads would not be heavy and, for a senior full professor, much of this might be done in graduate seminars.

Moving to the liberal arts college model, there are two concerns that chairs might have in staying prepared to resume the role of faculty member. First, a teaching load reduction is usually included with the offer of the chair position. While this may provide some space for new administrative work, the expanding responsibilities of the position probably will make for a much busier schedule than before. This will diminish time previously available for upgrading and modernizing the remaining courses taught. Time for personal scholarship has already been shown in many surveys to be the element of faculty work that suffers most. Both of these situations pose a dilemma for the new chair who may not be planning to make a career of leading a department.

Undergraduate education is going through its own array of transforming experiments, including the use of technology and strategies for active learning. The appropriate uses of these new approaches are not always self-evident to the novice practitioner, and much trial and error is often required to find out what works and what does not in a given setting. This type of work is taking place at many types of institutions, but where the focus is on the delivery of undergraduate education and where the primary reward structure is based on teaching, there may be a higher level of experimentation. Chairs pressed for time to meet the requirements of the administrative side of their positions may not be able to engage in such experiments and thus will fall behind others in the department who are becoming more expert in instituting new pedagogical approaches in their classes.

The push to increase the emphasis on research and scholarship is found not only in traditional research-intensive institutions, but also in comprehensives and in liberal arts colleges. This has reached the point where there are scholarship expectations for promotion and tenure and, again, the common refrain that "it is scholarship that really counts in merit and promotion and tenure decisions" is heard from faculty members. While that discussion is not appropriate here, research and scholarship are becoming more prominent elements of faculty work at liberal arts colleges. The new chair realizes this and will institute a variety of measures to promote this activity among faculty members. However, chair research is the first casualty of administrative responsibility. Most other aspects of work function on deadline or scheduled bases. Reports and personnel appointments are examples of the former and meetings and classes are examples of the latter. Moreover, chairs are expected to be responsive to the needs of a variety of constituents including faculty—with no appointment necessary. As an example of this, about 20 years ago my department conducted a search for a new chair. One of the finalists had a strong research program he wished to move and continue at our institution. He realized that this work would be in jeopardy unless he assigned a portion of his time to work on it. He explicitly stated that he would not be available two days a week, so he could focus on his work. This was not well received by some faculty who felt the chair should be accessible when needed. One can easily see why a chair's research agenda is so vulnerable. Getting back to the new chair at the liberal arts college, how does this individual not only maintain research viability but also increase output as is expected of the other faculty while performing the work of chair?

The situation for chairs in comprehensive institutions has some similarities to those in liberal arts colleges. There is more research infrastructure to support continued chair research, but again the research expectation is ratcheting up. Chair work here is complicated by much higher student-to-faculty ratios, restricted budgets, and a high proportion of at-risk students. Thus chairs spend much time and energy in hiring and monitoring adjunct faculty, encouraging and participating in fundraising, and developing strategies for improving student success. In many cases the sheer size of programs can be a detriment to personal scholarship.

With these possible backdrops to assuming the position of department chair, what strategies should the soon-to-be chair consider before or shortly after assuming the position? These strategies should ensure that he or she remains viable as a disciplinary practitioner such that the standard career can be resumed if the chair position is not to one's liking or if others (faculty members or the dean) do not appreciate the effort and a return to the faculty ranks is necessary.

Strategies for Staying Professionally Viable

A chair at a liberal arts college might not be able to keep pace with pedagogical advances in undergraduate education or have sufficient time to address the increasing research or scholarship expectations of the institution. One strategy to address the former is for the chair to team-teach with members of the faculty who have become adept at new teaching methods. The chair may be able to collaborate with an experienced mentor without needing to repeat the "experiments" done to define the details that lead to real effectiveness. For example, one semester the chair might team-teach with someone adept at integrating technology and another semester with a colleague who has been successful using active learning approaches. This strategy is applicable to other faculty members as well and promotes collaboration among department faculty. Another strategy, and this is best done at the time of appointment, is to negotiate with the dean for some development funding that allows chairs to attend conferences, workshops, and seminars to keep abreast of developments in teaching and scholarship. This is best arranged outside of traditional department resources so that the chair is not seen to be self-investing at the expense of faculty.

Maintaining and enhancing the research or scholarship profile while chair are not easy things to accomplish in this setting. Again, collaboration with a colleague is a possible avenue. Summer sabbaticals at research institutions or at other advanced organizations are possibilities as long as the work of the chair does not command a majority of summer time. Most liberal arts institutions offer limited summer programs, so that component of the operation is lessened. This might be part of the package negotiated with the dean.

The possibilities for maintaining a research connection are greater at a comprehensive university. Some of the advantage is based on sheer size. There are likely to be more individuals with whom to collaborate on research in this environment. Prior to assuming the chair, the individual likely had a research program in place so the challenge here is to find a way to maintain it while serving as chair. I have seen this take place successfully and I have seen it fail. It is successful in smaller departments where the work of the chair is presumably lessened in some areas. It also works in cases where the individual has a well-established research group that includes senior personnel. These colleagues may be permanent employees or transitionary personnel, such as graduate students. Senior graduate students can be immensely helpful but, alas, they will eventually graduate. Unless the group is well funded and can afford permanent senior personnel, sustaining a high level of productivity is difficult. Other successful models I have witnessed are those that are sustained through collaboration. In one case a modest research agenda was interrupted by many years of service as chair with no research activity. Upon return to the faculty, the individual teamed with another faculty member and enjoyed a very productive research career until retirement. For long-term chairs returning to the faculty, a yearlong sabbatical for retooling seems to be an excellent investment by the institution.

Summary

Faculty members who move into chair positions will make sacrifices to do so. Surveys of chairs show that time available for teaching and scholarship is reduced. The exception to this is in high-profile research departments and professional schools where assuming the chair position comes with a support package that can actually expand the scholarship work of the chair and allow for delegation of other department responsibilities. Teaching is not usually part of the equation in such settings. Chairs in liberal arts colleges and comprehensives must attend to the oversight of undergraduate programs and address management and leadership responsibilities while trying to maintain some connection with their research or scholarship activities. The latter would be required in comprehensive institutions upon return to the faculty, while liberal arts colleges are emphasizing this aspect of faculty work to a greater extent.

Chairs can keep in touch with pedagogical change in instruction through team-teaching with colleagues experienced with new approaches to student learning. Scholarship can be maintained through collaborative work with others in the department or on campus. For faculty members considering seeking chair positions, negotiating conference development funding or mini summer sabbaticals with the dean are also ways to keep the chair up to date and in a position to be competitive when returning to faculty ranks. Arrangements like this are possible for current chairs but are much easier to arrange during the appointment negotiations. For long-term chairs returning to the faculty, an in-house or traditional sabbatical for retooling is highly recommended.

4

THE CHAIR AS KEEPER
OF INFORMATION

The title of this chapter may at first seem unusual, both in its implications and its inclusion in this book. However, the information-managing role is vital to many of the topics that will be discussed, as it has an impact on dealings with deans, other administrators, and external constituents as well as with individual faculty and the faculty at large. It also impacts student-related considerations such as recruitment, retention, and follow-up after graduation (i.e., alumni relations). Other applications will be revealed throughout this chapter.

The basic premise is that information, whether in the form of raw data or analyses derived from data, is essential for effectively representing the department to its internal and external constituents. The forms of information necessary for these uses are many and varied. Data are collected in different places by different offices, thus requiring planning and forethought by the department for assembling and archiving. This, of course, means that the chair must take responsibility for having the appropriate information at hand for a variety of applications. To expect all of the desired information to be neatly filed in the chair's office may not be necessary, but the chair should know where to find institutional data on short notice. Department-specific data, especially that collected by the department, would be expected to be filed locally. The types of data to be collected, the constituents who might request or be influenced by the data, and matching these two variables will be discussed in this chapter. Ways that these customized datasets may be used to effect change, improve performance, promote success, celebrate achievement, and counter criticism will also be considered.

Data to Collect

Some types of academic data are always available in the form of bulletins describing degree programs and courses. Included will be options such as honors programs and special opportunities such as service-learning, internships, and undergraduate research. There are other types of data that are often difference-makers in some applications. Examples might include student success rates (degree completion) and placement (jobs, professional school, graduate school) after graduation. Also important are student support services such as tutoring, mentoring, and advising. Graduate program data might include number of applicants, number of acceptances, profile data on accepted applicants, graduation rates, and placement.

Department data in terms of course and total enrollments, number of majors, number of graduates, and changes over time are important in requests for new positions, monitoring program demand, and identifying opportunities for growth. These data are usually collected centrally but are available to departments. Departments can add interpretations and explanations for growth or diminished results in certain components of the information. Departments also have direct access to faculty workload data including such items as one-on-one directed work that sometimes is not included in institutional data. Other aspects of faculty work are derived from annual reports. These include productivity in research and scholarship and activities in departmental, institutional, professional, and community service. In addition, efforts to improve teaching that are not reflected in teaching load analyses are listed in these reports but usually not elsewhere. There are many items in some of these categories, and chairs should know where to go to retrieve this information. There are other types of atypical information that can be valuable to departments. An example might be how alumni view the impact of their educational experience on their career. Departments can sometimes get this information through their own alumni surveys or through those used by the institution. Should the latter be the case, the department needs to be aware that this information is available.

Data Customers

What constituents might request or be influenced by information provided by the department? There are many, and they may be generally categorized as internal or external. Internal constituents may be faculty—including those in the department. Faculty members are often unaware of many of the department's operations, a problem that manifests itself more in large, complex units. They may have pieces of information derived from reports and announcements but do not internalize this information unless it is necessary for their use when they receive it. On other matters, they may have opinions but not the complete information to support those opinions. Even basic information about the accomplishments of the colleague next door is often not known.

Other internal users of department information include the dean and other administrators. They have global information on department operations, but are frequently unaware of the reasons behind or nature of enrollment trends, student placement data, student accomplishments, and faculty-student interactions. Other campus units may have an interest in department data. For example, a professional school such as medicine or dentistry may have an interest in science departments that prepare students for application to their schools or may be seeking research collaborations among faculty in both schools. Current students are another constituency with whom departments may wish to share data and other information. An example would be graduate program opportunities.

The array of external constituents that may request department information or that may be targeted by the department to receive such information is extensive and diverse. Potential students, either high school or current college students elsewhere, would be sent an information set with the intention of recruiting them to the department as undergraduate or graduate majors. Similarly, departments may contact professionals in the K–12 system to inform them of local academic opportunities. Administrators and counselors could pass this information on to students who are considering choices for continuing their education. Former students may be sent a different dataset to demonstrate department improvement and additions with the hopes of reengaging them through service on advisory boards or as mentors and perhaps as a precursor to soliciting them to contribute in some way to department projects and programs.

Some external constituents fall into a group that might be labeled political or quasi-political. These would include governing boards or trustees, legislators, and accreditation organizations. The latter typically gather certain types of information that the institution and department can anticipate. Political groups may ask for isolated pieces of information and datasets that are incomplete in scope and thus can lead to misinterpretation. Special care must be taken such that requests from organizations whose members are not derived from the academy are met with accurate, complete, and appropriately interpreted information. This is a challenge because the report must be short and focused—not routine characteristics of some of our work.

Other possible external stakeholders who might receive or request information from departments are parents of potential students. They would be interested in specialized pieces of information, such as student support services available in the department or employment trends for recent graduates. Peer institutions would be interested in department information that enables them to compare their programs and gain ideas for their own development. Collaboration and exchange programs might result from this type of information sharing. Finally, employers may be interested in knowing how the department has prepared its graduates for the workforce. The focus for many will be on what students know and what they can do. The data here might include information on technical skills, experience with instrumentation, oral and written proficiency, team projects, and problem-solving skills. With some careful thought, these data can be culled from student experiences and assembled in ways that allow distribution to potential employers. Strong programs that meet these expectations will likely see improved student placement results and perhaps new or expanded internship programs that will make graduates even more attractive to employers.

Assembling Relevant Datasets

Outlined thus far have been many types of data and information on the department and many possible end-users. Each constituent group would be interested in a unique subset of that information, and it is important to omit extraneous information; otherwise the reader could lose interest before getting to crucial parts of what has been provided. This makes tailoring the vast body of data an important exercise. For example, a governing board might be interested in the number of students in the program, trends over time, graduation rates, student placement, and costs per student. The latter would be information from administration that is not of particular interest to other groups. On the other hand, high school students may want to know about career opportunities, student organizations, internships, undergraduate research, international programs, and what students in the program have to say about it. Accrediting groups would want to know about faculty productivity, reference resources (institutional data), program effectiveness (assessment data), graduation rates, and curriculum content. Print or electronic newsletters are still effective ways to communicate with alumni. While none of these is complete, the concept of partially overlapping yet distinct sets of information and data would be called for, depending on the intended audience.

Using Distinct Datasets

Packaging information and datasets into usable formats results in the development of several instruments. For the purposes of attracting attention, there are brochures, web sites, and posters that may be displayed at various events. Departments, schools, and institutions usually prepare annual reports containing some of the information that has been discussed. There are also specialized uses for the data collected, such as self-studies for program reviews, grant applications, accreditation reports, and random requests from school or local media and public relations departments, as well as requests from trustees, legislature, or higher administration.

Disseminating relevant department information and data to constituent groups, both internal and external, happens in many ways. For some constituents, students particularly, print materials are largely obsolete due to the extensive use of the Internet. However, contacting parents with a similar set of information may still be done effectively with brochures. Others may gather preliminary information from web sites but also want a permanent copy to keep for review. At this time, it seems that both modes of distribution are important. Internal transmission of department information can be accomplished through department and school annual reports. These are still largely print reports, although the move to electronic versions is inevitable. The specialized reports mentioned previously would be print versions or one-time electronic assemblies of selected information. Regardless of the outlet mechanism for department-relevant information, constant updating is necessary.

While the entire responsibility for assembling and parceling out this information into constituent-relevant packets does not fall to the chair, the chair should either possess or have access to the bulk of this information. For the rest, knowing who to call or who to request to obtain the information will be essential. Trust that faculty will not know most of this. Web site and brochure development and report authoring can be delegated to others who have been provided with the appropriate information resources.

Improvement Resulting From Data Dissemination

In addition to the benefits derived from providing appropriate information and data to external constituents, there are other benefits that can accrue for the department. One benefit involves faculty members as the primary data customers. Just as many faculty fail to be fully informed about their colleagues' contributions, they are also unaware of department operations that do not directly involve them. For example, they may not know how many majors the department offers or whether the department is adding or losing majors. Some of the data collected can be used in concise ways to keep faculty informed. Solid data are convincing and will draw the attention of department colleagues. For example, diminishing enrollments in an elective course for majors or in a nonmajors offering may alert the department to look at scheduling patterns, instructor assignments, enrollment trends in other units, course content, new competition, and other variables that may impact enrollment. Similarly, alumni surveys indicating lack of preparation in certain knowledge and skills areas should stimulate curricular revision.

Good information can also lead to renewed efforts for improvement when the dean and higher administration respond to department information. Appropriately formulated and organized department data can demonstrate how the department is working effectively toward campus goals and objectives. It can also indicate areas of opportunity that will not be realized without new investments. As will be discussed in Chapter 10, programs, data, and even interesting anecdotal pieces will be noted by deans and other administrators and used as sound bites in speeches, campus addresses, and interactions with the media. This is great publicity for the department and a boost to morale.

Summary

Department chairs represent the focal point for information flow into and out of the department. The chair role in sharing information with department faculty members will be discussed elsewhere; the primary interest here is the concept that the chair is the hub through which information about the department and its operation flows to campus and external constituents. Long-term and internally appointed chairs should naturally assume this role while chairs newly appointed from outside will spend a good deal of time and energy assembling or identifying the repositories of department data.

Most requests for department information come to the chair. Some information may be held in the personal files of the chair while other datasets may be kept by others on the faculty or by institutional offices. Thus data is a file or phone call away. Important categories of data are those on students and academic programs, research productivity, and professional service and civic engagement activities. There are many subcategories of these broad areas.

Requests for department information or information that the department takes the initiative in dispensing may be targeted to a wide variety of constituents. What is assembled must take into account the proposed audience and the purpose for providing or sending the information. Assembling a dataset for the governing board or an accreditation agency will consist of different data and have a different purpose than an information piece designed to recruit undergraduate students. Chairs must have or be able to direct those assigned to assemble data to appropriate information sources. While advice on how to present data and market it appropriately can be sought from external experts, the department must take ultimate responsibility for what is provided and how it is presented.

5

QUALITY ASSURANCE

Chairs are responsible for assuring quality in the department. That statement may not produce many dissenters, but it should raise many questions. What does quality mean? What defines quality in our departments? How do we go about measuring quality in what we do? These are not easily answered questions. The complexity of this issue is intensified by the fact that many departments have unique missions that require different evaluative measures as evidence for meeting quality goals. Beyond the variables of differing unit missions, the concept of quality is defined in variable ways by faculty and administrators, which can be problematic for chairs as they try to articulate this idea. Faculty might define a quality department as one with excellent faculty, based on scholarly achievements, who deliver excellent academic programs. Administrators may define quality departments as those that deliver products related to the larger goals of the academy. These may include high enrollments, rising graduation rates, multiple examples of civic engagement, and similar measures that certainly have favorable quantitative dimensions but do not necessarily guarantee quality.

While some of the measures mentioned may constitute elements of quality, a much larger view involving multiple measures is needed for assessing the quality of an academic unit. Wergin (2003) thoroughly defines quality in academic programs and delineates institutional cultures that promote reflection and faculty collaboration as ways of monitoring and maintaining program quality.

The types of mechanisms used to measure quality are highly variable and can include a number of concrete as well as environmental factors. This chapter will discuss two universal mechanisms commonly used by higher education to assess quality. The effectiveness of both of these mechanisms relies on the thoroughness of those who collect and report the data and the scrutiny with which the information is analyzed. These methods involve ways of documenting where the department was, where it is currently, how it arrived there, and what steps it might take in the future.

Assessment

One of the most common methods used to measure the quality of department academic programs is learning outcomes achieved by its students. Some of the principles of this type of assessment also apply to other elements of department function. The assessment of learning outcomes is largely targeted toward undergraduate degree programs or individual courses. An exhaustive review of learning outcomes assessment is not possible here, nor would it be necessary with the wealth of books and articles on the topic by recognized experts. Instead, some general features of assessment will be presented along with suggestions on how to start this process and some insights on what to expect from the department.

If assessment is defined as a mechanism for determining the quality of an academic program followed by changes that seek to improve the findings, then assessment can be extended beyond student learning to include many other functions and services the department seeks to deliver. For example, if the department defines itself as a research department but assessment of the research function reveals that the number of publications (a measure of research productivity) has declined 40% over five years with the same number of faculty members, then there is data to drive discussions to improve the situation.

One of the basic tenets for assessing student learning outcomes is that the process be faculty-driven as opposed to administratively prescribed. After all, who better is there to define what students ought to know and be able to do than those who design and deliver the curricula? While this makes sense at one level, it must be realized that most faculty were not educated and prepared in an environment where they learned how to teach, and they may feel that whatever was good enough for them should be good enough for the present day. But that was before the accountability movement. The demand that faculty think about expected outcomes (beyond exams and term papers), design measures to determine whether objectives have been met, make changes for improvement, and then repeat the cycle is difficult for many of them to accept, especially when their responsibilities continue to expand. An interesting note is that faculty members recognize that the major proponents of innovation in assessment do not come from the traditional disciplines or from research-intensive (except perhaps in assessment research) units at major universities. Thus there is a credibility issue regarding assessment in some academic cultures. Faculty involvement in assessment, while it seems natural, is not always necessary. Many large institutions realize that assessment does not need to be overwhelmingly burdensome. They use staff to deal with assessment, and oftentimes faculty may be unaware it is taking place.

Those who work in assessment realize that not all faculty members will participate and that assessment can be done without full buy-in. There will be some faculty who welcome the opportunity to see how they and the department are doing. Another larger group will be neutral but cooperative in the effort. The few who are staunchly opposed will not matter. The role of the chair is to seek and support those who would be interested in this work and to let faculty know how important it is. Even if all do not value the exercise outright, they can at least value the concept that conducting an assessment will free them from criticism, sanctions, and persistent requests—better known by faculty members as harassment—and allow them to do the things they really value.

In defining desired outcomes for student learning, it should be noted that this is not a process that sums the total of all outcomes to be expected from a single lecture in one course. Such lists may be useful for directing student study in preparation for exams and as examples of outcomes for an entire course, but the list of outcomes for one program cannot be hundreds of items. In fact, 10 to 12 are about the maximum. Surely faculty can define a dozen big-picture concepts that can be converted into statements detailing what students should be able to list/recite/diagram/label/explain/create/demonstrate/perform, and so on. These are plain and simple statements with one action about one item. The next step is determining how to measure whether the desired result has taken place. This can be done by a variety of techniques, some of which are questions imbedded within exams. Other methods are through performances, portfolios, specialized tests, assignments, capstone courses, and culminating experiences such as internships and research.

The final piece to effective assessment—and one frequently forgotten—is using the data generated to inform the improvement process. That is, you desire an outcome and find it in seven cases out of ten. What changes can be made in the program to increase learning in this area to eight or nine out of ten? The objective is to become involved in a process of continual improvement.

Program Review

Program review was presented in Chapter 1 in the context of chair responsibilities and will appear again in Chapter 22 where effecting change is discussed. This chapter will consider ways to ensure that the strenuous and time-consuming process of undergoing a program review is regarded as an opportunity for validation and advice on improvement rather than just a large amount of work done to satisfy administrators. Chairs play a crucial role in shaping such faculty attitudes and in presenting the department so that the ways that the review team addresses and evaluates the department can lead to improvement in how the department is viewed or can provide advice for overcoming obstacles to its success. It is crucial that the department approach program review as something beneficial to the unit and its faculty and not simply as an exercise in complying with an administrative mandate. This latter concern has been cited by Wergin (2003) as one reason why program reviews frequently do not result in quality improvements.

Program reviews can be considered as a component of assessment. They usually evaluate far more than the effectiveness of the undergraduate curriculum by evaluating the department work in research and scholarship, service of all types, graduate programming, and other relevant activities. Exceptions to this are targeted program reviews where a department is evaluated in a very specific dimension of its work, for example, an evaluation of program strength relative to the appropriateness to enter into graduate programming. A typical program review would include evidence of curricula effectiveness and course or program-based learning outcomes. In addition, it would have more global measures of effectiveness resulting from alumni and employer surveys and student placements in professional and graduate programs.

Emphasizing the assessment element of the program review will not win the enthusiastic support of many faculty members. Usually those who support outcomes assessment realize this and are pleased when a few faculty members champion the cause and generate useful data to document effectiveness and direct improvement. Program reviews ideally provide the department with ideas and advice to improve what exists; identify new opportunities for department growth; identify or make a case for new external and internal resources, respectively; suggest fiscal gain potential through cost saving or new revenues; and even provide advice on new workload distributions to enhance overall productivity in areas recognized as top priorities. The list here can be modified by the addition or substitution of other items that may resonate with the objectives of a given department. Using this approach, the prospects for gaining faculty buy-in for participating in a program review are likely to increase.

Another outcome for a program review that may interest faculty members is related to certification or validation of unit strengths. The exceptions, of course, would be departments torn by disagreement and dissension and departments, identified as not performing to expectations, that refuse to take steps to change for the better. These types of departments are often mandated to undergo a program review for exactly these reasons. Academic departments and their faculties tend to become insulated in their own domains. While they may have colleagues at other institutions where conditions differ, these variables are usually a mix of plusses and minuses. For example, the home department may have a small budget with the funds for part-time instruction provided out of the dean's resources. A colleague's institution may have a much larger budget but may also be responsible for part-time instructional costs. Direct comparisons are very difficult to make. The point is that most departments do not really know how well they are doing under their working conditions relative to other units where the conditions may be much different. An effective program review team will bring a variety of perspectives to the review and may be able to identify aspects of department work that are particularly meritorious. For example, the chemistry department may be commended for providing undergraduate student access to sophisticated equipment in its lab courses despite a meager budget, or the religious studies department may receive accolades for its scholarly output despite demanding teaching loads. Just as a department may not realize where they stand in a relative sense, other campus units and campus administration may be unaware of the real achievement of some its units. A thoughtful program review can validate this excellence.

The Review Team

The first step in preparing for a standard program review is to appoint a team to conduct the review. Institutions may have certain guidelines for this, but if they do not or if department input is allowed, several factors might be considered by the department in making its team member recommendations. The assumption is that the department wants an honest evaluation and some help in identifying the next steps in its improvement or evolution. Because most teams have some external members, the advice is to select one or more seasoned professors or chairs from sister departments at similar institutions that are regarded as more advanced, that is, institutions already at the point to which the department may aspire. Presumably these other departments were once at the same point as the department under review and have found ways to move ahead successfully. Others who may be asked to join the team could be community individuals who might employ graduates and provide a perspective on the usefulness of the education offered by the department. At the same time, the department can share its activities, interests, values, and culture with an external constituent to promote collaboration and understanding. Our institution does this and also includes at least one campus representative on program review teams. This promotes cross-campus information sharing and allows other units to learn more about the educational opportunities available to their students through other departments.

Preparation

The next step in the process, and the most time-consuming and critical to overall success, is preparation of the self-study. Preliminary considerations in this work are the motives for the review—what do the department and the institution want to derive from the review? The goals may be common to both, totally different, or some place in between. If institutional guidelines dictate the content areas of the self-study and information relevant to depart-

ment interests cannot be accommodated, permission for appendixes or a second document may be sought. Once this has been
established, the relevant information about the department is collected and assembled to construct the self-study.

Gathering the relevant data, combining it with appropriate
text, and posing questions and requests for advice to the review
team are major tasks. Writing the self-study typically falls to the
chair, although delegation of some segments to specific faculty
members and sometimes even staff may be possible and wise. For
example, a section on assessment may be best assembled by the
department faculty member serving on committees that define
disciplinary outcomes, collect the data, and monitor changes
made to achieve improvement. The section on graduate programs
where admissions data, retention, and graduate placement data
are presented may best be completed by the director of graduate
programs. The chair should oversee all elements of the report to
ensure continuity of presentation and style. Since faculty members
will want to have some involvement in the process, inviting comments on drafts of the study is an appropriate way to accomplish
this. This document reflects the contributions, challenges, needs,
and aspirations of the department community and input from all
members should be invited.

An important consideration for planning the self-study is to
balance the need for providing information with the absorption
capacities of the review team members. There is nothing more
frustrating than reading a final report that laments the lack of
information on a topic that was presented in exquisite detail in the
self-study. There is a danger that if readers become bogged down
in the detail of one section, they will skip it and peruse the text.
Thus it is best to present a document where the most important
data are presented in tables or figures accompanied by crisp text
that indicates trends, explains positive and negative features, and
defines other factors that influenced the data. If there is additional
data that provides more detailed insight, it can be presented as an

appendix found in a separate document. In this way the reader will continue to be attentive to the primary information and will consult the secondary data only if there is strong interest or time.

The final preliminary consideration for preparing the self-study is to keep in mind who will read it. Readers include the review team, faculty, the dean, and other campus administrators. Other department chairs may request a copy as a model for their upcoming program review or copies may be distributed across departments to inform others about the department's work. In preparing the report, be aware that it will serve as an educational piece for multiple constituents. It is also a document that will elicit suggestions, recommendations, and evaluations for the department and its higher administration as to what needs attention, what resources are necessary, and what the department is doing well. Since improvement is a major impetus for the review, the report should document areas where the department is weak. For example, if the department wants a vigorous graduate program but is unable to attract many qualified applicants, then it should ask for suggestions to improve graduate recruiting.

The Self-Study

Before outlining content areas for the self-study, it will be assumed that the program review is an inclusive one rather than targeted to a specific area of department responsibility. A helpful starting point for the document is to present the mission statements for the institution and for the department to specifically state how that particular discipline hopes to contribute to the college or university. At larger universities, intermediary statements of mission at the school or college levels may be included. These statements help the team place the work of the department within the context of the larger institution. (The lack of a department mission statement may indicate that it is time to develop one.) Mission statements can be followed by an abbreviated history of the institution and department, including the findings and results of its last program review.

Arrangement of the information may take many forms, but the overall contents described here are fairly standard. The section on academic programs might include a listing of all degree and certificate programs offered and instruction that provides service to other units. The latter reflects the department's contributions within the overall institution. Reporting student enrollments in department degree programs is essential, and these data should be presented in a timeframe so trends are evident. This section might also list degrees conferred, graduate placement data, and alumni surveys. Because some of these datasets can be extensive, a summary might suffice for the self-study with more detailed data presented in an appendix. Within this section the report may make future projections based on history and the advent of new programs. It may also ask the review team for advice on continuation of programs with flagging enrollments and the likelihood of success of courses or programs the department is considering for development.

Another standard section introduces department faculty members to the team and provides an abbreviated look at the contribution of each to the department. These are not full curriculum vitae; those would be found in an appendix. However, the section would contain research areas, disciplinary specialization, perhaps a listing of active collaborations, and other noteworthy features including major service or administrative assignments. A separate listing relating curricula offerings and faculty contributions would illustrate teaching workloads relative to research or scholarship contributions. Here the types of instruction (lectures, labs, clinical, studio, graduate or undergraduate, etc.) should be identified so readers will know the level and extent of each contribution. The rationale for differential workloads, if they exist, should be provided as well as some information about the criteria used for hiring, promotion, and tenure and merit increments. The latter can also be combined in a separate section. In addition, there may be a section on staff if the department is a large one with specialized technical and support personnel.

There will usually be a research and scholarship section in the self-study. This will be particularly prominent in departments where there are major expectations in this area of faculty work. Data illustrating faculty productivity in this area would include publications of various types, professional presentations, performances, invitations to other campuses and professional meetings, consulting activities, patents, and similar scholarly contributions. Of particular importance to disciplines in technological and scientific areas is external funding, which represents success in highly competitive arenas where the quality of the ideas and the track record of the applicant are the major determining factors. As in the case with student data, these types of information should be listed annually with corrections made to reflect the number of faculty contributing in a given year. Trends again become important considerations for the review team members to consider in their assessment and in the formulation of their recommendations.

Another section of self-study might include information on the service activities of faculty. This may be a particular interest in those disciplines where community service is a common and critical component of its contribution. Examples would include units in nursing, education, and social work where much of the faculty members' professional work is done external to the institution. Faculty appointments to national and international boards, editorships, and professional societies are also reflective of faculty stature in their fields.

Two final sections of the report of great interest concern quality indicators and resources, including finances or the budget available to the department. Thus far, lists have contained data on numbers of students, types of degrees, faculty assignments, research productivity, and other department activities. The only academic quality information is that derived from alumni and employer surveys and faculty quality data derived from listings in curriculum vitae. In the section on department quality, the survey data may be included along with assessment information and other measures used by the department to monitor and document its effectiveness. Summary data on student satisfaction surveys, other measures of teaching effectiveness (graduating student surveys, peer evaluations, peer review of instructional materials, etc.), and student placement in graduate programs and professional schools can be listed. In addition, a listing of faculty awards in all areas of faculty work could be derived from entries in curriculum vitae to provide a measure of the faculty quality and recognition across all areas for faculty work and interest.

The final dataset to consider is department resources. Department productivity, quality, and morale are often linked to available resources. Modest accomplishments may be particularly noteworthy if achieved with very meager resources. Resources include factors beyond dollars in the department budget, such as clerical, technical, and student services support, space, equipment, and community connections. The variable elements of these resources are many and cannot be listed here. A listing of resources and their levels should allow the reader, regardless of discipline, to determine whether they are luxurious, adequate, or limiting.

Information on the department budget will require some explanation in the text. All chairs are familiar with department budgeting in their own schools. However, there are many budget models, so to simply report a dollar number representing what is available to the department will be insufficient to the outside members of the review team. The budget model in place at your school or institution needs to be explained in terms of what is and is not included in the department allocation, how budgets are determined, what drives them down or up (are there incentives), and how department funds are expended by generally recognized categories. For example, a $4 million budget in one department may not be as lucrative as a $1 million budget in another equal-size department if it includes responsibilities for all faculty and staff salaries and fringe benefits, all part-time salaries, and all graduate assistant support and if the department with the smaller budget can tap other resources for these expenses. Another variable is whether budgets are constructed based on negotiated amounts in specified categories or are given as totally flexible dollars. The final tabulation of budget should again be historical, reflecting changes over at least the most recent years.

Compensation is clearly a part of the budget. Because they are public employees, salary information for faculty and staff at public institutions is often available to the public. Some institutions make this information easily available while others do the opposite. Private institutions may have different philosophies on providing salary information to the general public. In any case, it is inappropriate to list individual faculty salaries in the self-study. If the review team wishes to see these data, they may be made available upon request either before or during the campus visit. Average salaries at the different faculty ranks is usually sufficient information. Such a request may be forthcoming if unusually high numbers of faculty are taking positions elsewhere because of compensation concerns. A listing of the most recent salary range for new hires and what type of sign-on package is offered to new hires should be included in the study. The package goes beyond a startup fund and can include reduced teaching load, assistants, space, and other resource concessions. This will give the review team information critical to making suggestions to the department and its administration as to whether their offers are competitive enough to achieve their stated goals.

The Review Team's Visit

The self-study and accompanying appendixes are made available to members of the team several weeks before the scheduled campus visit. Department efforts to identify areas for growth and improvement will be diminished if the review team does not meet with key individuals during the visit. The visit is typically a whirlwind affair with meetings scheduled continually along with social functions where other ad hoc pieces of information are shared. Department chairs play instrumental roles in selecting campus individuals to meet with the team and are the frontline individuals in this phase of the review. Depending on institutional structure and intent of the review, meetings may be arranged with groups of department faculty (random, by rank, tenured and untenured), chairs of departments whose students are served by offerings of the department, individuals from research, admissions, and graduate offices, and perhaps some community organizations. The lead-off meeting may be with campus administration when institutional issues to be addressed are reiterated. The chair usually will then have an initial meeting in the department with the team where questions are raised regarding the information in the self-study and new information may be requested. At this time, the chair reiterates what the department hopes to learn from the team. After the visit is completed, there is usually an exit meeting where the team will offer a preliminary report as a precursor to the full report.

The Final Report

The final report will present several observations and recommendations for both the department and the institution. It should be shared with the faculty, and the chair should invite faculty responses to the review team's recommendations. The team may report on some controversial issues, such as teaching loads and faculty productivity. Faculty responses to such items should be compiled and distributed to them so all gain a sense of community sentiment. There will be recommendations with which the department will not agree because the team does not fully understand the issue or because of differing institutional cultures. For example, the review team may be more or less supportive of research than the institution and make recommendations that would distort institutional and department missions. In an example from a program review report in my department 10 years ago, the committee challenged the value of undergraduate research, stating that the learning curve for undergraduates was too steep and the return on investment too small to justify the activity. We chose not to make any changes and now see how undergraduate research has been shown to have many positive impacts on student engagement and success.

Administration will also have a copy of the report, and there will be some recommendations to which they will have to respond. Ultimately, a meeting between the chair and campus administration, including the dean, will occur to review the findings and recommendations of the review team, outline a plan for those that will be addressed, develop a rationale for not addressing some of the suggestions, and discuss what this means in terms of resources. The external members of the team were selected because they had experience at similar institutions considered more advanced than the home institution, thus they had been where the department was and had successfully moved forward. These team members can provide insight on what it will take to do the same. This is not just a new resource issue but may involve policy change and elevated expectations for current faculty. In many ways this is a reality check for all parties concerned. They will indicate that a high-quality department can or cannot be built on the current budget with the present number of faculty, the graduate program can or cannot be expected to grow employing the same stipend level, faculty scholarship can or cannot flourish within the current space limitations, teaching loads are or are not too high, and so forth. In the end there will be things for everyone to feel good about, things for everyone to work on, and a rethinking of goals based on current resources, policies, and values.

Summary

The department chair is responsible for assuring the quality of the work done by the unit. Academic departments are responsible for productivity in teaching, research, and service. Within each of these there are many subcategories that can be subject to quantitative and qualitative measurement. Quality of academic programs and student learning are of particular concern as evidenced by the current emphasis on assessment. The concept of assessment will not be embraced by all members of the faculty, but chairs should realize that full participation is not necessary to create an effective program. The basic principles of assessment are those that are routinely used in other aspects of our work. We establish programs to achieve certain outcomes and use end measures to see how we did. Once feedback has been gathered, it is analyzed and used to direct changes in the program. Translated to the program or course level, the first decision is to determine what students should know or be able to do, measure these within courses or through other means, and adjust elements of the program or courses to address weaknesses in achievement. Because assessment is best rooted in the work of faculty members, the role of the chair is to emphasize the importance of the activity, to reinforce the ease with which it can be done, and to recognize the work of those who lead the effort in the department.

Overall department quality is assessed by program review. This exercise will also include student learning outcome data obtained through the assessment program. Program review is typically expanded to include all aspects of department responsibility. The process is usually administratively prescribed at certain intervals, and the administration usually has an agenda or set of criteria that it wants the review team to evaluate. This set is not often the same set that department faculty think are the key elements of unit quality. Thus there is sometimes a lack of faculty interest in the process. Chairs play the major role in motivating faculty interest and participation by setting a department agenda for the review. In preparing the self-study, the chair should invite faculty input and participation in reporting the work of the department and should utilize the expertise of the review teams to comment on group achievements, unit direction, and long-term aspirations while also seeking advice on overcoming obstacles to future success. In this way the overall institution will receive a more comprehensive view of department quality while learning what must be done to improve performance.

6

STAYING LEGAL

As in the world at large, legal issues are a concern to department chairs, more so now than only a decade ago. An increasingly litigious society means it is necessary to adhere to institutional policy. Policies and protocols are contained in the ever-increasing amount of institutional documentation, usually handbooks or similar compilations that provide chairs with a comprehensive document to consult before action is taken. In addition to print or electronic information, chairs must have an identifiable set of human resources, including institutional legal counsel, to consult when critical issues arise or when they are uncertain about how to proceed.

In many functions, the chair is an official representative of the university, and what the chair does can be construed as accurately representing the policy position of the institution. However, some actions a chair can take may place the institution at risk, such as inaccurate statements to university personnel or to external constituents. The chair is also charged with enforcing a variety of university policies and informing others in the department of these mandates to ensure that the entire unit is in compliance. An example would be human resources policies in hiring. While some of the hiring is done by the department and is a direct chair responsibility, at many institutions there are faculty-initiated hires associated with technical and professional positions funded by external grants and contracts. Although funded by others, these hires fall under institutional policy, and thus the chair must make certain that searches and hires comply with the rules in place.

Another area where chairs must be vigilant is in maintaining confidentiality, especially with regard to student information. Student files must be kept in a safe place, and faculty must be informed that the old practice of posting grades with official (name or full identification number) student identification is no longer acceptable. Attention needs to be paid to new policies governing the use of human subjects. While many policies emanated from work in the medical field, there are now safeguards that extend to survey research and the use of data collected from classroom research. These may be subject to limitation under the new regulations. This situation is usually handled by filing a description of the proposed work with a review committee that will determine whether any limitations need to be placed on the work to protect the subjects. Another area concerns policies requiring the disclosure of conflict of interest. This policy is the result of situations where funded research appears to benefit a corporation in which the researcher has a significant investment. Many federal agencies will not review an external proposal from a principle investigator unless a complete conflict of interest disclosure form is on file in the research office of the institution. In these cases, it may fall to the chair to inform the faculty and to monitor their compliance with disclosure.

There are some academic legalities worth mentioning here. What we offer to students in terms of curriculum and expectations for a degree may change over the course of a given student's time at the institution. Upon arriving on campus, a student may have received a brochure, visited the department web site, or been provided a course bulletin at orientation. Any updates to requirements must be promptly included in these materials and clearly noted as replacing the old. This is more of a problem for printed material than web material. At the time of advising, students should be provided with updated information verbally and in writing. Many institutions have policies regulating how requirements may change for a student already enrolled. Typically, the old requirements are grandfathered in for a specified period of time unless the student elects to follow the new requirements. If the student wishes to remain with the old requirements, and one of the courses required is no longer available, the department will need to identify a reasonable substitute.

A potential area of concern for some institutions is whether course syllabi are legally binding documents. One issue is whether a faculty member can replace a segment of the course with new material after the semester has begun. Such a change can be well-founded based on current events that may place the new content in a highly relevant context. Another example might be when time runs short and the final topics are not discussed in class. This may result from class periods lost to inclement weather, a more engaged student audience with much to say, or to poor pacing by the instructor. In any case, there are situations where some students will try to make the case that they have not received what they expected and paid for. As result, many faculty are now titling these documents as "tentative" syllabi.

Personnel Issues

There are no more delicate issues in an organization than ones that deal with people and their careers. In an academic department this can mean dealing with staff and faculty members regarding merit compensation, advancement, and dismissal. While legal aspects are more likely to involve the last, there are also grievances resulting from merit pay and promotion decisions.

Staff

Staff present a distinct situation from that encountered with faculty members. Personnel issues for staff are typically governed by policies established by institutional human resources departments. For unionized campuses, the regulations are established through collective bargaining. Staff pay rates are established within certain parameters based on their employee category; staff are promoted only after a job function review by human resources, and their termination is allowed only under specific guidelines established outside of the department. Thus the scenario of a new chair bringing in a new staff team to run the department is unlikely to happen. There are instances where changes are allowed if an existing position can be eliminated because it is no longer necessary, and a new one, with new qualifications, can be created. The incumbent may or may not be qualified for the new position. If a staff member is not performing up to expectations, the chair must keep detailed documentation of the inadequate performance and provide written evaluations reiterating the need for improvement in order to ultimately remove a staff member. Chairs are encouraged to conduct regular staff evaluations and maintain close contact with human resources to make sure that cases of poor performance are appropriately documented and all appropriate offices receive copies.

Tenure Candidates

The probationary period preceding the tenure decision is one of the most anxiety-filled times for faculty members. Candidates are working to achieve the milestones they have been told will earn them the prize, and department faculty are hoping for success as validation that their original hiring decision was correct and that the institutional investment will earn dividends. This seems a reasonable scenario for most colleges and universities. There are, however, instances where a hire does not work out and tenure is denied or a non-reappointment decision is made prior to the tenure decision. These are difficult decisions for all parties involved, and can sometimes lead to a string of internal appeals and, ultimately, legal action. It is very important that institutions have carefully crafted policies on faculty evaluation and documentation of performance and that the chair and department committees follow them in all cases to avoid any legal ramifications of a negative decision. There is an abundance of examples where inadequate review and feedback or not meeting the requirements of due process have led to the overturning of tenure denial. That unfortunate circumstance can cost the college financially or saddle it long term with a faculty member whose performance has been deemed insufficient.

Faculty Tenure Decisions

In recent years there has been a renewed commitment in the form of absolute requirements for faculty annual reviews. While this has been prompted to some extent by new policies on post-tenure review (a review process directed at senior and other tenured faculty), it presents an opportunity to look at this process relative to what is expected of faculty members and what departments can do to enhance faculty productivity. While aspects of the annual review are developmental, there are summative applications as well. The tenure decision is probably the most important summative point; at this time, the decision will be made whether, after 5.2 years (the standard period nationally) in probationary status, enough has been accomplished to warrant a positive tenure recommendation.

The annual review process should provide a roadmap to tenure, outlining what has been done and what remains to be done. The review should not be automatically glowing and positive but rather honest and to the point regarding both accomplishments and deficiencies. Some institutions also have annual reappointment reviews with or without more formal third-year reviews. These reviews are conducted by appointed or elected faculty committees. The summaries of these committees must also be honest in delineating successes or providing accolades where warranted and in identifying shortcomings that must be addressed. If annual review feedback is not consistent with reappointment committee feedback, the chair needs to convene the department to reconsider its expectations to ensure that probationary faculty members receive a consistent message. An almost certain overturning of a denial of tenure or reappointment will occur if all prior annual reviews and reappointments reports are filled with positive statements until the final axe falls the next year. The advice here is to be unabashedly positive about the faculty member who has done in three years more than is required for 5.2 years; to be cautious and focused on the required objectives of faculty on track for success; and to be frank with someone who is lagging behind schedule. In this way the department is prepared to adapt to change (improvement or deterioration) in future performance and is likely to have its decisions upheld upon appeal.

Should a recommendation denying tenure or reappointment be rendered regarding a faculty member in the department, remember that it is just a recommendation, the first step in a long process. The chair is either part of this recommendation or makes a separate recommendation. The case then moves up through the dean's office and possibly to other school or campus committees until it reaches upper administration. Documentation in support of the recommendation is usually required to accompany the paperwork and may include past annual and/or reappointment reviews. The history of the case, how the faculty member was evaluated, and how he or she was directed to corrective action and offered support to achieve the required results will be a part of the record. The documentation will reveal as much about the developmental work of the chair and the senior faculty members on the review committees as it does about the faculty member. It should be recognized that as the case moves further from the department, reviewers will be less familiar with the individual and the expectations of the department. Thus accurate documentation becomes their primary tool in determining whether to support the decision. While there are several people involved in the process, it is the chair who must make certain that all parties are evaluated equitably, documented carefully, and recommended thoughtfully for this process to serve the institution and its faculty.

Departments and Students

There are also legal issues that arise between departments and students. Cases can involve the chair directly or indirectly through a faculty member. One type of interaction is a student appeal because of unfair treatment that usually, but not always, is an issue about grades. Parents can sometimes intervene on behalf of sons and daughters and will call the chair if they do not receive satisfactory information from the instructor. There are some guidelines to keep in mind with these cases. Chairs know that there are rigorous courses in the department evaluated according to strict guidelines precisely described in the syllabi. And there are always students who just miss the acceptable grade cut-off and those who "have always been A students," thus implying or stating that something is wrong with the instructor. In these cases the chair is polite, measured in responding to the concerns, and does not promise anything but to check into the situation with the instructor. In the vast majority of cases, the grade will be fairly given, and the chair will report that to the student or the parent. It is inappropriate to discuss the student's individual scores with the parent without the consent of the student, thus restricting the detail of the report to a parent. Other cases may involve instructors who have some history of being less precise in accounting for grade distinctions, thus requiring a more detailed conversation with the faculty member to make certain everything was evaluated in an equitable manner.

Academic Misconduct

A far more profound chair- or faculty-student interaction with legal ramifications is the one that results from a charge of academic misconduct. Misconduct includes being disruptive in class, cheating, plagiarism, falsification, facilitation, and similar dishonest behaviors. Many believe that these actions have been on the rise in recent years, driven by diminished student engagement, lack of appropriate work ethic, and the convenience of the Internet to assemble materials for assignments. The sanctions for such behaviors can go beyond a failing assignment or course grade to include dismissal. Because the stakes are high, some students will take legal action to avoid having their academic career, and possibly work career, permanently tainted.

Experiences with cheating and plagiarism vary among institutions, but there are set procedures to follow when students are charged with such offenses. Chairs should be familiar with or have at hand these procedures for themselves and for their faculty, both full- and part-time, who may allege such charges. Protocols may vary, but the first step is usually a meeting called by the faculty member with the student or students involved. Some students will admit to the transgression, allowing the faculty member to place any one of a number of possible sanctions against the student(s). The dean of students is also notified of the case. Other students will deny the charge, forcing the situation to the next level. This may involve the chair or it may involve the dean for academic affairs with a notice sent to the dean of students. The next steps may include a hearing before a committee of faculty members and perhaps some students, as well as other steps, on up to and including campus administration.

These steps are designed to provide due process for students. However, each step resembles a hearing, and the faculty member must return to present the evidence and respond to questions. Cases may drag on for months and can be overturned at any time, leaving the faculty member no recourse. When students in the class learn that a student who has cheated (and students know far more about this than the faculty) escapes sanctions, it diminishes the integrity of the institution and its policies. The honest students are the real victims in these cases. The seemingly endless appeals allowed have a quenching effect on the faculty member's enthusiasm about enforcing honest behavior, and it must be realized that many instances of cheating, and to a lesser degree, plagiarism, are not pursued by faculty members because of fear of being over-turned and a reluctance to spend months pursing the case.

Recommendations here are for more than chairs. Chairs need to know the procedure and support faculty who have uncov-ered and want to pursue bona fide instances of misconduct. The integrity of the institutions must be preserved, and students who honestly do their work must be supported. For institutions, the recommendation is to streamline the policy and procedures for such cases to support the enforcement of academic integrity on campus. While having a hotly contested case "go away" with no sanctions may provide some short-term relief to the institution, not rooting out and sanctioning dishonesty will result in a negative long-term image.

Sexual Harassment and ADA Issues

Two issues with serious legal ramifications deserve special men-tion, one because its many manifestations will appear regularly and raise many questions, and the other because of the potentially serious impact it can have on the department and institution. The issues are those related to claims of sexual harassment and to the needs of those requiring accommodation under the Ameri-cans with Disabilities Act (ADA). In both cases, chairs need to be vigilant about how members of the department handle iden-tified instances where requests or complaints are lodged. Chairs may also need to take leadership roles in helping faculty and staff interface appropriately with those on campus assigned to facilitate and investigate potential cases where violations may exist.

Sexual Harassment

Sexual harassment occurs when there are unwelcome behaviors of a sexual nature or with sexual overtones. There are two recog-nized categories of sexual harassment. The first is the quid pro quo (this for that) form where there is a defined exchange of what is expected in order for a benefit to be received. A sexual favor is what is expected and would be rewarded with a job, a promotion, a raise, admission to a program, a favorable recommendation, a course grade, and so on. A single incident of this type is sufficient to constitute sexual harassment. The second category is hostile environment sexual harassment where there are persistent environmental conditions of a sexual nature that prevent a student or employee from working effectively. Examples may include a work area where suggestive print materials are on display, where coworkers persistently make objectionable remarks and tell suggestive jokes, where someone makes continual overtures of a romantic nature, and where other constant verbal, physical, and/or written advances that seek an intimate relationship are made. These are not single events; those would not constitute sexual harassment. There must be repeated events to constitute a hostile environment.

The common element all sexual harassment cases have is that they involve a power differential. That is, one person has some type of power over the other and can therefore use it for sexual gain or to attempt sexual gain. In higher education, positional power is the major differentiator rather than physical power, often the factor in other settings. Examples might include a professor and graduate student. Graduate students need the approval of professors for their degree, may need favorable letters of recommendation for admission to new programs or to gain employment, or may need the professor's approval to maintain visa status. While some may believe such cases that are gender-constant, this is not always the case; it is the position differential that identifies the perpetrator and the victim.

The chair's role in dealing with sexual harassment occurs at several levels. The first is in being specific and adamant that this kind of behavior will not be tolerated in the department. This stance is demonstrated by providing new employees with written materials or conducting/promoting workshops and seminars for new faculty, staff, and instructors that emphasize the seriousness of the issue, as well as providing guidelines for dealing with cases that may emerge. In addition, moving quickly to fully investigate every instance of sexual harassment will also convey the urgency with which this matter must be addressed. It should be noted that many of the court sanctions against universities in sexual harassment cases result from the universities' failures to investigate charges, hoping they will simply disappear.

In dealing with reported cases that may constitute sexual harassment of the hostile environment type (inappropriate comments and jokes, repeated requests for social interactions, etc.), the chair first needs to tell the victim to let the other person know that this type of behavior is not welcome and that he or she insists that it cease. The excuse that such behavior was not intended in a threatening way is not how the legal system will look at it. Rather, it is how action is perceived by the victim that will carry the weight. Beyond verbal requests to stop a behavior some recommend that the perpetrator be sent a letter requesting cessation and that the victim keep a log of incidents that contribute to the hostile environment. The chair may also have a conversation with the perpetrator, especially if that person is a member of the department or known to the chair. The campus office responsible for dealing with charges of sexual harassment, usually affirmative action, should be notified of the complaint and the steps taken to address it. That office may provide other steps to be taken by the victim or the chair.

There are two final considerations about this issue that warrant discussion. The first concerns the demographics of the higher education environment. Consider the major population present—students. There is reason to speculate that there are more instances of sexual harassment among students than there are between students and faculty or staff or among the populations of full-time university employees. Clearly, those involving university employees get the most attention. Sexual harassment among students is difficult to detect because it may take place outside of the classroom and away from the oversight of faculty and staff. Instances may become known when the victim confides in a faculty or staff member or when an acquaintance of the victim reports the situation. Another way to learn of these situations is through teaching assistants or other young helpers who may work in large classes. These individuals are easier for students to approach for obvious reasons. It is important that teaching assistants and other similar students receive training in steps to take in reporting and dealing with instances of sexual harassment that are brought to their attention.

The second consideration is taking steps to avoid false claims of sexual harassment. Sexual harassment is a high-profile issue and cases, whether real or manufactured, generate a great deal of media attention. They bring significant embarrassment to the university and to the individual against whom the claim is made. Even if untrue, such claims can have severe professional and personal consequences for a faculty or staff member. Most faculty members and staff are aware of this potential, but it does not hurt to remind them to meet with students with office doors open, to avoid any physical contact, and to keep the conversation away from any suggestive topics even if prompted by the student. If a student has made suggestive remarks in the past, future appointments should be made only with a trusted third party present or nearby.

The Americans with Disabilities Act (ADA)

Institutions of higher education and their employees are familiar with the mandates of this law, yet there are some areas that can be controversial in their application. The law applies to individuals with physical or mental disabilities or those perceived to have such conditions. The law forbids discrimination against individuals with such conditions with regard to employment, admission, promotion, and other career decisions. This does not mean that general conditions for these career advancements have to be modified but rather that physical or mental disabilities cannot be used to exclude them if they meet published criteria. In the academic setting, this means that those with disabilities are to be granted access to programs and that reasonable accommodations be made to facilitate their completion of those programs.

All chairs are familiar with the accommodations and renovations made to allow those with physical disabilities to have full access to what they need to be successful. Examples include changes made to assist those who use wheelchairs and other mobility assistance devices, signers used to communicate class materials to those who are deaf, and other types of assistance to provide verbal descriptions of visual material to those without sight. These and other similar accommodations are typically arranged for through a campus office charged with such responsibilities. There are some department-specific accommodations that can arise, primarily in those disciplines where laboratory and other types of active learning environments and special facilities and equipment are used. A common example might be a chemistry lab where benches are set three to four feet above floor level. A student who uses a wheelchair would not be able to work at such a bench. If a permanent lab station set lower does not exist, the department will have to accommodate the student by bringing in a temporary, mobile bench to allow the student to complete class assignments.

Other elements of the ADA where some confusion and resistance remain are those related to accommodations for those students with mental disabilities. The culture of higher education has been one that, at least to some degree, is designed to direct student learning and then to assess student success in that process. Successful students are expected to demonstrate both intellectual ability and hard work in order to be certified in that process. Professors seek to have students compete equally with each other or against a common standard with all students having access to exactly the same support, consideration, time, and guidance. The ADA changes this equation for some students. Hence, there is some overt resistance and some acquiescence that is based upon compliance rather than buy-in. In addition, there are some individual situations that trouble faculty from time to time. The solution here is to find better ways to work together and promote deeper understanding of the issues behind accommodation and academic standards. The following examples may illustrate why there is continuing tension between some faculty members and campus offices where decisions regarding allowing and defining student accommodations are made.

Student A is enrolled in a professor's course, does not perform well, and withdraws at the halfway point. The student reenrolls in the subsequent semester, this time with documentation from campus indicating the need for extra time on exams as an accommodation. The following semester, the same student enrolls in another course without the accommodation paperwork. This is perplexing to the professor—either the student is eligible or not. This raises the question as to whether the assessment for accommodation is provided according to sound guidelines that will protect academic standards and integrity. In another related example, a professor agrees to extra time for an exam and sets up a time for a proctored exam that allows 90 minutes instead of the usual 60 minutes. The student appears, completes the exam in 35 minutes, and leaves. The professor wonders whether the accommodation was necessary or appropriate.

All faculty members realize that they cannot ask the nature of the disability requiring the accommodation. In some instances, questions as to what standards of evidence are acceptable for an accommodation are answered with statements that this information does not have be disclosed. These types of responses cause some faculty to wonder whether accommodations are being made simply to be in compliance on a just-in-case basis or whether real, consistent justifications for accommodations are required. Other students in classes have raised questions about what they consider unjustified and unfair accommodations that are granted. While these cannot be taken at face value in all cases, there are instances when the students

receiving accommodations are well known to some of their class-
mates as being questionable recipients of special considerations.

What is the answer to this continuing problem? There needs
to be open communication between campus offices that determine eligibility and the academic units that make the accommodations. Faculty members need to learn about the types of
disabilities encountered and why specific accommodations are
appropriate. They also need to know the verification standards—
who makes the determination, what evidence must be submitted—for a disability to be certified. Without informed exchanges
where academic standards and equity are part of the discussion,
it is likely that these tense encounters will continue to take place.
What does not work is threatening faculty with legal action
unless they comply. Chairs might consider inviting representatives from the appropriate campus office to discuss some of these
issues. There will need to be open consideration from both sides
to make real progress.

Summary

The legal environment in higher education has changed in the
past decade. This is partially a reflection of a more legal-conscious
society and partially the result of new policies and regulations
that impact college and university operations. Department
chairs, as the result of their signature authority, have always had
an official status at the university that might be subject to legal
entanglements. Many of the underlying issues are concerned with
academic requirements, degree approvals, and other aspects of
student academics. Student misconduct issues are on the rise due
in part to the availability of technology that makes cheating and
plagiarism more tempting.

Legal aspects related to personnel have become more complex
due to new policies on leaves, employment, faculty evaluations,
and post-tenure review. Chairs need to be familiar with all of these

policies as well as the standard policies in reappointment. New regulations on the use of human subjects in research and conflict of interest policies require chair vigilance and certainty that all department personnel are aware and in compliance.

Two areas where legal ramifications have become more prominent are those dealing with sexual harassment and accommodations mandated by the Americans with Disabilities Act (ADA). American colleges and universities have had a history of turning their heads when charges of sexual harassment have been lodged, which has resulted in several successful, high-profile lawsuits. Chairs must be very public about their intolerance of sexual harassment and must back this up with prompt attention to any accusations that may be lodged. Close contact with campus offices charged with investigating and dealing with such charges is essential for chairs.

Chairs also need to work closely with the campus office responsible for assuring appropriate accommodation under ADA. Faculty members are usually informed of their specific responsibilities by a campus office. Resistance will sometimes be encountered as a result of real or perceived decisions on accommodations that are uneven or arbitrary. Chairs may need to bring faculty and ADA personnel together to better understand the issues and requirements so that accommodations can be extended to those entitled without violating what faculty feel are sound and fair academic practices.

7

STAYING SANE

The title of this chapter may be an oxymoron to some because seeking or accepting the position of chair is already symbolic of having surrendered some sanity! However, there are real benefits to serving as department chair as the concluding chapter of this book describes. Those currently employed as chairs and those considering or aspiring to the position need to know that the job can be overwhelming at times if care is not taken to anticipate the workload, find ways to dissipate pressure, and discover outlets where chair work is acknowledged and appreciated. In assessing chair positions at other institutions and even some on the same campus, it appears—and this could be wrong because one never knows unless one walks the walk—that some chair positions are more demanding than others. Some have more natural complexity. For example, running a science department is, in the words of a recent visitor to my department, like running a hospital. There are no patients, but there is a major equipment base for both teaching and research that must be maintained and managed. Another variable is disciplinary change, which is more evident in computer engineering than in philosophy. Those units with graduate programs bring a set of responsibilities not found in those without graduate offerings. Perhaps most significant are those departments that have a major undergraduate component—they are more challenging to operate than those that are graduate and professional only. With these variables in mind, three areas of concern to chairs and possible ways to deal with each will be discussed.

Avoiding and Dealing With Burnout

National surveys rating professions that are particularly high in stress indicate that administrative-professorial positions are among the top few. Continued high stress can lead to what is referred to as burnout, although the borderline between the two is undefined. Describing the characteristics of great stress or burnout may remind us of how we have felt from time to time, but the permanency of either condition is variable. In other words, there are situations where high stress reigns and department chairs may feel burned out but they may return to modest stress levels as conditions improve.

Chair burnout is characterized by poor relationships with others resulting from an inability to give them appropriate attention and consideration. Burnout produces low personal productivity and a self-perception of a lack of accomplishment. The effects of these conditions result in feelings of despair and ineffectiveness. While certain situations may cause some of these reactions, such as a particularly difficult series of interactions with a faculty member or the dean or the feeling that your administrative work will never allow you to finish a particular project, real burnout happens when all of these are present for an extended period of time and one dreads the trip to work each day.

Several aspects of chair work have been identified as contributing to stress that can build sufficiently to result in burnout. It should be recognized that the degree to which these situations affect a person depends on the personality and experience of the chair. For example, some people can dismiss a difficult confrontation or recognize it as another version of events experienced in the past. Rookie chairs and others with more sensitive personalities may not manage such situations as easily. Other stressors include insufficient time to complete assigned work, frustration with the loss of opportunity for scholarship or teaching, encroachment on personal and family time, annoyance with seemingly unnecessary bureaucracy, and over-commitment.

Recognizing stress before it leads to burnout is critical to taking steps to alleviate it. There are textbook steps that one can take, and here they will be placed within the context of the work of an academic department chair. One is to define the scope of chair work so that overcommitment is controlled, ensuring that time remains for those activities the chair values. Chairs, however, must be flexible because new assignments cannot easily be declined and others have far too much value personally or departmentally to ignore. Choices may be made individually by the chair or in consultation with the faculty or the dean. Delegation of tasks may be necessary. The job may be altered to be more like the department structure used by chairs who seem to work efficiently and with little stress.

Managing time is another approach used to reduce stress. Perhaps this means closing the office door for two hours a day to devote time to big projects and work through stacks of paperwork. While access may be denied to faculty, staff, and others, a frank discussion at a faculty or staff meeting to explain the reason for this is usually acceptable to one's colleagues. Another aspect of this concept is to set priorities and chronologies for meeting expectations. Finally, in structuring chair work, plan something that is fun. This might be a department social event on or off campus. This can help the stressed chair reconnect with faculty and staff.

One final "cure" for stress, and one that I use routinely, is taking special care to ensure good health. This includes healthy eating, getting sufficient sleep, and stress-reduction activity. While I sometimes stray from the first two, I am absolutely committed to a regular exercise program. That program preceded my time as chair and is likely rooted in some form of overcompetitiveness. Still it serves me well as a way to reduce stress. At this time my routine consists of early mornings at the gym from Monday through Friday—three days of vigorous aerobics and two days of weight lifting. Previously it was running and, after injury precluded that, it was cycling. My work as chair did not allow the time commitment that cycling required, so the switch was made to workouts at the gym. Alternatives may be walking, hiking, swimming, martial arts (also handy during annual reviews), and other similar activities. Hobbies can be effective stress releases. I have colleagues who paint, collect and operate model trains, fish, and hunt for collectibles on weekends.

Delegating Responsibility

This is of particular interest to me because I have not been successful in this area. What is even more disturbing, I know I am bad at it, need to change it, but never seem to get around to transferring work to others. I have made some efforts, though, and have some ideas on how delegation may be done in ways that not only relieve some of the workload assigned to chairs but can also help faculty return to a visible "full employment" and foster faculty career objectives. For the most part, however, I have taken on more than I need to as chair so that faculty can have the time and freedom to be productive teachers and scholars.

Chapter 1 of this book outlined traditional chair responsibilities, listed newer ones, and predicted increasing emphasis on another set for the future. Like much in higher education, nothing is taken off the table in order to accommodate the new assignments. The expectations of faculty have also increased as new responsibilities are added or recommended. For example, how many faculty members knew they would be responsible for assessing student learning outcomes when they applied for their first academic positions? Certainly no one who has been teaching for more than a decade anticipated this would be a work expectation. Another example is the ever-expanding set of compliance requirements that need approvals for a variety of things, tests to do certain types of work, and personal disclosures. Doing this work is complicated enough but also having to serve on committees that review and approve all of this extra effort has added to faculty responsibilities. Chairs, of course, have the new job of making sure that faculty members are compliant and that committees have appropriate representation.

Models for the Delegation of Administrative Work

Two models may be considered for the delegation of administrative work at the department level. One is the department executive committee. Executive committees are usually found in large departments or in departments with strong research missions. Exceptions to this are smaller units that use an executive committee structure. In most cases executive committees are advisory in nature and can be used as sounding boards for policies developed by chairs, upper administration, or other department committees. Membership on executive committees is determined by chair appointments, by faculty election, or by policy designating specific categories of representation. The latter may be the case in large departments where each academic program or research focus area is represented along with other standing committees.

The second is the associate chair model, where a faculty member serves, usually as the result of appointment by the chair, as a replacement at chair functions and completes some routine tasks of department administration. A common associate chair assignment is to hear student complaints. Other functions associate chairs may fulfill include interviewing and placing adjunct faculty, managing routine paperwork, and completing ad hoc tasks assigned to the chair by the dean. I have a long-time colleague in another department who fulfilled this role for his chair. When the chair received an assignment to complete an economic model for department operation or conduct a faculty workload analysis, I knew he would get the assignment and call me to find out what he was supposed to do. While these models have value to the chair from the perspectives of gaining advice and off-loading some work, both models could be significantly enhanced to improve their impact on department operations and provide more developmental opportunities for faculty who serve on executive committees or as associate chairs.

Improved Delegation Models

Beyond reducing chair workload, the associate chair model might be reconceived with the intention of also improving the functioning of the department and providing opportunities for the individual taking the position. In the case of the former, consider all of those things you would like to do as a chair but simply do not have the time or energy to begin. Perhaps you would like to set up a peer tutoring program for your majors or an early intervention scheme to identify freshman students who are faltering in the first weeks of the semester. These ideas have potential positive impacts on student success and retention and could be models for others at the institution and beyond. These are also ideal assignments for an associate chair. While they do not reduce chair workload, they do improve the department. Other discrete assignments that may be delegated include grant writing for large projects involving several faculty or departments, providing orientations for adjunct faculty or graduate students, and creating marketing materials.

The idea that the position may afford opportunities for the individual, beyond the title and perhaps extra compensation, is an interesting concept. There are two types of faculty members who would make ideal associate chairs. One is the senior faculty member looking for a change from the routine of teaching the same classes or fighting the hard battle to keep a competitive research program funded and productive. This individual would be a respected and productive person looking to contribute in other ways at this career point. Thus, when one looks at changes over a career and considers the concept of differential workloads for faculty, a move to more service in place of some teaching or research work may result in real gains for the department. The second prospect for the position of associate chair is the faculty member with an interest in pursuing the administrative track. In some cases faculty members will reveal this interest to the chair while in others this aspiration may be revealed in annual reviews if the chair has been paying close attention to the work interests of such faculty members. In this situation, the chair may be more deliberate in suggesting assignments that provide experiences relevant to serving as a college or university administrator. For example, delegating the responsibility for scheduling classes taking into account student needs and faculty preferences may be an instructive exercise to include in this portfolio.

A critical element in the reconceived associate chair position, regardless of the type of faculty member who accepts it, is that many of the assignments should be discrete activities for which the associate chair can take full ownership. In fact, very creative associate chairs may even be able to define their own assignments. Some routine activities would continue, of course, such as representing the chair at functions and meetings when he or she is unavailable. However, success in special projects can clearly be attributed to the associate chair, making a significant difference in the eyes of others and acting as positive reinforcement for the associate chair. It also allows for delineation of activities as associate chair on the curriculum vitae. Imagine a listing as a single line item of "Associate Chair, 2001–2004" versus one where concrete products and activities are listed under that position. A case in point is that of an associate chair in my department. This individual volunteered to be associate chair and had some projects she thought would be of value to the department. They were accomplished quickly and they significantly improved some of our operations. Unfortunately, this successful stint as associate chair made her an attractive candidate elsewhere, and she left to lead her own department and has since moved higher in administration. This, apparently, is one of the downsides of effective chair delegation.

Modification of the executive committee model also has potential for relieving chair workload. Executive committees are more likely to be advisory groups than working groups. If that is the current culture of an existing executive committee, it may be difficult to convince the membership to actually take on some responsibilities. However, if the concept of an executive committee is new, there is an opportunity to outline some of its responsibilities. Advice to the chair can be one responsibility, but special projects to enhance the department and a mechanism to have a rotating plan for chair representation can be other responsibilities charged to the new group.

An advantage of this model over that of associate chair is that there would be a wider array of talent available to the chair because of the number of faculty members participating. Special assignments can then be delegated by matching the varying expertise of group members. The overall potential of this model to reduce chair workload is probably less than that of the associate chair model because full commitment to administrative work is not guaranteed from any member of the committee. It does, however, have potential for expanding department services and achieving improvement if the special tasks are challenging and can add something positive to unit operations. Exceptions may occur where there is a subset of members who have an interest in service and administrative work. This model also has less impact on career building and fewer opportunities for those interested in administrative career tracks.

A key point a chair should consider when choosing one of these models for workload delegation includes delegating some highly visible and important projects that will be widely recognized as worthwhile. Both models should be treated as development activities for the participants that may introduce them to new opportunities on campus, provide introductions to alternative career paths, and create new value work for faculty who are stuck. The chair can reinforce the value of the contributions by the associate chair or the executive committee by recognizing this work in the merit reward system and by regularly highlighting the accomplishments of the individual or group in reports, meeting agendas, and other venues.

Maintaining Motivation

At first, being chair is a new experience, with many people offering congratulations and everyone giving you some space to set your path and develop your agenda. This is called the honeymoon. It lasts longer if you are an external appointment because no one will be able to read you for several months, and most individuals do not have the courage to press you on issues. If they do, the easy answer is that you have not been here long enough to fully understand all the ramifications of whatever is being questioned. An internal appointment is well known, and it will not take long to discern whether you will act like your old self or someone new. Faculty will also be more comfortable approaching you for responses to important issues. Of course, the "I am not yet familiar enough with . . ." deflection will not work.

Rather than being overwhelmed upon taking over in the middle of an academic year, I actually had the time to do many things I could not schedule today. As an internal appointment, I knew several things I could change quickly for positive results and real impact. This was a major boost to morale and instilled confidence in the faculty that the new person actually had some worthwhile ideas and the initiative to put them into play. Now over a decade later I can say what I like about the position and what I do not look forward to doing. For example, the first set of annual reviews conducted was a revealing experience and everyone, including me, was cautious in their behavior. Over time this process took on a distinctly different cast as some reviews were viewed as meetings to look forward to and others were interactions where frank and difficult discussions would have to take place. There are many other examples of routine and extemporaneous (like student complaints) experiences that can become drudgery and lead to a loss of vigor for the job. The challenge is to find the things that are invigorating, exciting, challenging, and rewarding to counter the routine and less than fulfilling ones so there is a balance between the positive and less appealing elements of the job. Of course, having a net positive is always the best situation. There are some considerations that may be helpful in maintaining motivation and interest in continuing to lead an academic department. Some of these ideas are overlapping ways of achieving similar ends.

Goal Setting

Goal setting with faculty is a crucial activity that will be fully discussed in the context of the annual review process in Chapter 16. Goal setting with faculty members can be a component of the improvement process where this is necessary. More important in this discussion is using goal setting to sustain and enhance interest and motivation. In a faculty context, this is an essential element in maintaining vitality such that successful faculty can reap the rewards associated with increased success and recognition. Successful chairs over time need more recognition than knowing that their faculty and the dean appreciate their efforts, that they have filed all reports and other paperwork accurately and on time, dealt with all inquiries and complaints, taught their classes, conducted what scholarship their schedules and duties will allow, and other routine accomplishments.

In thinking about new goals, the process may be either internal or involve the dean. Because chairs are expected to help faculty identify appropriate goals and because they have had opportunities to hear the creative goals that successful faculty members set for themselves, they can be expected to creatively direct their own future achievements through goal setting. Involving the dean in this process is an interesting concept and may have some value. Whether this is possible or likely depends on the process of chair review by the dean. I can say that this has not been a regular event in my stint as chair, so formal goal setting was an internal activity. In situations where annual reviews for chairs take place, goal setting in consultation with the dean may be a beneficial process.

If goal setting is used to invigorate the chair and provide a real challenge for future accomplishment, then it must include objectives beyond the routine ones. For example, if the dean proposes more extensive written reviews for faculty or additional reports on student progress, the chair is not going to be very enthusiastic about work projected for the coming year. If, on the other hand, the chair comes to that review with concrete plans for new objectives that will likely have positive outcomes for the department and institution, then endorsement and encouragement by the dean can be a boost to chair commitment to the new task. Goal setting can be effective without dean input, and many chairs enhance their effectiveness using this as a guide.

Make Something Measurably Better Each Year

Chairs who have been in place for a decade or more will remember good years and bad years with regard to available resources. The good years probably were not viewed as such at the time but, relative to present times, they are miraculously transformed into good years. Available resources often place limitations on what can be accomplished in a given year. The challenge of improving some aspect of department function or accomplishment each year can be met regardless of resource issues. A new instrument for teaching or research can be a way to achieve this when the fiscal climate is favorable, but in tougher times, submitting a collaborative proposal seeking resources for that instrument might be a new goal. Other examples in difficult times might be the development of an online self-advising system to assist student progress, the development of a new degree option in an interdisciplinary area involving existing courses from two or three departments, or the development of a new instrument for student learning assessment. In each of these examples, the monetary costs are minimal, the products are tangible, and the outcomes move the department forward. Success through the chair's leadership in facilitating these ends can be a positive stimulus to ensure continued interest and engagement. Another positive gain is that the entire department can be invigorated by these efforts.

Professionalizing Academic and Administrative Work

The research/scholarship tradition of the academy is universally recognized as one that produces new knowledge, applications, or interpretations. There are predictable processes by which such innovations are reviewed and disseminated. Reviewing these is neither necessary nor appropriate here; however, the underlying principle is worth examining more closely. Scholarship is defined by new ways of doing things, new applications of existing methods and approaches, new understandings of processes, innovative interpretations of existing assumptions, sources and creations, and a large variety of other contributions that add to current repositories of facts, thoughts, and ideas. The bottom line is that scholarship takes many forms and is accepted as scholarship after rigorous peer review that validates methodology, data collected, interpretation, and other elements of quality. Once the peer review process is cleared, the results are then disseminated so that others can benefit by access to the new information that can direct the future scholarship of others. These considerations, while accepted practice in the realm of traditional scholarship, are frequently not recognized in other forms of accomplishment beyond traditional disciplinary work.

Scholarly contributions are now more recognized in the area of teaching through the emergence of a more extensive array of peer-reviewed media, both print and online. While there is still a way to go in getting universal recognition of these contributions as "equivalent" in their impact and importance relative to traditional disciplinary contributions, they are nonetheless appearing more frequently on curriculum vitae and promotion and tenure documentation of faculty members at universities where traditional research has been the sole mark of scholarship. Even as these new venues for sharing innovation appear, there are many aspects of real contribution that remain unshared.

Chairs not only need to encourage faculty members to share the results of their projects through professional presentation and publication, but also to do the same with the work produced through their administrative roles. This book continuously reinforces the important roles that chairs play and the increasingly complex work of chairs in higher education. While there are no absolute prescriptions for dealing with individual challenges that chairs and departments may face, there are many strategies, programs, and structures that have had success. Identifying and utilizing professional venues for sharing the results of these efforts can be a way for chairs to professionalize their work, invigorate future work, and create personal and institutional visibility.

Using an example from the previous section on improving some aspect of department function each year, a successful web-based self-advising system may yield positive results in the form of fewer final audit problems, high student satisfaction data derived from appropriate surveys and interviews, and more efficient use of existing advisors to solve nonroutine problems. The advising instrument and the data supporting its effectiveness would constitute a proposal for attending a national conference as well as the elements of a publication in a journal dedicated to effective practices in higher education. The chair might be the presenter/author or co-presenter/author with other contributors. Other examples include department efforts at improving retention, new models for workload delegation, and approaches to formative faculty evaluation. While the venues for these will differ, they do exist. The point is that new approaches to solving the challenges chairs and departments face, innovations that improve department operation and productivity, improved ways of recruiting, retaining, and serving students, and identifying new income streams are all subjects that will be of interest to those in higher education, including other department chairs. This concept will be developed further in Chapter 23, where chair development is discussed.

Identifying New Challenges or Projects

With the increasing workload for chairs, this suggestion does not seem like one that will promote mental health and contentment with the job. In fact this criticism can be levied at some of the other sanity-preserving suggestions made previously. The response is one made by analogy. In the weeks before April 15, a tax accountant will work extremely long hours and interact with many constituents expecting the miracle of large refunds. The long hours and high stress lead to exhaustion and the need for the vacation scheduled to begin April 16—a week hiking steep mountains at high elevation. Clearly, this is not what one would expect as a cure for an exhausted person, yet the accountant returns reinvigorated and ready to resume work. The secret is not reduced work and increased leisure, but the diversion of hiking. Similarly, personally selected, versus routine and mandated, new projects for chairs can be a diversion from typical, standard stress sources and provide positive and invigorating experiences.

Other examples might include reinvolvement in a disciplinary research project that had to be set aside in the past or starting a new one in collaboration with a colleague within or outside of the department. Such a venture would not be considered outside the work realm of a chair, so its products would be seen as real contributions to the department. Such projects would obviously require time and effort but are similar to the way that hiking at 8,000 feet would require time and effort. The value is in the reinvigoration one gains from the diversionary aspects of the new work. In doing some things like this, the hangover from a particularly long and difficult season of faculty reappointment deliberations can be balanced.

Using Peer Resources

Some articles have promoted using peer mentors for new chairs. The benefit here is that experienced chairs can alert the novice to heavy workload times in terms of reporting and reviews, provide some advice on how the dean likes things done, and share anecdotal information on dealing with staff and faculty issues. Formal programs for new chair mentoring no doubt exist, but at most institutions this type of interaction occurs informally, occasionally, and on an ad hoc basis. During my time as chair, I have seen several new chairs in other units come and go. Some will occasionally call to see how I handle a particular situation, ask advice for dealing with an issue that has arisen, or inquire about how my new budget fared. But other new chairs will never ask for advice, choosing to handle things themselves. It should be noted that challenges faced by chairs are not always unique, and local chairs have seen most of them. Having private conversations about chair issues can provide multiple perspectives and demonstrate that there are many acceptable answers to routine problems. Having as much information as possible is advantageous to the chair, whether the advice is followed or the chair chooses to pursue his or her own solution.

Another model for chair support is through institutional organizations for department chairs. All institutions have chair councils or similarly identified bodies that are a part of the college or school administrative infrastructure. These groups meet weekly to monthly under the leadership of the dean and may operate in different ways. The common model is that they provide a point for the distribution of information from upper administration and from the dean's office, for requests made to departments for information or for new activities, and for planning of school events. However, this is not the type of organization that provides learning opportunities for chairs or supports their work.

Small institutions may have a single chair council where all campus chairs know each other. At large, complex campuses, those doing chair work have different titles and a chair may know only a small percentage of one hundred or more chairs. While there may be great wisdom among both groups, they rarely meet in an environment where sharing can comfortably take place. In the case of complex campuses, additional perspectives regarding school and unit contributions and unique issues facing chairs can be largely unknown to others on campus. This neither promotes understanding nor the potential for collaborative interactions.

Community of Chairs

A community of chairs is a group consisting exclusively of department chairs (as defined by their responsibilities) that exists for the purposes of improving communication among academic units, sharing values and goals, and solving common problems. It generally is comprised of a small group drawn from multiple schools on campus. Those most likely to be initiators are the more globally visible chairs on campus. Others are peri-odically encouraged or invited to attend meetings. Deans are not involved in the community of chairs. These groups work best when there is no identifiable leader, that is, there is no "chair" of the community of chairs, and when there is no formal listing of this group as a committee or council. This means that there is no way for administration or others to assign tasks to the group and no one who is listed as a "contact" for the group. Operat-ing under the institutional radar allows this group to commit its energy to sharing and identifying issues that affect them as department chairs.

Meetings are typically arranged around the group's indi-vidual schedules and are hosted by members on a rotating basis. There is rarely an agenda, so discussion is free form. There is usually a brief introductory period where everyone unloads his or her most recent woes. Once this cleansing has taken place, the members realize that they are not in this alone and that others may have even more difficult challenges. These con-versations would not happen in other more formal venues but are possible here because of the trust that has been established among members of the community. Occasionally there will be issues that impact several members, and the group may develop strategies to address this. The positives here are that more than one unit supports the solution, and those approached realize that this is more a campus issue than an individual one. For the most part, in these meetings, participants learn about the cul-tures of other schools and of new models for doing things that may represent improvements to processes in their own units. They also share their own experiences in dealing with com-mon issues and information relative to chair work that they may have learned at other venues.

There are two things one should know about such chair communities before initiating one on campus. The first is that some deans may be suspicious of such groups. Department chairs who meet without the dean may be a disconcerting concept to some deans, but usually reassurances from chairs that this is not a mutinous group will be a sufficient solution. The second is that the community of chairs will have a finite lifetime. The core group that initiates the community will begin to dissolve as members retire or move on from chair work. Replacements are not always as enthusiastic as the founders, and attendance will begin to diminish even though special recruitment meetings (a special topic agenda with food) have been held. Remnants will remain, however, as a loosely knit group of individuals who call each other on an ad hoc basis to exchange information and provide advice.

Summary

The position of chair will be a stress rollercoaster. There will be times when things run smoothly and the workload is manageable. There will also be times when the chair wonders if all the deadlines, both routine and out of the blue, can be met. Periodically, there will be times of high contentiousness (an appeal of a negative tenure decision, a serious complaint, the annual review season, a difficult difference of opinion involving the dean). These situations will raise the stress level for the chair, and continued high-stress levels can lead to burnout. It is much easier to deal with stress than the burnout that may follow. Chairs need to be conscious of time management, wary and vigilant of overcommitment (some chairs have a tough time saying no), and make a concerted effort to maintain good health. The latter requires attention to diet and sleep as well as stress releases in forms of exercise or other hobbies.

Ways for chairs to deal with some workplace stress include considering models for the delegation of discrete aspects of chair work. The department executive committee or the associate chair models may be adaptable to this function. One stress release may be a department social function where all can interact in informal ways detached from the pressures of the workplace. Setting goals with faculty members is a valuable exercise to show interest in and direct their work. The same can be achieved for chairs, alone or in concert with the dean. This process helps to focus work and creates a way to acknowledge success, in this case your own. Other techniques to maintain chair interest and motivation are to extend the hard work done on projects into professional presentations and publications and to engage in diversionary work. In the former, there is acknowledgement of value in the work completed; in the latter there is new work, but it is pursued without the entanglements of the routine. Finally, interactions with peers and other department chairs can be therapeutic in the lessening of chair stress.

8

COMMUNICATION

Productive interactions depend on good communication. Restricting the conversation to higher education narrows the topic somewhat, and focusing on department chairs places this concept within a critical administrative layer in colleges and universities. The first definitive statement about this topic regarding department chairs is that they need to be able to communicate with many constituents, although interactions with faculty, staff, and the dean receive the most attention. Department chairs are the link between administration and the faculty. Deans expect department chairs to make certain that administrative policy is followed, that requests for information are met, and that the campus mission and goals are addressed. Faculty members expect chairs to be untiring advocates for the department and to protect them from undue interference (sometimes referred to as harassment) from administrators and others. That may be strong language, but I have heard this term used many times. The idea of advocacy is common in most books about department chairs in higher education, and even welcomed by the dean, but the shielding concept does not seem to get as much attention.

Communicating With the Dean

The preceding paragraph implies very delicate balances that chairs must achieve in bringing important issues from the administration to the faculty and in articulating to the dean and other administrators where some of their ideas might need revision or even withdrawal. Each of these situations present real communication challenges for the chair. There are mandates and other policies and requests from administration that the wise chair recognizes as things that must be carefully addressed for the benefit of all. The chair must provide faculty-friendly justifications, indicate paths for compliance that are not overly burdensome, and project positive outcomes for the department. This may require some careful forethought, but putting a positive spin on yet another administrative incursion into faculty life can lead to peaceful acceptance.

The function of the chair as faculty protector has several manifestations, but all are based on the chair's intimate knowledge of department operation, individual and collective faculty work, and overall unit goals. In Chapter 10, the idea of *compartmentalized thinking* by university administrators will be discussed. This is a tendency to momentarily assign overwhelming importance to a single aspect of university responsibility or activity and can be attributed to several factors. First, administrators may become "infatuated" with an idea that works well in one venue and may insist that everyone adopt it. Examples might be service-learning and distance education. Deans and other administrators are from several to many years removed from traditional faculty work. Some may occasionally teach, but they do mostly administrative work. Faculty work evolves just as any dynamic entity does, and administrators sometimes lose track of what faculty do, what they have to contend with, and what their personal motivations are. Upper administrators can also be pressured by boards, legislators, and other external groups to address problems, real or perceived, within the institution. These may be as far-fetched as undergraduates never having full-time faculty as their course instructors or faculty playing golf every Wednesday. More realistically, there may be claims that not all faculty members in the department teach first-year students. In trying to dampen criticism, top administrators may pass on to deans the mandate that all faculty become involved in first-year instruction.

When such mandates reach chairs, they know exactly what consequences will occur if such a plan is enacted. The response should not be "we will not do this," but rather should be data-based and delivered in several forms (at least in a face-to-face discussion with written or email follow-up to prolong impact) that describes the effects of such a radical change on instructional responsibility. A relevant point might be that reassigning faculty will leave critical upper-division classes unstaffed, thus slowing the pace of student degree completion. Alternatively, increasing teaching loads to accomplish the new instructional goal may jeopardize scholarship and recruiting new faculty. The chair's task is to place the initiative in the context of the unit's overall operation and the entire set of institutional and department goals. In addition, an alternative plan to meet the objective of the proposed change can be very helpful in crafting an acceptable outcome for all. The bottom line is that chairs must be creative and sensitive in how they communicate some pieces of information both to their faculty and to upper administrators.

The other side of chair communication with the dean seeks to inform the dean of the department's contributions and its potential and, on selective occasions, request investments in the department to further its excellence. These requests may be perceived as asking for resources, but their real intent is to offer an opportunity that is difficult to refuse. This is the advocacy piece of chair work and is expected by deans. Consider a dean of any school. This individual will come from an academic discipline that is usually represented in that school. However, there will be other disciplines with which the dean may be unfamiliar. A dean of arts and sciences from the English department may have little understanding of the needs, culture, and operations of the chemistry department, for example. The ways instruction is delivered, the cost to deliver a credit hour, space and equipment requirements, and how scholarship is conducted are but a few of the ways that English and chemistry departments differ. Deans will depend on department chairs to educate them about the nature of the various disciplines and the changes that occur in those disciplines over time. While there may be a temptation for some to take advantage of a new dean for short-term gain, the ultimate relationship will depend on the chair's credibility.

The concept of investment was used in the preceding example as a way to communicate need. Two considerations related to investment come to mind here in formulating a proposal for new resources. One is payback for the investment that comes in the form of direct or in-kind replacement. For example, requesting additional funding for adjunct hires or even new faculty lines to meet student demand in a new program in the department or expansion of programs for other campus units can generate additional fiscal resources for the school and essentially pay for themselves. Meeting campus need and expanding unit programs may also carry political value. A request for additional space for research in a hot area can be justified by the promise of increased external funding (presenting examples where this has happened will be convincing) that will bring new overhead dollars into the school. Department chairs have the relevant data from which to make appropriate projections about the indirect and long-term returns of such endeavors. The second consideration involves requests that are linked to institutional, school, and department missions. These types of connections can be very difficult for administrators to ignore because they will make the front page on the university's agenda. For example, if the institution's mission statement prominently mentions its commitment to civic engagement, then the theater department's request for a shared hire with the local performance company to create programming for inner-city children will be a very attractive proposal.

Good communication with the dean is essential to department success. Getting relevant information to the dean will depend on personality, and the chair must know, or learn if it is a new relationship, how to productively approach the dean. Some deans expect and even welcome casual drop-ins by chairs. Some expect a firm appointment with a known agenda. Others are more social and prone to accept invitations—to lunch, for example. Find the best route to have a full conversation, then lead with a description of the "problem" to be solved by the new initiative and follow with possible solutions. Data supporting the alternatives and revealing the weaknesses and negative consequences of the original state of affairs can follow, if necessary. If the resulting solution addresses the issue to the satisfaction of all parties, then the lunch will be a welcome "business expense" for the chair, even if it is paid with personal resources.

A corollary to effective communication with the dean is to get to know his or her staff very well. This includes associate and assistant deans as well as professional and clerical staff. Not only can these individuals help gain the chair a favorable audience with the dean (the secretary will know about the mood of the dean), but they can also be conduits of useful ideas and information that may predispose the dean to more effective approaches to the problem during the meeting.

Communicating With the Faculty

The challenge here is the many individual personalities that cannot all be approached in the same way. So chairs need to develop several effective strategies to deal with different personality types. The first step in communicating with faculty is to create and maintain an atmosphere where the free exchange of ideas is allowed and encouraged. It is well recognized that this type of open and respectful consideration is very important to underrepresented faculty. Beyond that, it is important that all be heard and that all opinions be respected and debated impartially. Without this type of environment, it will be difficult to create a unit of shared responsibility and full participation.

An important concept to remember is that no matter how much and how frequently information is offered, much of it is assimilated by faculty only if it is of interest to them at that moment.

This is not a condemnation of faculty but an awareness that their lives are complex and their minds are occupied with many things. Still, frequent and even repetitive distributions of information by the chair are worth the effort if for nothing else than to provide evidence that the information was made available when claims of lack of information are made. When I have been criticized for not informing faculty, in most cases I have been able to print copies of meeting agendas to show that the information was provided.

The avenues for communication with faculty are many. Announcing new information to faculty such as successes and awards is discussed elsewhere in this book. This type of information as well as other relevant pieces of data can be distributed in similar ways. Items of particular importance can be listed on agendas for department meetings or targeted committee meetings. As agenda items, they are reiterated and explained at the meeting, thus providing an opportunity for faculty input and questions. When the meeting is over, faculty have a hard copy to take with them, and some will actually file these documents. Special memos and written announcements may also be effective for reaching faculty. The use of email is on the rise, and many faculty members are very open to information sent in this form. I believe that sending data as an attached document rather than imbedding the information in the email message is somewhat more effective. If faculty go through the extra step of clicking on the attachment, they seem more likely to take the time to read its content. Regardless of whether the document is distributed electronically or in hard copy, crafting it in an attractive, organized, and succinct format also contributes to the likelihood of its being read.

Over the years, there have been articles extolling the virtues of chairs wandering through the department as an effective management tool (Mallard, 1999). At first this sounds absurd, but upon reflection, I realize that I actually do this regularly. But it is more than wandering. On some of my excursions, faculty members who see me cruising the hallways joke that I am taking attendance.

Of course, I'm not, but I never let them know this! Some trips are just to get away from the office or the computer screen. Others are initiated with the option of joining a faculty discussion in the hallway or at some other location or to initiate one with someone encountered along the way. There are also opportunities to greet undergraduate or graduate students, technical personnel, or other professionals who work in the department.

Encounters of this kind often lead to informal information exchanges that take place in both directions. Chairs learn what faculty members are doing at the moment, including a new research finding, a proposal or manuscript in preparation, or a new classroom strategy. Listening and remembering these topics for a later conversation—that is, "Was that manuscript accepted for publication?"—conveys chair interest in individual faculty work. Additionally, these random encounters allow for an informal, relaxed atmosphere in which to share information with faculty. The setting is a welcoming one for candid faculty feedback. While not all faculty members will be informed of everything using this method, those who do participate will spread the word, prompting other faculty members to drop by to confirm or provide commentary. This method will be further discussed in Chapter 9 as a way to isolate conversation of a controversial issue and help to overcome resistance. In controversial situations, strong personalities can sometimes dominate, and these encounters can allow for a full discussion with faculty members who are not as aggressive or are uncomfortable sharing in open meetings.

Other important chair-faculty communication areas are those related to hiring and career progress. At the outset, the department through the chair must communicate expectations for reappointment to new hires. The message should be consistent and reiterated at regular intervals both verbally and in writing. The message should also be compatible with institutional policy and with the findings of faculty review committees. This theme continues through the promotion and tenure process and extends to merit-based rewards. For example, telling a faculty member what is expected for receiving tenure in five years and then denying tenure using new criteria will rightfully represent a losing case for the department upon appeal. Inappropriate or poor communication can have legal implications for the chair.

Communicating With Students

Depending on the nature of the institution and the size of the department, chairs may have extensive interactions with students or very limited person-to-person interaction. In the former situation, chairs will have a regular teaching load, may participate in academic advising, and could interact with students through social organizations and professional clubs. Chairs of this type will also complete much of the paperwork associated with admission, auditing progress, and approving degrees as well as hearing student complaints. In larger, more complex departments, student interactions may be limited to graduate students and the most urgent of emergencies related to degree conferral or serious cases of misconduct. Chairs in these departments typically delegate student-related paperwork and routine complaints to staff or other members of the faculty.

All chairs have extensive impact on students through department policy and requirements. These impacts are communicated through brochures, web sites, bulletins, and other official documents and postings. Included are degree requirements and perhaps department-specific policies related to grade petitions, withdrawals from classes, make-up exams, and other matters that affect students. It is critical that these policies are clearly articulated and in compliance with university-level policies. Appeals of irregularities or challenges to vague policies can be time-consuming for the chair and embarrassing for the department. Worse yet, such errors can have legal consequences.

Communicating With Staff

This aspect of chair communication can be overlooked, but a careful review of the work staff members do for the department will reveal that staff are the primary frontline people in much of the work of the department. Staff members do everything from fielding and directing calls to the appropriate resource people, to advising students, to preparing complex materials related to instruction. They may be involved in fielding complaints and solving problems relative to student transfer credits and to academic auditing errors. Staff members are frequently the primary individuals responsible for compliance to policies on safety, animal use, building evacuation plans, and accommodations. Staff members also play important roles in managing budgets and balancing accounts, hiring adjunct faculty and other personnel, and responding to financial audits. They file paperwork for travel reimbursement, a function we all appreciate being done accurately and promptly. Just from this partial list, one can see that much of what the department does can be compromised when regular and clear department policies and expectations are not communicated to staff. Good communication with staff can also reveal morale issues and other points of concern that arise among this distinct group in the department. Chairs must also be vigilant in making certain that faculty and others do not abuse staff. Again, this relies on open communication and an atmosphere of mutual respect among all members of the department team.

Summary

Surveys of department chairs and those who deal directly with chairs routinely list communication skills as one of the most important characteristics for successful leadership. Because chairs play a delicate balancing role between bringing administrative expectations to faculty and functioning as a faculty advocate, this skill is critical to keeping both sides satisfied and to maintaining good working relationships in both directions. On the administrative side, the chair must interpret policy and present it in a way that faculty will give it a fair hearing. On the other hand, chairs may have to negotiate modifications for policy implementation in order to preserve other positive features of unit operation. In both cases, careful communication is a key ingredient to success. The chair must also have an open communication channel to the dean for effective advocacy. The dean will depend on the chair for disciplinary understanding, and the chair must provide honest justifications and requests in order to ensure that future dealings will enjoy full and open consideration.

Chairs must also have regular communication with the entire faculty body and with individual faculty members. General information may be dispensed to faculty members through written and electronic memos, meeting agendas, and verbally at group meetings. Keeping copies is a handy way to counter any claims that information was not provided. Individual communication with members of the faculty is more complex and based upon personality differences. Faculty members may have to be approached in different ways and on different occasions. One effective way to foster open communication between the chairs and members of the faculty is for the chair to be available to faculty by walking the shop floor, that is, passing through faculty congregation areas whether they be a line of offices, labs, cafeterias, coffee rooms, or mailboxes. The random (or planned) encounters allow for information exchange in relaxed, informal settings. Much can be learned in both directions.

Chairs communicate with students in the same way as faculty members do, but they also communicate through department policy. Chairs represent the university in an official capacity as they set guidelines for transfer credits, course substitutions, withdrawals, grade changes, and the like. Chairs are also responsible for information found in bulletins, class schedules, brochures, and department web sites. Finally, chairs must regularly apprise staff of policy changes because staff members are frequently the front line of information to those who call or visit the department. Providing accurate information and referring visitors to the appropriate individual or office are necessary to garner a positive reputation for the department.

9

WORKING WITH FACULTY

Interacting in positive and productive ways with department faculty is essential to unit excellence and to the overall professional and personal success of the chair. Just as a dean is only as good as his or her department chairs, it is equally true that a chair's success is determined largely by the good works of the faculty. Chairs do receive credit in a sense for the performance of the department's faculty. While some individual achievements are clearly the result of faculty efforts, when they take place on the chair's watch, the chair's reputation is enhanced. Some chairs will even list collective accomplishments on their curriculum vitae to demonstrate their leadership abilities. However, before one becomes concerned that chairs may take undue credit, remember that deans, provosts, chancellors, vice presidents, and presidents do the same on a different scale. As long as the elements of success are appropriately attributed and the chair has instigated or supported the initiative, then this type of ownership is justified. Leaders encourage and foster good work in many ways that provide a supportive and enabling environment for success.

Before we consider how to create a productive department environment, it is instructive to discuss the challenges of learning about individual faculty so that the chair has a credible influence on their work. When talking about faculty members, multiply that challenge by the number of faculty in the department. If that number is more than 25–30, the process will be difficult and time-consuming. This task is alleviated to a good degree if the chair is an internal appointment and thus familiar with many if not all department colleagues. There will be much variation in temperament, motivation, collegiality, interests, values, and abilities among faculty in a department. The chair must know how to effectively deal with a majority of them to get them working together as a team while preserving and supporting their individual professional goals.

Personality Types

In planning this book, I thought it would be interesting to identify some of the personality types I have observed among faculty. Just as writing about deans is a sensitive issue because a good deal of what one might say comes from personal experience, writing about faculty traits is rooted in the same experiences. Thus there is some discomfort in the thought that members of my faculty may read this and recognize themselves or their colleagues in some of the descriptions. I will say at the outset that all profiles are based on faculty I have heard about in other departments and that any that may be interpreted as having a negative context are always accompanied by many positive traits. The solution is to be able to work around the negative and magnify the positive. Beyond the types listed here, there are many other combinations.

The Quiet, Respectful Type

This is a colleague who may address the chair as doctor or professor. This formality can be loosened up with requests for first name usage or sending emails and memos signed using only your first name. Quiet faculty members often do not tell the chair everything he or she should know. This may be a component of the personality of the individual or fear of repercussion if there is bad news to report. This simply delays the inevitable as well as the ability of the chair to suggest avenues for improvement. Chairs need to check in routinely with faculty of this type to learn what is necessary. Examples may include faculty members who are having trouble in the classroom. If they disclose this early, the chair may be able to direct them to someone or something that may help. Waiting until a semester or year is over and evaluations have been done delays intervention and creates an undesirable permanent record. In another situation, a quiet faculty member who submits a proposal for external funding that is unsuccessful may miss valuable advice to meet the next deadline if the chair is not promptly informed.

The Open, Honest Type

In contrast to the quiet, respectful type, this faculty member shares everything, including an assessment of the strengths and weaknesses of his or her work. This person is open to suggestions and actively seeks to emulate the approaches of other successful individuals. This type of faculty member needs a regular meeting with the chair, and the chair should anticipate this by occasional drop-bys and other "chance" meetings. There are not too many people in higher education who regularly display objective self-assessment.

Those Who "Just Know"

Faculty members of this variety are incredible assets to the department and pleasures for chairs to work with. When told at the outset what is expected of faculty, they just plain get it. It is as though they wrote the book themselves. They understand the nature of the contributions expected in teaching, research, and service, and they have a sense of when to help when extra assistance is needed. An example I have observed on more than one occasion provides a good illustration. One semester, a member of the faculty becomes seriously ill and is unable to meet classes for a period of time. Some faculty will make themselves scarce in order to avoid helping out, but faculty who "just know" are immediately in the chair's office volunteering to do their part even if the course is not directly within their expertise. This example has been repeated several times, and each time the faculty members who step forward are among the most productive and effective in all areas of faculty responsibility.

The "It's All About Me" Type

For some chairs, this is one of the more difficult personalities to work with. It is seen in actions that are transparently self-serving. Most of these types are not very effective about masking motive, and other members of the faculty recognize why they are taking certain positions. What they fail to realize is that their colleagues automatically begin to question everything they say, even when the statements are not self-directed. This type of personality can also evolve into arrogance. Rather than try to manipulate outcomes that will favor them, this personality type will state outright that they are the best, most accomplished, undervalued, unappreciated, widely recognized, or some combination thereof and therefore should receive special consideration, recognition, or favorable treatment. Chairs will be very well aware of this characteristic because they are frequently confronted with examples of self-proclaimed excellence. Even when great accomplishment and recognition are valid, I expect that most chairs would like that accompanied by a dose of humility.

The High-Maintenance Type

These are faculty members who require guidance for everything they do, who are exceptionally active and inquisitive, or who tend to become involved in controversy more often than average. Sometimes this trait comes with a positive slant, and at other times one that is not so positive. In some instances the constant need for guidance reflects a lack of confidence that can disappear with time. Inquisitive, active types will continue to ask questions, seek advice, and move ahead in all aspects of faculty work. Chairs should be pleased to be available when faculty members like this come calling. The final example are faculty members who seem to be out of phase in certain aspects of their behavior, and as a result annoy students through their comments in class or offend faculty or staff in the department or from other parts of campus. Chairs may have to pick up after them through apologies and may have to schedule advice sessions on how to critique an idea without insulting its source or how to encourage better student performance without challenging intelligence.

While this is not an exhaustive list—most readers could contribute some types of their own—it at least illustrates that working with faculty members is a complex and highly variable exercise. All of these personality variables impact chair work and affect sensitive interactions that chairs may have with members of the department. As different and idiosyncratic as faculty members may be, the characteristics they all share are that they are bright, well-educated individuals. It is their set of talents that must be harnessed to make the department run smoothly and productively.

Assessing Skills and Talents

While awareness of personality type may be very important in approaching individual faculty members, assessing their skill sets and interests is key to assembling the working team of the department. Departments with undergraduate programs operate under the traditional model where faculty members contribute in teaching, research or scholarship, and service. The way these three areas are defined and the way they play out in a given unit can vary. In some units, the research or scholarship is very prominent with specific outcome expectations for faculty. In others, research and scholarship are entwined with teaching and there will be different expectations. Teaching may have parameters of several courses per semester and may emphasize new course development. Service expectations at one institution may favor professional service, whereas at another, institutional service is more highly valued. In some settings, it may be defined primarily as guiding graduate students. No matter what the institutional or department culture, the chair has two primary responsibilities to ensure that the department meets its mandate in an efficient manner. The first is to lead faculty in discussions that define their abilities, interests, and motivations in these three areas, which will also impact faculty evaluations. What is important in teaching, research or scholarship, and service not only provides the basis upon which faculty agree they should be evaluated, but also provides a blueprint for how department work might be apportioned among faculty members.

Armed with the knowledge of faculty skills and interests, the identification of the output expectations of the unit, and an understanding of the obligations of the department to students and others, the chair can now do some matching. While workload assignments may have to follow some guidelines at the individual level, there is usually some flexibility available to the chair as long as the unit meets its overall objectives. The second chair responsibility or goal is to assign everyone a full load of work but with different fractions in the three areas based on strengths, weaknesses, and interests. This is the concept of differential workloads and will be discussed in Chapters 15 and 16. For example, a department with a graduate program may not be best served by having every faculty member teach a graduate course or mentor graduate research students. Faculty members who have not been engaged in discovery in the discipline for some time may be best assigned undergraduate courses. Both are essential and valuable, but individuals are placed where they can contribute most effectively and are not forced into uncomfortable assignments or those they are not prepared to assume. In this model some faculty will teach more traditional classes than others, some will direct more graduate students, others will conduct more research, some may do more student advising, and others may assume more administrative responsibilities. If all these tasks are understood by faculty to be important to department goals, then different can be equal.

Creating an Environment for Success

The next question is what steps the chair might take to create an environment in which faculty can do their best work. This idea may very well be the primary role that a chair plays in higher education. Perhaps it is also the primary role of deans and other administrators, though a good deal of the time they are distracted by other pressing issues. After all, the real products of the university—student instruction leading to a degree, research and dissemination of its products, and institutional and disciplinary organization building—are accomplished by faculty members. If administrators do not regard their primary role as supporting and providing services through a variety of campus offices, then one has to question their perceptions of the positions they hold. Chairs are not as likely to have their feet held as closely to the fire as other administrators because they, too, are faculty members and do some of the same work that department faculty members do. Thus chairs are more likely to be aware of issues related to an appropriate environment for successful faculty work.

What types of behaviors and strategies might a chair employ to get the best their faculty have to offer, create an atmosphere where faculty members feel they are working toward common goals, and create an attitude among faculty that the chair will support their efforts? While it is understood that administrative responsibility may reduce the chair's participation in faculty work, it is important to faculty members that the chair knows what challenges they face. What better way to do this than by working side by side with faculty doing real faculty work. For example, chairs of large departments in research universities may not teach, meaning they are not directly in touch with changes in student populations over time—and the student population has changed dramatically during my career. For years I worked for a dean who did not care if I taught. In fact, other chairs of large departments in the school rarely met classes. However, I continued to teach the same load as research-active faculty members, an activity that has not gone unnoticed by faculty surveys reviewing chair performance. Likewise, chairs expecting faculty members to support a culture that expects research and scholarship to be externally funded may want to submit the first proposal.

These are all examples of the age-old approach called leadership by example. It still works.

Another element of creating a favorable environment for faculty productivity and positive attitude is that of respecting in both obvious and public ways each member of the department community. This means everyone's opinion is heard fully. This does not mandate agreement with all that is said, but that everyone has their say. This is not always easy to ensure because some faculty will be less apt to engage in certain discussions due to personality type or other variables such as rank, gender, and minority status. It is critical that these voices be heard and that their input be considered when establishing department direction and policy. One can understand that the new assistant professor might be more comfortable allowing a discussion of curriculum reform to be pursued by veteran faculty members who have been overseeing program development for years. However, an outsider's fresh ideas might introduce new avenues for consideration. The issue of gender is particularly sensitive in disciplines where women have not been well represented. There may be subtle ways in which meetings are conducted that do not invite full participation or generate responses, indicating the input is not weighed equally with that of others. Similar types of messages, even when not intended, can be sent to members of other underrepresented groups. Departments can miss out on unique perspectives and may develop retention problems with these individuals if special care is not taken to make them welcome and full participating members of their deliberations.

Chairs need to be vigilant about making certain that everyone participates. One way to do this at meetings is to call out, after the more vociferous faculty have worn out their lungs, those who have not yet commented by asking how they feel about the subject. The chair can then synthesize the statements made indicating how they agree, contrast, or interface with others made and what new interpretations they provide. In cases where faculty status may preclude the desired level of participation, there are facilitators and other resources available on conducting inclusive meetings. They may be well worth the time and effort if they bring all aspects of faculty thought into the conversation.

Public acknowledgement of unit and individual success by the chair is a true reward for many faculty members, and in these days of fiscal restriction, it may be one of the few rewards they receive. There are several facets to support this idea. First, what products and successes are valued in the department? This can be as simple as being nominated for a school-level teaching award, getting a new course through the approval process, or being appointed as the director of a campus program. On a different scale and in a different aspect of faculty work, landing a $1 million grant and even a $2,000 award may be noteworthy and something that the recipient should feel good about. If these types of outcomes are part of what the department values and good examples of unit goals achieved, then this type of accolade plays the dual role of reinforcing goals and expectations.

There are many ways that success can be celebrated, including special memos to all faculty and the dean, emails, and inclusion on department meeting agendas where an accomplishment can be recognized before the entire faculty. Another way to celebrate success is by nominating faculty to various school, institutional, or even external awards, although some caution in doing this is warranted. The chair must ensure that the individual's performance warrants the award sought; otherwise a nominee's disappointment may be accompanied by a loss of credibility for the nominator. While the disappointment can be explained as tough competition, losing credibility can have lasting effects that jeopardize a stronger subsequent nominee. Finally, chairs should not forget to include staff in these announcements, and they should also recognize the value of celebrating overall department successes such as a record number of degrees conferred, the largest percentage increase in external funding, the most scholarship recipients in the incoming class, and so on. These considerations can boost community and individual morale.

Another way that the chair can help to create an open department atmosphere is by being accessible and visible. Yes, this costs chair time and conflicts with getting routine administrative and faculty work accomplished. Chairs who sequester themselves behind closed doors for at least part of each day will get more of their personal and routine office work done much more efficiently than a chair with an open-door policy. The chair who preceded me even erected barriers in front of his door so one had to make special efforts to see if it was open. This and his disappearance most afternoons discouraged faculty from visiting. This uninviting situation sent the message that he was not too interested in faculty problems or in hearing about faculty plans and ideas. The open-door policy is costly in both time and interruptions, but it is worth following. Although faculty members may become used to this environment and take it for granted, they will miss it when a new chair decides to do otherwise. Thus chairs should get used to scheduling 30% of their day while the rest is reserved for the ad hoc events of faculty, staff, and student visits, and other extemporaneous events.

Another aspect of chair accessibility is being seen in places other than the main office. In Chapter 8, the concept of management while walking around was discussed in the context of using impromptu drop-bys to learn about faculty attitudes, projects, activities, and concerns and to make trial runs for new ideas. An added benefit to this idea is that it makes the chair visible in the faculty domain. The relationship between a faculty member and the chair need not always play out in the chair's office, the seat of power. There are more neutral and relaxed places for interaction. Just as walking around allows the chair opportunities to visit faculty members, the pass through by the chair allows faculty to initiate conversations, ask questions, or seek advice on their own turf.

Another way that the chair can favorably interact with faculty to promote department productivity is to acknowledge and value multiple contributions. If there are department chairs who have medium to large departments of exclusively high-producing faculty across all areas of responsibility, then there really is a Lake Woebegone. I think all chairs realize that their colleagues are at different career stages, with diverse talents, varying motivation, unique knowledge and skills sets, and a myriad of temperaments. To expect that they all contribute in preset percentages across work areas and at the same levels is unrealistic. The strategic deployment of faculty resources known as differential expectations allows for more work in areas of expertise and interest at the partial expense of areas where there is little motivation for participation and where the nature of the work is no longer compatible with faculty preparation. It is essential that faculty have expectations in all areas so they can interact with and understand each other's contributions. Thus faculty should not be excused from teaching, from contributing to the service mission, or from contributing scholarly work. Rather, what this means is that relative weights in these areas can be adjusted according to potential impact while making certain that everyone is expected to work 100%.

Even with the assignment of differential workloads, some faculty will be more productive than others. There is always the question about how a chair might deal with such a case in the evaluation process and for consideration of merit increases. After a period of time and several reviews where productivity is discussed with a faculty member performing at the margin, the chair may realize that this level of contribution is about all that can be expected. This is not poor or problematic performance, but it is mediocre. How individuals like this might be treated with regard to merit increments has attracted more attention in recent times when dollars are scarce and rigid productivity models are followed. In some quarters merit increments are awarded only to those who perform at defined levels or those who are among the top X% in the unit in terms of performance. The danger here is that providing zero in raises will often result in diminished performance and some faculty who will just give up on making improvements or reduce their effort and output. These will become the faculty who come to teach their classes and slip away until the next manda-tory session. While these reward-the-stars schemes hope to cre-ate significant incentive for high performance, they can also cause separation among the faculty. Others models use relative merit systems where all contributions are weighed and provided reward based on level. In a differential workload system, the chair can recognize merit proportional to the preset workload distribution, thus acknowledging the work of all. The stars will still be the most highly compensated, but lesser merit will still see some reward. All of this assumes we are weighing contributions across the three areas of responsibility.

Chairs can promote an environment of opportunity in the department by being vigilant in identifying new opportunities for faculty to expand their professional interests. Frequently, such opportunities come from outside the department and can be campus- or community-based. While faculty members can and often do learn of these possibilities, chairs probably spend more time interacting with constituents external to the department and thus will be exposed to more potential opportunities. (In Chap-ters 19 and 20, the chair as campus and external entrepreneur will be discussed in more detail.) Bringing new ideas in team teaching across disciplines, the potential for research collaborations, or new mentoring opportunities can benefit faculty and alert them that the chair has faculty in mind as he or she makes the rounds outside the department. Making these external connections also raises the profile of the department on campus and identifies the unit as one that values collaboration.

A final point on how a chair might foster an environment that will be maximally conducive to excellent faculty work is to actively and continuously promote collaboration and the idea that indi-viduals will succeed only if the department community succeeds. Star players never win the ring unless the team excels. The concept of collaboration seems to run contrary to many of the expecta-tions of higher education, yet incoming faculty want to become members of an intellectual community. That membership concept implies that members of this group will work together in ways that advance and promote the discipline and the department. However, many academic cultures regard collaboration as individual weakness and dependence. The unfortunate outcome of this viewpoint is that department accomplishment becomes a summation of isolated, individual contributions that are often disconnected, especially when it comes to the delivery of academic programs. In addition, the individualistic attitude makes it impossible to take advantage of the synergy that collaboration can bring.

Promoting collaboration must be approached with care by the chair. It is well recognized that faculty have their primary affiliation with their disciplines and that their primary peer group consists of the recognized leaders within that discipline. (As discussed in detail in Chapter 14, the practices of higher education promote and mandate that such affiliations be present.) After all, most institutions will not tenure and promote members of their faculties unless they obtain the objective testaments from experts in the field about the quality of their contributions to the discipline and the excellence of their work within that disciplinary context. So why should they not expend significant time and effort in impressing and cultivating high-profile disciplinary peers?

Chairs will recognize that department advancement and improvement and the coherence of its academic offerings will depend on faculty working together. In scientific and technological research environments, chairs will also be aware that many current problems require the expert contributions of individuals with different training and skill sets. The challenge here is to promote collaboration without jeopardizing faculty careers and advancements. The dilemma is that reality requires collaboration and policies on tenure and promotion require independent excellence. This contradiction has been partially offset by institutional mission statements that recognize and promote collaboration. While such statements go beyond research ventures to include service functions, school-to-school relationships, and relationships with external entities, they nonetheless provide a framework for helping the internal culture to not only accept but to value collaborative work.

Because my institution lists collaboration in its mission statement, when new faculty are recruited, the potential for department- or campus-level collaboration is an important factor in the selection process. We realize that new faculty members will have a very difficult time succeeding if they work strictly on their own. As we fostered this approach to hiring and guiding faculty, we knew that tenure and promotion language still favored the independent research model. As way to transition to more progressive thinking, probationary faculty were counseled to engage in collaborations where a real opportunity existed but also to have other related projects that were uniquely theirs. Thus, when the tenure decision was due, there was evidence of independent work and collaborative work. While the former needs no interpretation or explanation, the latter is subject to questions about who is really the major mover on the project and who is along for the ride. In this situation, the chair needs to counsel the candidate to delineate in the documentation the unique contributions of all participants so that independent evaluators understand that the amalgamation of talent has produced something that none of the individuals could have brought to fruition alone.

Collaboration can manifest itself in academic programming through team teaching and the development of interdisciplinary curricula. These opportunities create a situation where what goes on in the classroom is more widely known and will influence other courses, resulting in a more coherent experience for students. Another effective way to get faculty members to work together on issues around academic programming is by strategically instituting reviews of curricula content and delivery when new instructors are integrated into key courses. Faculty members will sometimes resist curriculum revision when they infer that it is motivated by some level of dissatisfaction. The instructor transition removes this consideration and faculty are able to have frank discussions about what they are doing in their classes and what they expect in the prerequisites for their courses. These moments are also perfect times to introduce assessment data into the mix so that discussions will consider strengths and weaknesses and institute plans for improvements in meeting core objectives.

All efforts to encourage collaboration will have diminished impact unless the system recognizes collaboration within its reward structures. The transitions to new models in research have been discussed. Many of these are outside the direct control of the chair, although he or she can be instrumental in managing, documenting, and supporting the process. At the department level the chair can support and encourage collaboration through the merit system. The process of including collaboration in measures for faculty evaluation will begin with its endorsement by the faculty. Once accomplished, the chair can count collaborative work at full value for both or all faculty contributing. This includes research publications, grants applications, and new courses or programs developed. Initially there may be a few objections where some individuals feel the single piece of work should have a unit value of 1.0 and that contributors should split that value. If collaboration is considered an objective of value, then there needs to be incentive to promote it. Any effort that gets faculty to work together, exchange ideas, negotiate solutions, and solve problems helps to create a community attitude within the unit.

A final idea on presenting the department as a community rather than a listing of individual contributions lies in how the department reports its accomplishments. Although there are other examples, let's use the annual report to make this point. Should individual accomplishments be presented or community accomplishments or perhaps a mix of both? Degrees conferred at the undergraduate level have no individual ownership, so there is no decision to make there. Graduate degrees may be the result of specific faculty effort that will change from year to year. Publications, presentations, and other measures of scholarly productivity might be listed numerically, with individual names and bibliographies listed alphabetically in an appendix. Grant funding might be listed as totals rather then as individually awarded amounts. While some faculty members may complain they are not getting the recognition they deserve, this type of presentation reinforces the idea that the department is a community and that it will present itself as such.

Summary

Working with faculty members constitutes the primary work of a department chair. For internally appointed chairs, many of the faculty members are long-term colleagues, collaborators, and personal friends. Among the faculty may be the present chair's predecessor and perhaps potential successor. Some will be supporters and others may be detractors. All of these possibilities make interacting productively with this group of individuals a complex challenge.

Personality types among faculty members should be considered in how a chair might approach individuals and in predicting how individuals will react to certain situations. Seeking assistance from a faculty member who understands the overall obligations of the department versus a faculty member who is highly self-directed and protective of personal time are two different experiences. Personality type can also dictate how much chair time might be devoted to a faculty member, which faculty members must be sought out for information, and which freely share it.

With all of this variability, faculty still share the common elements of working in the same discipline, being well educated and highly intelligent, and having a set of responsibilities to foster their career achievement and to contribute to the success of the department and institution. Chairs need to create environments that capitalize on the first two to ensure that the latter is met.

Chairs can create positive work environments by performing the work faculty members are expected to do—setting an example is still an effective leadership tool. Chairs should strive to solicit and respect the input of all faculty members in setting policy, developing curricula, conducting research, and other activities where differences of opinion may come into play. Chairs should publicize the good work of faculty members based on their individual excellence and their contributions to unit and institutional objectives. Chairs create a positive environment when faculty members realize they are present, accessible, and working toward the department's goals. Chairs also generate goodwill and elevate morale when they can bring new opportunities for expanding professional work to faculty members.

10

WORKING WITH THE DEAN AND OTHER ADMINISTRATORS

Just as the preceding section placed me at risk with my faculty colleagues, this section could jeopardize me or reveal to the dean some of what I've been up to over the years. I served 12½ years under the dean who hired me until he retired and was succeeded by an external hire in fall 2004. My perspective of working with campus deans is shaped largely by the first of these two experiences and less by the second and interactions with other deans.

There are no major revelations about how to work with the dean to get what you need—if I had such tried and true approaches for influencing, manipulating, or convincing a dean, I would consider them proprietary and patent them! Rather, I hope to share information that will reinforce how important it is to have a good working relationship with the dean and how equally important it is to operate in such a way that the dean is comfortable with what you are doing, even if he or she does not know what you are doing most of the time. This is the trust factor. Some of what is discussed will work for most deans while some elements will be determined by individual personality. For the latter, chairs need to learn from their own interactions as well as from those who know the dean, including more experienced chairs and former dean colleagues or dean peers.

The first requirement is that chairs must be able to work with the dean, and vice versa. If this relationship does not work, the department will not thrive and the college or school will not achieve its full potential. Thus, even though faculty at colleges and universities feel that they ought to choose the department leader, it must be recognized that the appointment is almost always made on the recommendation of the dean. An astute dean will not appoint a chair whom the faculty will not tolerate, and faculty need to recognize that it is not in their best interests to insist on a chair who is incompatible with the dean. There are cases where chairs and deans have not been close prior to the appointment of one or both; however, once that relationship exists, it is essential that they learn to work well together.

What Deans Do Not Want or Like

Late or Inaccurate Paperwork

Paperwork is a management function, and it must be done correctly and in a timely fashion. Some paperwork functions are the direct responsibility of chairs while others belong to the department, but the chair is responsible for all paperwork being completed. Chairs are responsible for faculty appointment paperwork, annual reviews of faculty, budget and merit raise recommendations, forwarding paperwork associated with tenure and promotion, and routine or special requests for reports from the dean or upper administration. Many of these items can have legal ramifications and generate negative feedback from those above the dean, who, of course, will hear about them before the chair does. Other items where the chair may have delegated responsibility to faculty or staff members includes class scheduling, approval of degrees, student admission paperwork, and award nominations. It is obvious if any of these things are done in error or done too late, that a number of important constituents can be sufficiently disenchanted to call the dean.

Overspent Budget Accounts

Most institutions regard schools or divisions as budgeting units with deans allocating resources to individual departments. In many cases, deans reserve a portion of the budget to cover unanticipated costs, take advantage of special opportunities, or entertain special requests. This reserve can be thin, and an over-extended department can deplete it very quickly. To assume that the department will be bailed out may not be unrealistic if some of the projected department expenditures are for contracted services. To avoid legal proceedings or to make certain that student progress is not jeopardized, the dean may need to cover the shortfall or ask upper administration for a special allocation. Deans do not like either solution.

Hearing Department-Level Complaints

This is true whether complaints are from students, parents, or other constituents. There are several aspects to this, the most obvious of which is that the dean or his designee, an associate dean or a staff member, has no knowledge of the details of the precipitating incident. There are cases where students, parents, or others go straight to the president, who then forwards the complaint to the appropriate dean. In these situations, the chair has no knowledge. Most of the time, however, complaints will originate within the department. It is important to deal promptly with complaints—ignoring them can lead to going outside the department. Chairs or their designees experienced in such issues will know whether they have satisfied the complainant. If satisfaction is not achieved, then the chair needs to provide a warning to the dean. Should this incident then be appealed to the president and passed to the dean, he or she will already be familiar with the case.

Surprises

Surprises like those just described are not welcome, and the warning recommendation is a good place to start. A faculty member who is upset over a merit raise, is passed over for promotion, or receives a negative student evaluation may storm from the chair's office and head for the dean. Here, a quick call may be the only warning possible unless the chair has anticipated the response and had time to provide the dean with the background necessary to understand the issue fully.

Being Out of the Information Loop

That is, they do not like to hear about department activities from their bosses. This is applicable to both good and bad news items. A significant achievement by a faculty member should not be shared with the provost without telling the dean, too. Simultaneous announcing is usually acceptable in cases like this. For items that involve negative impact, it is best to bring them to the attention of the dean first so that common strategies for upward dissemination can be agreed upon.

Continued Requests for Resources From Chairs

This can come in the form of requests for budget increases, new positions, more space, funding for special activities, and the like. This is not a blanket statement—deans expect chairs to be department advocates and to plan for department improvements, including new programs that mandate new hires, new staff to serve students, and events to raise the visibility of the school and department. However, there is a line between justified advocacy that is backed by solid planning and predicted outcomes and persistent requests for resources because someone else received them or because the department wants to squeeze very possible dime out of the dean. It seems logical to assume that each unit will get a certain number of favorable audiences with the dean regarding requests for resources. Chairs must make sure that the requests are legitimate and backed by sound data, are nontrivial (i.e., high cost), and are for what the department cannot do alone—for example, when a valuable faculty member receives an offer from elsewhere and the counteroffer needs to include a salary adjustment. Even when the overall amount is not high, departments typically cannot arrange for these adjustments. The advice here is to pick your shots and make sure you are not the one always asking. Having a list of things you have done yourself to achieve improvements is always a helpful way of demonstrating self-investment, department-style.

What Deans Want

Deans typically have signature projects, goals, or visions that they articulate regularly to their constituents. Even in the absence of a formal strategic plan, new deans will show their hands in terms of defining certain objectives that will continue to mark their tenures. Some examples may be a drive to increase external funding, develop new degree programs, promote interdisciplinary work, achieve greater diversity among students and faculty, or increase scholarship funding. Deans will talk about their initiatives regularly, both inside and outside of the school. Departments that are able to provide examples of progress in such areas should communicate their successes to the dean. Much of the world in higher education is driven by key words and phrases. A couple of examples, ones that did not exist in the higher education thesaurus two decades ago, are outcomes assessment and civic engagement—and look where we are now with these concepts. The point here is to frame successes within one or more of these buzz words such that the dean realizes the department is onboard with the school's agenda and that all are working toward a common set of goals. It would be crass to link this type of framing to resources, but the positive attitudes generated cannot hurt the department's image and institutional value.

External Funds, Including Gifts

External money can come in the form of grants and contracts or from philanthropic fundraising. This is not to imply that deans are money collectors, but rather it is a recognition that often this type of new monetary resource can make the difference between success and failure. Individuals above and below the dean, including chairs and faculty, also appreciate what external support can do for academic and research programs directly and indirectly by freeing up internal funds for new initiatives. External funding is seen as a measure of unit quality and allows for greater visibility and enhanced attractiveness to potential faculty members and students. The overhead from grants can add to school and department budgets. Gift money is not included in the general budget at public institutions, thus offering greater flexibility in how it is spent. Institutions also may have interschool bragging rights concerning the amount raised or the amount garnered per faculty member. The dean will enjoy winning these competitions.

Recognition for Their Good Work and Wise Decisions

Although cynical faculty members may be reluctant to admit this, deans, and even chairs, can occasionally have good ideas that turn into successes. Deans also are frequently involved in successes achieved by academic departments. In fact, it seems that this should be their main responsibility. Such involvement may occur by providing funding, new faculty or staff positions, lobbying higher administration, arranging for collaborators, or helping with an external proposal. When administrators are successful, I have heard faculty say that it's just part of their job, so no special recognition is required. This is a mistaken notion. Faculty members have responsibilities in some mix of teaching, scholarship, and service, and when they do a particularly good job they are rewarded with promotion, tenure, merit increments, and personal accolades. It seems that parallel, high achievement, not just ordinary work, for administrative successes should also be recognized. Chairs should be aware of this and provide credit where it is due both with department faculty and others outside of the department.

Things They Can Brag About

These are the types of items that find their ways into convocation and commencements speeches, special requests to higher administration, and addresses to external constituents, including those from whom gifts are solicited. The "things" referred to range from major, innovative programs and accomplishments to small anecdotes or human interest stories. Imagine what a dean would do with a program developed by the Department of English with a consortium of local businesses to offer a new degree program in applied writing in business. One can hear the speeches with sound bites emphasizing collaboration, enhanced enrollments, external funding, and civic engagement. Then there are the human interest stories about the mother of four who commuted 60 miles round trip each day to earn her degree and gain admission to the medical school. If you have stories like these to share, let the dean know and you will likely hear them repeated elsewhere. The astute dean will give appropriate credit to the origin of the story.

Effective Interaction

There is not much concrete information or advice to provide on how to effectively interact with the dean. Chapter 8 discussed communication with various individuals, including deans. Much of what is the best way to interact and share information with a dean is a function of personality. That works on both sides. Some deans do not mind chairs and sometimes faculty walking into their offices (with open doors, of course) and reporting information or just touching base. Some, in fact, like this. The absence of the chair, except for scheduled group meetings, for an extended period of time can lead deans to wonder what chairs are up to. Other deans like to scrupulously partition their time and want appointments made for specified periods of time with set agendas. On the other side of the issue, some chairs prefer more structured meetings and will not be frequent impromptu visitors. Some deans will set aside time for a discussion that is more social than business, a propensity that can build strong personal relationships and create more of an open door atmosphere. Others have more set agendas and want to focus more on academic business. Other models and behaviors exist within the range described. When there is a new dean, chairs will need to be attentive to the way the dean prefers to interact with chairs and adjust the strategy for approaching accordingly.

Some issues will need to be negotiated between chairs and deans. A chair may have to approach the dean about a new staff or faculty position or to ask permission to replace a vacated slot during times of fiscal restriction. There may be requests for instructional help to cover new sections created in response to student demand or for the purchase or repair of essential equipment. Of course, there is the expected budget request and negotiation that takes place at most institutions. The following offers some considerations on how to approach these meetings to improve chances of success and create an overall better working relationship in the future.

These meetings need not be adversarial or demanding. Civil behavior in a relaxed atmosphere, perhaps with a touch of humor, may be one way to disarm any oversensitivity resulting from other negotiations and to lower defensive protections so that rational arguments will be heard. Those arguments or justifications should be well articulated, supported with data, and demonstrate that the chair has a forward vision for the positive impact that any investment may have for the department. For example, take a proposal for a new faculty line in a certain area that will create new student demand, including new majors to the institution, and initiate the development of a cross-campus interdisciplinary program. Citing data on existing student interest, the success of similar programs elsewhere, and the lack of competing programs in the region are all pieces of supporting evidence that can be convincing in these conversations.

Other considerations in dealing with the dean include the responsibility of the chair to think bigger than or beyond the department. Deans expect chairs to be strong department advocates. They also respond to chairs who recognize that some outside ideas or needs may take precedence over department need. In some ways this is thinking as a dean might. However, if there is greater need or greater potential impact in another idea outside the department, chairs must recognize and support this. Institutional vitality is a beneficial situation for all departments. As an example, some space becomes available in a school where space is a very limiting factor. A chair could use that space to consolidate department faculty, some of whom are in the building next door. This is certainly a good idea for the benefit of that faculty community. However, another chair suggests that the space be used to create an instrument center to house equipment used by faculty members in several departments. Further, the centralization of the equipment can also be used to attract new faculty without having to duplicate some of the items. Here the chair sets aside limited department advantage for the higher impact potential of the instrument center. Understanding the larger picture, being astute about appealing to greater needs, and knowing when to bow out are all attributes chairs might think about in their dealings with the dean.

There will be occasions for chairs to interact with other administrators on campus. Who they may be depends heavily on the nature of the institution. A small liberal arts college may have a dean who reports to the president or perhaps vice president. The layers from top to bottom in such an environment are few. At a large institution, however, the dean may be one of two or three dozen deans, and the institution may have a bevy of vice presidents, associate vice presidents, chancellors, and so on, creating a complex management system where authority lines become unclear. For simplicity, the assumption will be made that the dean reports to the provost and the provost reports to the president.

There are occasions, and chairs can make them take place with greater frequency, where chairs have the opportunity to work with or share information with the provost and even the president. The variable frequency is related to the profile the chair chooses to assume. (See Chapters 19 and 20 for a discussion of working outside the unit and with campus constituents.) Many activities can have high-profile outcomes that attract the attention of upper administration, and as a result, the chair may be assigned to a committee of campus importance. While this may be extra work, it also gives the chair a voice in issues of campus concern and provides an audience with upper administrators where other pieces of information can be exchanged. The exchange may be two-way and the chair can come away with deeper insight on campus policy and information that can be used to benefit the department. Provosts and presidents also like sound bites, anecdotes that reflect positively on the institution, and news on innovative programs of potential or high productivity. If chairs use these opportunities to pass favorable department information on to high-level administrators, they also need to make certain that the dean is informed.

One final topic about dealing with deans and other administrators is related to chair frustration with what may be called compartmentalized thinking by deans and others in administration. Chairs work in environments where they constantly think about and deal with issues in undergraduate and graduate education, teaching effectiveness, research and scholarship, and service functions, all of which have different dimensions. This places chairs in the best position to predict the impact of changing emphases within these categories on other aspects of department work. Deans have less of a perspective on these ramifications, while provosts have almost no idea about the ripple effect of doubling one commitment or assigning faculty or staff to new functions.

Deans and upper administrators deal with more global issues such as school and university budgets, actions and desires from trustees, requests from alumni and community groups, and other far-reaching questioins. Their detailed understanding of delicate balances among the myriad of things an academic department does is limited. Thus they frequently deal with whatever the issue of interest is for their present audience. Some examples may be helpful. There is a special campus symposium organized around the topic of the value of undergraduate research. Clearly, this is an important and timely topic. The dean attends, listens to the reports on the successful work of faculty around campus, and leaves enthusiastic about the importance of his or her school becoming more active in this work. At the next meeting with chairs, the dean states that all undergraduate students must be mentored in research by department faculty. This clearly creates a challenge to the work balance in the department and may jeopardize other important department work if additional resources are shifted to work that is individualized for many students.

The story continues a week later when the dean hears the institutional research report announcing the amount of external dollars received by faculty and returns to the school with the goal that faculty members submit more grant proposals to support research. Again, balance is disrupted and faculty are confused about what direction to take. Chairs, of course, know that the department will have faculty members who are suited to and interested in working with some undergraduate students and faculty members who are effective and committed scholars who routinely write grant proposals. However, the sheer number of students involved, as well as the fact that many will be unprepared for research work, places huge burdens on the faculty members. Another aspect of this administrative focus is when major addresses are given by administrators that focus on a limited array of the work of the institution or school. These presentations are usually the result of targeting the subject matter to the audience at hand. Chairs need to understand that their superiors can be led to focus on single aspects of faculty work without considering these within the context of total work and responsibility. Deans and other administrators must recognize that faculty work as orchestrated at the department level is a complex, interrelated tapestry, and it is worthwhile to step back and take in the entire picture before suggesting changes.

As in the earlier case for calls that all faculty members be involved in the instruction of beginning students, chairs must negotiate new demands with deans and administrators in a way that overall campus goals can be met. While there is value in undergraduate research, not all students in large departments can be meaningfully engaged in it. Limiting this demand to selected degree programs or to experienced upper-class undergraduates may be a consideration. Chairs should present alternatives within the context of the unit's other responsibilities and goals to demonstrate how faculty time will be impacted and what items may be shortchanged in order to accommodate the new initiative.

Summary

Probably the most important single relationship that chairs will establish is the one with the dean. The relationship must be built on trust and mutual respect and be productively functional. If disagreements become the dominant aspect of the relationship, the department and institution will both suffer. Of course, it helps if the two people genuinely like each other.

The chair must be cognizant of what the dean does not appreciate as well as what the dean seeks from the departments. Deans do not like budget overruns, being uninformed about important issues, having to respond to complaints that should be dealt with at the department level, and chairs who constantly ask for new resources. How deans may respond to surprises depends on whether they are good news or bad. What deans like is new revenue streams, examples of department success that can be used in school reports and addresses, and credit for making the right decision. If the dean has created two new faculty lines that allow a department to launch a highly successful program, then somewhere in accepting the accolades for this success, the chair and others should mention the foresight demonstrated by the dean in making the investment.

Approaching the dean formally or informally is accomplished based on knowing the dean's preferences. Some prefer informal, unannounced drop-bys and are happy to put aside their work to discuss pressing matters or just to touch base with chairs. Others prefer to have set schedules and will hold discussions only by appointment. Chairs will learn how to best approach the dean through trial and error or by asking. Chairs may also be able to communicate indirectly through other members of the dean's office and can also gain information from the dean's staff regarding what might be good days or times to approach the dean. If the dean is approached with a major request or to discuss an issue of significant controversy, being well prepared with supporting information is a must. Requests should be justified based on their contributions to the department and institutional goals. Controversial items where there is likely to be disagreement must be discussed in a civil manner, always remembering that two people can agree to disagree.

11

INTERACTING WITH STUDENTS

Department chairs may have differing degrees of direct interactions with students. Because most readers will be affiliated with departments that have undergraduate students, the types of interactions described will be within that context. Most, but not all, chairs will have some student contact through teaching. While this may be graduate-level contact in some instances, chairs will at least have undergraduate responsibility related to teaching that may include scheduling classes, assigning instructors, overseeing and leading improvements in the curriculum, and monitoring effectiveness. These contacts with students and others that arise in the classroom will be not be discussed here in favor of some old but still high-profile student interactions and some newer considerations that are receiving a good deal of attention. These issues are ones where chair leadership is essential for improvement and success.

Student Recruitment

The idea that academic departments would become involved in student recruitment is a given in departments with graduate programs. Extending the concept to undergraduate students in that department, however, would not be accepted as easily. Graduate recruiting is a department-level function with someone in the unit acting as the admissions office. All application materials are received by the department and reviewed by a faculty committee. The recommendation for admission goes to the graduate school or to a school-level committee for final approval. Candidates are often invited to campus and are eagerly interviewed and courted by faculty members. Faculty will also travel to graduate recruitment fairs and visit other institutions in hopes of luring quality undergraduates to their graduate program.

The situation with undergraduate student recruitment at the department level is quite different. This function is handled almost exclusively by the campus admissions office or some derivative of that office. These staff members maintain contact with area (area can be local to state to regional) high schools, visit and display at college recruitment fairs, send out multiple mailings, purchase lists of student test scores for targeted contacts, and do a myriad of other things in a generic, institutional effort to bring new students to campus. Once specific information from perspective students is known, more targeted contacts are made with information or materials relevant to disciplinary interests. These efforts are supplemented by other campus offices dealing with scholarships and financial aid, career opportunities, and campus life. The direct involvement of academic departments is rare. They may provide brochures and other materials and construct web sites useful to campus-level recruiters, but they do not usually participate in active outreach to potential undergraduate students.

This scenario is now changing. Small liberal arts colleges are in competition with each other for high-performing students with the resources to invest in the high tuition and fees required. Public institutions are feeling the pinch of flat or reduced public support and real or political caps on tuition hikes. Their only avenue for further revenue enhancement is increased enrollments with the hope that new students can be accommodated on the margin. Other public institutions are seeking to raise their profiles and increase retention by admitting a better-prepared student body. This means they will have to lure students who would normally enroll elsewhere. While these new initiatives can be accommodated to some degree within the traditional recruitment framework, the sharpening competition will require more personal and targeted approaches to prospective students and will involve academic departments.

Departments have been or may be asked to develop recruitment initiatives to attract more undergraduate applicants and actively recruit those who follow through with applications. For the former, departments will have to work with campus recruiters to make certain they have updated printed and electronic materials (web sites and CDs) and that campus personnel have department contacts so they can respond to student questions. Local and area recruitment fairs benefit when faculty or other academic individuals, not just staff, are on hand to answer questions. Campus events also present opportunities for tours of the facilities and other hands-on experiences. Another idea, one I have seen from schools trying to recruit my children, are personal letters from faculty members in the department of interest listed by the prospective student. These are personalized letters that mention the student's name within the text and are actually signed by a faculty member. I am certain such letters are form letters generally extolling the advantages of the department or a program. Such documents can be prepared by staff with student-specific names and addresses. Students like the attention from letters, and the personalized touch from a faculty member impresses both students and their parents. Finally, some schools use current students to call prospective students to encourage them to enroll, invite them to campus for visits, and generally promote the virtues of the college or university. These calls must be scripted to some degree so that students do not provide incorrect advice or information. Other examples may exist, but departments should be prepared to become more active in assuring they have a strong pipeline of undergraduate students entering their programs.

Student Retention

Retention has always been an important issue, but the emphasis on it has increased dramatically in recent years as the competition for students has risen and as parents and legislatures have questioned the large, empty costs that result when students are unsuccessful and leave. Even private institutions, where retention is high in a relative sense, are concerned about students who do not return. From a department perspective, it is much easier and less expensive to retain an existing student than to recruit a new one. As a corollary, retaining students can help to populate upper-divisions courses where capacity exits at most institutions.

Retention has many dimensions that can be explored here only in a summary fashion. Consider the higher education enterprise 30 to 40 years ago. At that time, perhaps 20% of the population went to college. Plenty of good-paying jobs were available to those who chose instead to enter the workforce. A close look at what happened then will show that student success was not high. I recall my freshman biology class, initially containing about 100 students. In my senior year, there were fewer than 30 biology students enrolled. A few had gone on to professional school prior to graduation and others had switched to different majors, but a good number were part of the attrition that we still see today. I do not recall a public outcry over this phenomenon. Rather, I recall being told by my parents that college would test my ability and my commitment; some students would meet the challenge and others would not. It was understood that colleges and universities would set the bar, that some would clear it and others would not.

Today, perhaps 80% of graduating high school seniors go on to further education. This is the same top 20% of the past plus the next 60%. All things being equal, why would one expect the success rate to be higher or even the same? The answer is that times have changed as well as expectations, attitudes, and realities.

A college degree is now considered the minimum requirement for entry-level positions in the American economy. Thus access to higher education has become a matter of entitlement or social justice that provides an opportunity for all to compete in the pipeline leading to at least a middle-class life. And once these students arrive on campus there is a growing expectation that they will earn their degrees.

While the new expectations resonate as appropriate goals for a democratic society, they place real stresses on the higher education system. These stresses include those related to the culture of higher education and those related to standards and what a college degree really means. Before this conversation gets too far removed from the work of department chairs, it needs to be noted that these stresses will impact academic departments, especially those in public institutions. Thus they will require the attention and creativity of department chairs. Chairs must work to improvise support structures that facilitate student success and to convince faculty that the delivery of higher education must assume different characteristics.

Higher education has acted as a filter for hundreds of years. That is, students entered the academy, but only a portion survived the rigors and challenges of earning a degree. In the new world order, this is no longer acceptable. There are now the expectations of both access and success. While selective institutions retain high expectations that can be met by their continuing high student profile, public institutions confront these stresses in more pronounced ways. Veteran faculty members have class standards based on their instructional histories and the ways they were taught and evaluated. They made the grade and expect their students to match that if they, too, expect to receive the same degree. Those approaches will not be effective with the top 80% of all high school classes. The way we deal with the instruction of new freshman students, and all undergraduates for that matter, must change in order to improve student retention and persistence to earn a degree.

To set some parameters on what is meant by retention, one needs to study the accepted national measure for this statistic. That measure, the one used to evaluate and rank institutions, is first- to second-year persistence of fall, full-time, first-time freshmen. For some institutions this can be a very misleading data point because it does not include many of the students who may attend an urban public institution. A related statistic used in institutional rankings is graduation rate. The same cohort is used to calculate how many have graduated in six years. Thus, from a practical perspective, institutions have focused on this student group and what happens in the classroom during the first year. Upcraft, Gardner, Barefoot, and Associates (2005) provide a glimpse of the many aspects of the huge effort to understand and improve the first year such that overall student success is enhanced.

Improving retention is a daunting task because the nature of the student clientele populating the first year has changed dramatically. First-year student bodies are more age-variable, more international, contain more first-generation members, more racially and culturally diverse, more likely to have a higher percentage of members with documented disabilities, and more endowed with academically underprepared members. Again, these variables are seen to their fullest extent in urban, public institutions. Institutions focusing on efforts to improve first-year success are approaching this challenge in a time of diminished resources and in an environment where other aspects of university operation are competing for limited internal resources. To be successful, these efforts need to be recognized as critical to the institution and worthy of the participation and energy of its academic departments.

Chair Leadership in Retention Efforts

Just listing the diversity of the student populations in beginning classes demonstrates that improving retention is a tough problem and one that will require a multipronged strategy. The diversity of courses these students will enroll in further complicates the situation. The role of the chair in bringing the department to the table in these efforts will take on two distinct aspects. In order to be successful, the chair must first bring the urgency of this matter to the faculty. Many faculty members will respond to hard data—low retention rates or poor student performance in the department's beginning courses may stimulate a renewed sense of commitment to improving its status. A simple fiscal analysis of what is lost to the institution and to the department when a student does not persist to the second year can be persuasive, especially when budget constraints are limiting faculty replacement and diminish other symbols of department well-being.

The first aspect of the chair's role in improving retention is participation in global, institutional approaches to improving the first year. There are many possible manifestations of campus effort and a given department will probably not be able to muster the resources to engage in all. Those that seem to hold promise for the department based on its role in teaching first-year courses should be identified as participation points. Examples may include mandatory freshman seminars or the availability of upper-class student mentors who work in freshman classes. For the former, departments will have to contribute to the content of the first-year seminars and participate in their instruction. This may mean reconfiguration of instructional assignments. For the latter, faculty members teaching courses will have to work with campus experts in designing effective ways for mentors to contribute to student support and preparation. Chairs will also need to share identified best practices for improving student retention with faculty members. This may involve inviting key faculty members to special workshops or seminars on retention. It also helps if the chair attends these on a regular basis to emphasize their importance.

The second aspect of the chair's role is to lead the work that the department does internally to improve student success in its beginning courses. In the final analysis, retention efforts are not going to be successful without the contributions of the content experts who teach the introductory courses. Department-level changes may include restructuring course scheduling, adding new elements to sections of a course, and incorporating ancillary experiences as an addition to the course. For example, a recitation, quiz, or problem section could be added to a course. This section would be scheduled as a required component and perhaps constitute a credit hour. The extra meeting might be used to review material, take practice or real quizzes, promote student collaboration on problem solving, or provide instruction that reinforces content in the main body of the course. Whatever changes are made, they will require faculty input to ensure their relevance to the material to be mastered. These efforts are designed to enhance student success without diminishing traditional standards.

As a final comment on innovations to address the retention problem, I will raise a concept that will reappear later, the concept of turning innovation into scholarship. Developing a sound strategy that increases student success in a given course such that a higher percentage of students are retained is something others would like to hear about and try in their own courses. Successful results of such a strategy would also be the raw material or preliminary data used in a proposal for external support for dissemination and extension of the initiative. Effective strategies for increasing retention would be welcome contributions to the professional literature that features the scholarship of teaching and learning.

Student Advising

A special area where chairs have at least indirect interactions with students is in advising. Advising has been identified as a major area in student recruitment and retention. Advising is also a lightning rod for criticism, especially in institutions where the student population is highly variable and where student numbers far exceed those of faculty and staff. In such institutions, advising remains a sensitive issue with regard to student satisfaction, no matter what is done to improve the process. I will distance myself somewhat from the printed and spoken wisdom of others on how and by whom advising might be delivered and on what an advisor is actually supposed to provide in the way of service to students.

While virtually every written piece will list advising as a faculty responsibility or duty and recommend that it be given greater weight in evaluating faculty for merit pay and promotion and tenure, I take the position that advising is complex and intricate work and who is best suited to provide this service depends on a number of variables. This student service plays out differently depending upon institutional type, student-to-faculty ratio, and the changing expectations of students about what they can reasonably expect from an academic advisor. The following discussion will present advising activities and make some recommendations regarding who should do this work and how far academic departments should go in dealing with issues that students bring to their advisors. The focus will be on undergraduate advising.

First, the variable of institutional type should be considered. A small, private, expensive liberal arts college may claim a student-to-faculty ratio of eight to one. The numbers immediately suggest that the average burden of advising will be light, assuming a proportional distribution of students among faculty. Majors may not be distributed proportionally, so some load deviation may occur unless faculty are expected to advise in more than one academic discipline. Second, such institutions are selective in admissions resulting in homogeneously bright students who, with their families, have probably planned on college for many years. Furthermore, students are full-time and progress through their four years as cohorts. Faculty members at such institutions have substantial teaching loads in terms of sections assigned but generally teach smaller classes. The advising function sometimes becomes as prominent in their lives as scholarship. Everyone knows this from the outset and the process seems to work well.

In contrast is a large, public institution where the student-to-faculty ratio may be 20 to 40 or more to one. Add the unequal distribution of majors, and the number can climb higher in some units. Also consider the larger number of undecided or exploratory students, and another challenge emerges in the advising arena. Moving that public institution to an urban setting brings more complexity. Here, the number of underprepared students rises as a reflection of the mandate to provide access. The number of first-generation students also rises in such settings. These are young people who are the first in their families to go to college and who are at considerable risk because there is no family history in higher education—the process is a learning experience for them all. Finally, urban settings bring many part-time, adult, and working students to the university. All of these categories of students have special needs and unique issues that are brought to advising sessions. Advising is indeed a very complicated matter in these settings.

To set the stage for looking at advising models, I must return to my experiences before I became chair. At that time I was responsible for all undergraduate student paperwork including transcript evaluation, degree auditing, admissions, and assigning advisors. We operated under the recommended model that all faculty members have obligations to advise students, and new students were distributed on a cyclical basis so that the numbers would be the same for everyone. Because I also prepared the graduation audits (and because of some other information), I came to know who did a fine job of advising and who did not. I can recall approving some unusual degrees because of advisor errors. One that comes to mind is counting calculus as an arts and humanities course so a student could graduate on time.

Aside from advising errors, there were issues of absent faculty in summers when new students needed to schedule fall classes. Sabbatical leaves and other absences were also problematic because other faculty would be unfamiliar with continuing students they might be expected to serve. Ours is a research environment where faculty are expected to earn external funding for their work and their ten-month contracts could be supplemented with two months of summer salary from grants for 100% effort. These individuals could rightfully say that they held a university-endorsed contract to provide 100% of their effort toward the project which excused them from participation in orientations and other advising activities in the summer. Others had no summer funding, so were under no obligation to do university work. These occurrences became so problematic that I began to consider the student record before me to match it with an advisor. This would have been most inappropriate because it was grossly unfair to marginal students who would be assigned the disinterested advisor. The only other option was to recommend to the chair that only certain faculty be advisors. Thus their reward for doing a conscientious job was more advisees. This system was obviously not working.

Let's now turn to student expectations in the advising function. I think those of us in the ranks believe that department-level advising is first and foremost academic advising. We need to help students select the appropriate classes for degree completion. We also need to steer them to the right degree options to meet their career objectives. This might play out differently in the philosophy department than it would in chemistry because the philosophy major probably is not headed for a career as a philosopher, but the chemistry major may very well be working in industry as a chemist. But there are other elements in the advising process that place the faculty advisor at a disadvantage and can lead to student complaints and low evaluations of advising.

Some students expect ad hoc advising, that is, they show up at a faculty member's office without an appointment and expect to be served. If the faculty member is not there, then the advisor is regarded as unavailable and is criticized for not meeting student need. I had a student call our office one July asking to see an advisor. The student was told that the advisor was not in that day but was due back the next day. The student was advised to call the advisor and leave a voicemail message about arranging an appointment. The student was irate and demanded advising that day, stating he would be driving to campus to receive advising. I asked staff to direct him to me if he actually appeared. I had no intention of providing advising, but was prepared to provide a lesson in professional courtesy.

Advising sessions can sometimes lead into areas where faculty have no expertise and where there can be some legal liabilities. Faculty members in my department have been asked for advice on dealing with unwanted pregnancies and domestic abuse. These are clearly outside the expertise of faculty and have potential legal ramifications. While there are campus resources prepared to deal with these kinds of issues, some students expect their advisors to help, rather than strangers in other offices. Not providing help with these issues when the student asks in confidence can also lead to student dissatisfaction with advising.

The final issue is one of time allotted to students and the circumstances under which an advisor should be meeting with students. Students who are advised as to course selection may return later to discuss the process one or more additional times, sometimes accompanied by parents. Students may have to withdraw and need an advisor's signature. But because they are frequently at the deadline for this transaction, they need their advisor's signature immediately. If the advisor is not available, the student approaches other faculty members or department staff who know nothing about the student or the circumstances. Finally, there are those students who really bond with their advisors and return several times in the semester to discuss a grade on a history paper or their preparation for an upcoming physics exam. While these are the kinds of personal interactions and connections we seek in some respects, they take significant amounts of time from individuals hired with other primary work in mind.

By now the reader is probably thinking that advising should not be done by faculty and that students always present unreasonable

demands on advisors. On the contrary, most students either successfully self-advise or see their advisor according to protocol and
schedule. At high-enrolling institutions, the number of exceptions
can be considerable, a situation that leads to survey results indicating that students are dissatisfied with advising regardless of the
institution's efforts to improve the process. So how might advising be handled at complex institutions where students outnumber
faculty by substantial margins? There are several models that seem
to work, and many can be combined to offer students sound, accurate advice as they work toward their degrees. To avoid making
the discussion too lengthy, I should note that each of these models
could be in place at several levels (institution, school, and department) at larger universities.

Selected Faculty Advisors

When the advising load is manageable, members of the faculty can
take on this task. However, it is important to recognize that not all
will be suited for or will effectively carry out this student service.
These variables are a function of personality and interest, respectively. In soliciting faculty for this responsibility, it must be clear that
not all will be involved and that those who do participate will not
be placed at a disadvantage in merit considerations and promotion
and tenure decisions relative to the nonparticipants. Because many
people consider advising to be an extension of the teaching process,
it can be one of the elements for evaluation in the teaching category. In institutions with substantial teaching loads and a healthy
number of students to advise, one course of released time may be a
reasonable consideration. When faculty evaluation is discussed in
Chapter 16, a recommendation is made to use multiple measures
in evaluating the various contributions that faculty members can
make in the areas of faculty responsibility. Advising can certainly
be one of these. Differential faculty loads are another way to allow
faculty more work in their areas of strength and ensure that all are
100% engaged in faculty work. These considerations must be shared

with all faculty members, with evidence that selections were made with exceptional diligence and effectiveness evident in the reward structure and in decisions for promotion and tenure.

Professional Advisors

This model calls for the hiring of a full-time (part-time if the student load is low and the position can be shared with a related department) professional advisor. This individual may be a graduate of the department or someone familiar with the discipline. Those trained in other areas can do this work, but there will be situations where they will be at a disadvantage. The current climate has been moving toward requiring at least a master's-trained individual for advising positions, which may drive costs higher. Professional advisors can be extremely effective, and they have several important advantages over faculty advisors.

Professional advisors see their primary professional role as a student advisor. Faculty advisors, no matter how well intentioned, will always regard teaching, research, or professional service or some combination of these as more fundamental to their careers and self-image. Thus the professional advisor will establish, as a priority, checking with other programs regarding changing requirements, will call other institutions to inquire about transferability of credits, will prepare requirement checksheets for all department degree programs and minors, and will perform a variety of tasks to keep track of the details required for effective student advising. Expecting individual faculty members to keep track of this or even parceling out pieces of this work and having them share results is not going to be nearly as effective. Creative professional advisors also can organize campus visits by graduate and professional schools for graduating students. Faculty would rarely do such tasks that would involve scheduling interviews and arranging for travel.

Professional advisors are more available to students. They may hold open hours and can be reached by phone. There is little

chance that they will be in class or involved in some type of scholarship project where they cannot respond. Professional advisors
are likely to be a 12-month appointment and thus available for
summer student orientations and pre–academic year sessions
for students. Because responding to students in nonclassroom
situations is their primary obligation, professional advisors are
likely to return calls and email messages more promptly than
faculty members busy with other things. Structuring time will
be important for professional advisors who have heavy advising
loads, but they are more likely to provide on-the-spot service
than faculty members.

For those still believing that faculty should do all advising I will
say that a disciplinary-trained professional advisor brings much
more in the way of convenient student services and represents a
single source of advising wisdom. That is, when errors do occur,
it is a one-stop process to correct them. Professional advisors not
trained in the discipline will initially be hampered by their lack
of understanding the nuances of the subject area. Hiring a professional advisor is an expense, one institutions may not be able to
justify. Some will say that faculty members are already paid, so the
advising services they provide are "free." The counterargument is
they are not free if advising is ineffective, if students are misadvised
and leave the department, or if the advising work diminishes faculty productivity in teaching or scholarship.

Peer Advising

This model is used in combination with one or more of the others
and is rarely used alone as a way to advise students. The model
uses advanced undergraduates in the department to do routine
advising of underclassmen. Appropriate training and oversight by
a faculty member or a professional advisor are essential for this
model to be effective. There are also issues of access to student
records by other students that may limit the work they can do.
An advantage here is that students will be very comfortable with

their peers. Another characteristic, and one the can be positive or negative, is that student advisors know the department, its curriculum, and its faculty from personal experience. This means that they can alert students regarding what to expect in certain courses and how to prepare for exams. On the other hand, they can advise students away from certain courses or faculty members because of their experiences when such a decision is not in the best interests of the student. Thus care must be taken in the selection and training of peer advisors, and they should only participate in the routine aspects of advising.

Group Advising

This model for academic advising may not be applicable throughout a student's stay at the university, but there are some defined circumstances where it can be used effectively. In smaller institutions where students are primarily full-time and move through a prescribed curriculum, a cohort of majors may be captured in a common course and some class time can be set aside to direct them in selecting the next semester's courses. In larger institutions there are two possible opportunities to take care of advising in the first year. One is during extended orientation sessions prior to fall classes where students are divided into groups based on prospective majors. Another opportunity is during freshman seminar classes. One theme of these seminars is the importance of advising and the responsibility students have for knowing the degree requirements, setting their own path to the degree, and utilizing advisors when they have questions they cannot answer for themselves. Freshman seminars are frequently thematic, and beginning students in the same major are often placed in the same section. This facilitates course selection. Even undecided students represent a connected cohort because they will be taking classes that meet general distribution requirements and perhaps an exploratory course or two. This model must be used in conjunction with one or more of the other models, but it still can save significant resources if extended orientations and theme-based freshman seminars are part of the institutional preparation and instruction of beginning students.

Technology

There are ways that technology can assist the advising process and reduce face time devoted to this activity. Electronic audits that will fill in course requirement grids as a student completes each semester are helpful with the simplest elements of the advising process. For more complex issues such as course transfers and substitutions and advising students on probation, students would still need a session with an expert advisor.

Other Considerations

There are other considerations chairs should be aware of in the advising arena. First, in larger institutions with the complexities already outlined, be prepared for student advising to show as a poorly rated item on student surveys no matter what models have been employed and how much energy has been expended. While students who properly use the services provided will have a positive experience, those who did not avail themselves of the service will rate advising poorly because they never received any. Survey items such as "I found my advisor to be helpful" will not earn a "strongly agree" or "agree" response when the student never made an advising appointment.

Second, if professional or faculty advisors are the models used, they should serve students primarily by appointment. These are professional people and should be treated as such. When an advisor does not know whom to expect, he or she cannot be prepared for that student. Appointment advising allows the advisor to review the file and notes from the last session. Some students will demand "drive-through" advising and be upset when told to schedule an appointment. Other students will make appointments and not keep them. There is nothing wrong with discussing the discourtesy of this behavior when they finally do come in.

Third, there will be students who soak up personal resources by appearing regularly at the advisor's door to discuss any number of issues. This represents a real connection that has been established, but it may prevent the advisor from serving others at peak time. In such cases advisors must offer only an abbreviated time while negotiating a future meeting when student demand has diminished.

Finally, there is the challenge of a reality check conversation with an advisee. We see this frequently because my department is the primary route for students seeking admission to medical, dental, and veterinary schools, all of which require very high standards of performance. No matter how delicately or sensitively an advisor counsels having a backup plan, negative comments about the advisor who dashed hopes for the only career they ever wanted or the advisor who said they were not good enough will appear on student surveys. I think we all understand that the advisor has done the right thing and the student may eventually realize this, but at the time it can be a devastating revelation.

Summary

The chair's role in interacting with students is manifested in several ways. Among the emerging expectations for academic departments are those associated with making certain that there is an acceptable level of student registration and that students who do enroll are increasingly successful in earning their degrees. Student recruitment is part of the equation. There are two main drivers for increased department focus on recruitment and retention. One of these is financial. While selective institutions have ways of ensuring an academically strong student body that pays high tuition for the full four years of study, public institutions, particularly public institutions in urban settings, have a vastly different student clientele. They are also faced with diminished state support and limits on tuition. Thus recruiting and retaining students at these institutions takes on special meaning. The second driver is political pressure to increase student success based on expected return on state and private investment. Again, selective institutions with strong students graduate a high percentage while publics with less resources and many at-risk students struggle. Recruiting a stronger student body and giving special attention to efforts to retain matriculating students thus are becoming new expectations.

Student recruiting has been largely relegated to staff in the admissions office and other campus offices. Departments will play an increasing role in having content experts on hand for certain elements of the recruiting process. In addition, specific personal outreach efforts to prospective students may become a regular department strategy to win the competition for talented new students. Increasing retention is important to all institutions but is particularly crucial to urban publics. At the national level there are several institutional-level intervention models that have shown some effectiveness in retaining students. In addition, there are possible programs and initiatives at the department level that can prove effective in seeing students through their first year on to graduation.

Chairs will play critical roles in both these efforts. They must be able to articulate to faculty the importance of student recruitment and retention. This may be done at several levels, including linking success in these areas to resources available to the department and to the ability of faculty members to do other work they feel is more aligned with their professional advancement. Chairs must also be selective in determining what campus initiatives the department will join and how they will contribute. Resources will likely preclude full participation, so those where the department can be particularly effective should be selected. The department under the leadership of the chair should devise its own strategies to enhance student success and recruit future students.

Student advising is universally important and an interaction that seems to result in negative satisfaction for many students. There are several models for student advising. The faculty model, one that some insist is the only appropriate one, seems to work well in departments with few students and at institutions with low student-to-faculty ratios. Once the number of students rises and the diversity of the student body increases beyond the full-time young adult, the faculty model suffers for several reasons. In such systems the professional advisor model seems to work best. This individual will see advising as the primary job responsibility and will be prepared to deal with at-risk students and other special cases that arise on a regular basis. Other models are possible, and combinations are frequently used to deliver student advising. Chairs should be aware of the various possibilities so that an effective advising system can be put into place.

12

STAFFING THE ACADEMIC DEPARTMENT

The most important activity a department does in terms of immediate and long-term impact on quality, culture, and focus is to hire new faculty members. Before beginning the recruitment process, the chair may have to make the case to the dean either for a new position or permission to replace a departed member of the faculty. In today's climate, approval is less certain and, if granted, may not be for the same type of position. While search and screen committees typically do the work of posting position announcements, reviewing the bulk of applications, and selecting the short list of candidates, the chair plays critical roles leading up to this committee work and is a central participant in selling the department, explaining its operation to candidates, and actually negotiating the details of the offer. In the early stages, the chair's role is critical in establishing the committee and in leading discussions as to the disciplinary focus of the new hire. Issues around the actual hiring process will be fully explored in the next chapter.

New Approaches to Hiring Faculty

Veteran chairs have no doubt already recruited new faculty, and those thinking about seeking a chair position know that they will participate in this process. But what many chairs fail to realize is the extent to which the nature of faculty hiring has changed over the last decade. A significant cadre (approximately 50%) of current tenured faculty will retire in the next 10 to 15 years, making the next wave of hiring crucial to higher education as it proceeds through fundamental changes in how it does business.

The traditional approach to replacing a retired or resigned faculty member has been to request permission to hire a tenure-track assistant professor or perhaps a tenured or tenure-track individual at an advanced rank. A new position allocated to the department would also have been requested on the tenure track. This scenario, however, has changed dramatically over the last decade, and there is every indication that these new trends will continue into the future. Increasingly more common is the likelihood that the replacement will be denied or approved with an appointment that is not on the tenure track. Chairs and would-be chairs need to know the positive and negatives of filling faculty lines in different ways as they develop plans for staffing their departments for the coming decades.

Factors Driving New Faculty Hires

Everyone is familiar with the increased dependence on part-time or adjunct faculty in higher education. This is certainly an element of change, but it is only a part of the new trend. A more recent trend has been the move from tenure-track hires to full-time nontenure-track hires. The major factor driving this change is cost. Full-time nontenure-track faculty members are brought in at salaries ranging from 75% to 50% of those offered to tenure-track hires. They are also expected to teach more, covering the expectations of the vacancy of a tenure-track hire plus some. Over the short run, this appears to be a good solution if teaching coverage is an important objective. In addition, faculty hires in science and technology areas at research universities require significant initial investment in terms of startup packages to get them in position to fund their research from external sources. These packages usually run in the hundreds of thousands of dollars and have been known to exceed $1 million in some disciplines at high-profile research universities. These costs are avoided with full-time nontenure-track hires.

Research expectations, whether at an established research institution or one that wishes to increase its research profile, have additional impact on the types of hires that are now being made. The surge in undergraduate enrollments at colleges and universities has come from an increased number of students who are not prepared for the rigors of higher education. Thus there is a focus on first-year experiences that are frequently offered as large, multisection classes. These are not attractive work assignments for faculty who are charged with producing in a very competitive research environment and who are expecting to teach at least partially in their area of expertise, probably at the graduate level where they can train their own students. At liberal arts colleges where the research expectation is on the rise, the administration must recognize that research cannot be done on the margin but must have time allotted to it. A reduction in teaching load is usually arranged for those who have research as a part of their professional portfolios. The teaching expectations that are emerging are not a good match for the type of tenure-track faculty that colleges and universities say they desire. Attempts to accommodate research expectations and the cost issue are the two major reasons for the move to full-time nontenure-track hires devoted to teaching as a complement to the standard tenure-track hires who previously contributed across the three traditional areas of faculty responsibility.

To meet the current and future needs of an academic department within the fiscal restrictions that will continue to be in place for the foreseeable future, chairs need to plan how their department should look in terms of an appropriate mix of faculty appointments. The plan will need to be forward-looking and account for enrollment projections, new programs, and department demographics. The plan must also be developed in ways that allow for flexibility to accommodate changing needs that cannot be predicted ahead of time. To be able to cover all the bases, taking into account many contingencies and the likelihood of fewer lines is the challenge. If this can be accomplished, the chair will be in the best position to make convincing arguments to the dean about the right replacement when a vacancy occurs.

Recognizing National Trends

Zimbler (2001) reported that among institutions with tenure systems, the number of part-time faculty and full-time nontenure-track faculty increased by 11% and 10%, respectively, in an 11-year period. Finkelstein and Schuster (The Future of the American Faculty, 2004) present more precise data from the National Center for Educational Statistics on nontenure-track hires relative to tenured and tenure-track faculty. From 1993 to 2001, the percentage of tenured faculty fell 6% while the percentage of those on the tenure track remained constant at about 20%. During the same period of time, full-time nontenure-track hires increased by about 7.5% to nearly 35% of all faculty. When isolating only new hires during the same time span, tenured hires remained constant at 6%. This reflects senior faculty moving from one institution to another with tenure. New appointments made on the tenure track dropped by 3.5% while nontenure-track hires increased by 4%. These data indicate a clear trend away from tenure-track replacements and toward full-time faculty not on the tenure track. With the bloom of faculty retirements just around the corner, continuation of this trend has serious implications for how the faculty staffing the higher education enterprise will look in two decades. The factors that have led to this shift will only increase the pressure on the staffing process, and chairs need to be aware of the types of hires they may have to consider to maintain faculty staffing that can meet the demands of the future.

Full-Time Nontenure-Track Hires

The Positives
The preceding paragraph is not meant to imply that the trends cited are necessarily negative. There are some positives about the move to nontenure-track hires that balance some of the negative aspects. Part-time faculty and full-time nontenure-track

faculty can bring individuals into the academy who would not ordinarily be interested in or eligible for tenure-track positions. For example, individuals with requisite preparation but family responsibilities that preclude them from attempting the requirements needed to attain tenure frequently show interest. There are indications that these positions are often sought by women and members of other underrepresented groups. This may be due in part to spousal issues related to family obligations or to credentialing issues where postdoctoral experience may be missing or may be a result of a lack of confidence to apply for traditional appointments. Finally, there are Ph.D.s whose only real driving interest is teaching. These individuals would not make good candidates for tenure-track positions if tenure is based on factors other than teaching.

An advantage to the institution and possibly to the department is that nontenure-track positions allow the flexibility to rapidly adapt to new conditions and change the focus of instruction. Adjunct faculty members are hired on a semester-to-semester basis and contracts may not be renewed when student interests change and enrollments drop. Full-time nontenure-track appointments are generally renewable annually, at least during the first several years, permitting a change to another expertise in response to lowered interest or a more promising opportunity. While these suggestions may seem impersonal, they do allow colleges and universities to respond to real-world conditions, something they are criticized for not doing in a timely manner, because when faculty members are tenured, such changes in direction can be delayed for decades. Finally, nontenure-track hires are major contributors to the teaching mission. Regardless of institutional type, full-time nontenure-track faculty teach many more sections than their tenure-track colleagues. They also teach primarily at the introductory level where need is the greatest and where some senior faculty are least interested.

The Negatives

Several negative aspects should be noted about new appointments that are not on the tenure track. The usual picture of a faculty member in higher education is that of someone who crafts and delivers a sound, relevant curriculum, pursues new knowledge or provides innovative interpretation in the discipline, and renders university, professional, and community service that improves society and moves the institution and discipline forward. The so-called triple-threat faculty member is not represented in nontenure-track hires where productivity is expected in only one or two areas (usually teaching or teaching and service) of faculty responsibility. As an extension of this concept, the idea that research and scholarship inform teaching in ways that are meaningful and enriching is weakened when increasing numbers of faculty are not in tenured lines. It is interesting to note that this split is occurring simultaneously with a strong national movement to enhance undergraduate research. Institutional and federally funded programs supporting and encouraging both students and faculty to become engaged in their areas of interest through the discovery process are proliferating. At the same time, they are threatened by the migration to faculty hires who will have no responsibilities in research.

A department profile that reflects the extent to which faculty are engaged in scholarship, and unit reporting that includes productivity measures in terms of publications, external funding, and other scholarship parameters, also suffer when tenure lines are replaced with nontenure-track appointments. For example, publications per faculty member or external funding per faculty member or even department totals of these measures may fall when fewer faculty are engaged in this type of work. Only if the new appointments allow remaining faculty more time and focus so that their productivity dramatically increases would productivity tallies hold their own. Beyond these quantitative losses, there is the perception that the model of higher education as a collection of communities of scholars would be lost. Taking nothing away from the important contributions that nontenure-track appointments make in teaching or service, there is the belief that the discovery scholarship of the community is diminished by the increased percentage of faculty whose areas of work are elsewhere. In considering the divide that may emerge along with the fact that the overall distribution of assignments and expectations are not proportional, one can predict the beginnings of different clusters of faculty within the same academic unit. Possible issues that this situation can create for the department chair will be discussed shortly.

Evaluation Issues

While the downsides of nontenure-track hires can create challenges for chairs, there are additional, personnel considerations that develop when academic units move to a mix of tenure-track and nontenure-track faculty. Chapter 16 discusses the use of faculty evaluation both as an accountability measure and as a mechanism for sustaining high productivity through goal setting and positive feedback and as a means for leveraging improvement. One of the hallmarks of an open evaluation system is that the department establishes a set of criteria used to evaluate each member. This paradigm would also be reinforced by promotion and tenure guidelines and considerations for merit that would reflect the same set of criteria. When a unit moves to faculty appointments that are limited in the areas of expected contribution, the schema for evaluation changes. Because research or scholarship is not usually expected, nontenure-track faculty would earn no credits and thus be at a disadvantage when it comes to merit assignment. Chairs will have to make certain that the evaluation grid includes both quantitative and qualitative elements so that teaching-focused faculty can earn additional merit based on their increased teaching loads. Alternatively, an entirely new evaluation scheme may be developed in those departments where there are large numbers of nontenure-track faculty.

Equity Issues

A related set of adjustments that chairs will have to make are those that fall into the category of equity issues. Equitable does not always mean equal. Nonetheless, some department practices will have to be adapted for new faculty, and how that is done may raise questions related to equitable treatment for all faculty members. For example, much of what is called faculty development occurs at the department level. In some cases, faculty members are allotted a small sum of money for their professional activities. These can be in teaching or research for the most part, and can be used to purchase materials, travel to a meeting, or pay a student helper. Perhaps more common is the model where the chair has funding that he or she is willing to invest in faculty. There may be incentives, strings for some, attached to such requests. For example, travel funds may be allocated only when the faculty member will be presenting at a conference or research seed funding will be granted with the understanding that an external grant proposal will be submitted within a specified time period. But how would the chair allocate parallel investments in nontenure-track appointments? The examples given were deliberately related to scholarship as a way to reinforce the point. There may be teaching innovations developed by a nontenure-track appointment that may be suitable for presentation at a conference that features advances in instructional approaches. Opportunities to invest in nontenure-track appointments should be sought as ways to improve performance, to provide professional stimulation, and to acknowledge the professional status of individuals who are members of the faculty.

When nontenure-track faculty join a department where formerly all faculty were tenured or on the tenure track, there are then two "kinds of faculty" in a unit with only finite resources insufficient to meet all needs, and certainly all desires, of the department and its faculty. What the chair may regard as equitable may not be seen the same way by all members of the unit. In these cases the chair must work to constantly highlight the contributions that all groups make toward meeting the responsibilities of the department. Departments with scholarship expectations will depend on one group of faculty to fulfill that role, while faculty assigned primarily to teaching roles will meet the needs of large numbers of students, thus allowing time for scholars to produce. This challenge is similar to and an extension of the one involving differential work assignments that are used to match faculty interest and talent to faculty work in order to maximize unit productivity. (See Chapters 16 and 22.)

Political Issues

There are also political issues that develop with this new mix of university faculty. Although these issues may be institutional in origin, many aspects are played out at the department level and resolving them is critical for full inclusion of new faculty appointments into the academy. One issue relates to voting privileges. While one might initially say nontenure-track appointments should have such a privilege, the issue becomes less clear when one considers the number of items on which faculty might actually vote. Should they vote to elect the tenure and promotion committee or to define the disciplinary expertise of a future tenure-track position, or even to select a tenure-track appointment? Should they play a role in evaluating the department chair? If yes, then how would this impact a department with a strong emphasis on scholarship where nontenure-track appointments outnumber the tenure-track lines? This could happen, and one only has to think of all the committees in the academy and ask whether it is appropriate for all types of faculty appointments to serve on each. Beyond voting privileges, there are also questions about rights and privileges afforded to tenure-track faculty that should be extended to these new colleagues. There will be mixed answers, and all of these questions have to be worked out both institutionally and departmentally to establish a set of operational policies that are clear and equitable to all parties concerned.

Possibilities for Nontenure-Track Appointments

Most in higher education could provide examples of nontenure-track appointments, but there are some more obscure types
and other examples where certain appointments are now being
used more universally. Because most readers either have such
individuals in their departments or will have in the near future,
it may be valuable to review the possibilities to help chairs plan
their departments.

Part-Time or Adjunct Faculty

The part-time or adjunct faculty member may or may not have
a terminal degree and will teach a load ranging from one course
per semester to the full allotment allowed by institutional policy. This individual may also teach at more than one institution,
thereby patching together a full-time job, though usually without
benefits. Adjunct faculty members are more common in urban
institutions where the local population is large and the number
of qualified individuals is high. Some may criticize this type of
appointment, but most chairs who employ adjuncts will say that
as a group they do a very good job. I will say that I could not
get the job done without them and that, in many cases, I doubt
whether full-time faculty could outperform them.

Adjuncts teach primarily in introductory courses and sometimes in courses where special expertise is needed. An example
of the latter would be in courses for clinical sciences where highly
specialized expertise is required. They often teach sections that
are offered at night, on weekends, and at off-campus sites, none
of which are prime choices for full-time faculty. Adjuncts are not
paid well—many are teaching because they have a calling and they
teach for the love of it. I sometimes believe that if we doubled the
salaries for adjuncts, we would get a new cadre of individuals and
the instructional quality would decease because money, not love,
would be the incentive for teaching.

There are downsides to employing adjuncts. Because they are usually on campus only for their classes, they are less accessible to students. They are frequently unable to attend training and orientations sessions as well as special events related to instruction. The need to have regular contact with the faculty member who serves as course director to make certain that course content is up to date. Care must also be taken to ensure that adjuncts are aware of all university policies regarding academic matters and that they are not capitulating to grade inflation pressures.

Lecturer

Another common nontenure-track appointment is the lecturer. This full-time position is characterized by a full teaching load (four to five courses per semester) with no responsibilities in other areas. In the majority of cases, the teaching is done at the introductory level. This appointee may have a terminal degree, but the master's is sometimes sufficient. The lecturer position is most commonly renewable through yearly reappointment and is not eligible for conversion to a tenure-track position.

Clinical-Rank Faculty

Those readers on campuses with health sciences schools will be familiar with clinical-rank faculty appointments. These faculty usually have responsibilities in teaching and service. Though complex, clinical-rank appointments offer some interesting possibilities for institutions considering or using nontenure-track appointments. The flexibility allowed by such positions has led to the adoption of clinical ranks outside of schools specializing in health sciences. For example, schools of education and engineering are now hiring clinical-rank faculty. In schools of medicine and nursing, clinical-rank faculty can be part-time, full-time, or volunteer. For brevity, we will consider them as full-time appointments. The position features ranks—clinical lecturer through clinical professor—so there is a defined career path with promotional steps. The promotion potential creates incentive for excellent performance beyond that linked to merit increments. Some schools offer the possibility for long-term contracts and for conversion to tenure-track status.

Academic Professional

A type of nontenure-track appointment that does not have a high profile in higher education is the academic professional. Academic professionals may make contributions in any area of faculty responsibility, including research. They are usually hired with specific roles in mind and do not work across all three areas of responsibility. For example, they may do some teaching and handle advising and internship placement for students in a specific program. Alternatively, they may do limited research and prepare reports and other products resulting from the work of the research group. From these descriptions, academic professionals occupy positions that bridge faculty and staff. Some have a terminal degree, allowing them to contribute at high levels in a variety of ways.

"Reinvented" Lecturers

Another type of nontenure-track hire is really a form of the lecturer position. My institution has developed this position as the result of a campus effort to enhance student retention by replacing adjunct faculty with full-time lecturers. The retention effort specifically targeted large enrollment courses taken by freshmen, resulting in many lecturer appointments in English, mathematics, and communications. The positions carry full-load expectations (four sections per semester) and modest responsibilities in service. The unique feature of these positions is the potential for promotion to senior lecturer. Once this status is achieved, the individual is eligible for a long-term contract, thus providing some job stability. This version of the lecturer incorporates some of the favorable characteristics of the clinical-rank appointment.

Planning for Future Staffing Needs

Given the various choices for faculty appointments, including those on the tenure track, and the fiscal realities now faced by higher education, a few institutions are developing staffing plans. Departments are asked to identify their needs for faculty coverage of anticipated responsibilities and institutional expectations and construct a pattern of hiring that will meet those needs. Like all plans, staffing plans are subject to continuous modification and adjustment as unanticipated changes occur. Chairs play the major role in this process as they are in the best position to predict future need and to understand faculty work in the discipline.

Predicting the future is a risky business, especially in our present climate of abrupt change. To see where a discipline may be in five to ten years will be particularly challenging in disciplines where change is common. Other disciplines have remained fairly stable over time, so the task is more manageable. Identifying the future state of a changing discipline is critical for ensuring that the right expertise is in place to accomplish a successful scholarship mission and to offer relevant curricula. Setting the future of the discipline within the context of real-world demand will help to make predictions on enrollments. Since enrollments drive funding for new positions, identifying programs likely to be attractive and those likely to fade is essential to constructing staffing plans. One must also be aware of changes in programs and enrollment patterns anticipated in other units whose students take courses in the department. In departments where a substantial portion of its offerings are in service courses, changes in employment patterns and the programs offered elsewhere on campus can have a major impact on the department's fiscal profile. As an example, my department, biology, has routinely taught about 75% of its credit hours as service to others. Some of the major users are students in pre-nursing, dental hygiene, and other health sciences. Other significant enrollments come from students in various schools who are fulfilling a life sciences course requirement, from returning degreed students changing careers, and from students in related science programs. A drop in demand for nurses or a change in the size of the undergraduate nursing programs can immediately result in a drop of 10% of the department's enrollment. Knowledge of employment prospects and programming changes allows the department to anticipate and prepare for these fluctuations and include the appropriate rationale for justifying requests for staffing in these areas.

The other critical category of data necessary for a predictive staffing plan is personnel demographics. Assessing the status of current faculty and staff, who is eligible to retire in the near term, and what roles staff members currently have are beginning points. The next step is matching this changing human resource category with the anticipated disciplinary and demand changes already discussed. Gaps representing unmet need may appear, so the plan will require a hiring strategy to meet those needs. For most institutions the hiring strategy will not include more tenure-track lines exclusively. That is not the recent history, and conditions are not likely to improve to allow a return to that model. Thus the chair must devise a plan to meet future need with a mix of faculty and perhaps staff appointments that will ensure coverage and deliver the quality that is expected.

Chair Issues Relative to a New Faculty Mix

One last concept relative to the role of the chair in overseeing academic departments with new mixes of faculty appointments will be important for a successful transition. Already mentioned were some cultural issues among faculty based on different roles, equitable treatment, and inclusion. While these issues involve chair planning to create a faculty that is variable yet marked by mutual respect and that works together toward a unified goal, there are new skills that a chair must acquire so that the new model continues to work successfully. With a faculty that will likely have one or more types of nontenure-track appointments, the chair must now be prepared to guide several career paths. If some nontenure-track appointments have promotional steps or eligibility for long-term contacts (forms of limited tenure), the chair must be prepared to guide and advise these individuals in ways appropriate for these careers. These will clearly be different from the guidance provided those in tenure-track lines. Likewise, the types of investments in career development will be different, as will be the professional outcomes and products. These considerations are tied to an equitable evaluation process for the new appointments. Chair and faculty interactions of these types are complicated personnel issues under any circumstances and especially so when the number of career paths is expanded.

Summary

Hiring the faculty that will deliver the department's curricula, produce its scholarly products, and contribute to service activities of several types is a responsibility that will have a long-lasting impact. Hiring trends over the past decade have resulted in a shift away from traditional tenure-track hires to part- or full-time nontenure-track hires. With the many retirements anticipated over the next decade among the present tenure-track positions in American higher education, continuation of this recent trend can significantly change the compositions of college and university faculties in the early part of the century.

Among the causes for these changes are the cost of tenure-track faculty and the increasing need to provide introductory coursework to student populations that are underprepared relative to peers of the past. In addition, such hires place the institution in a position to respond to rapidly changing needs by substituting different expertise among its nontenure-track positions. The increased dependence on adjunct faculty and the conversion of tenure-track lines to full-time nontenure-track lines are two of the major trends noted. Chairs need to be aware of the changes, why they are taking place, and ways they can plan department hires such that all responsibilities are met in the future.

Chairs also need to be aware of some of the criticism and challenges of bringing full-time nontenure-track faculty into positions formerly held by tenure-track faculty. Because their roles are targeted primarily to teaching, the new hires will not contribute to the scholarship element of the department, resulting in two types of department faculty. Chairs must be prepared to provide equitable evaluations and resources for both groups and must remind all faculty members of the important though different contributions of both groups. In planning for future department needs, chairs may find that a mix of traditional hires along with lecturers, academic professionals, clinical-rank, or other models of faculty hires will provide the best means to address department responsibilities.

13

RECRUITING AND RETAINING FACULTY

Once the decision has been made on how to fill a vacancy, meet instructional need, or open a new focus area, the process of recruiting the right individual begins. Let us assume that the dean has approved a search for a tenure-track faculty member. The first step in the process, either before or after the dean's approval, is to decide which specialty the new faculty member will represent. For example, will the department seek someone in early British literature or in creative writing? Once this is determined, the chair will form a committee, usually called a search and screen committee, to handle much of the day-to-day work of describing and advertising the position, collecting applications, and conducting initial dossier reviews.

Appointing this committee is the first step in which institutional policy may come into play and where the chair must make some important decisions. As an element of its commitment to ensure that the institutional objectives to promote diversity are met, an office on campus, usually the affirmative action office, may be asked to approve committee membership to assure that it represents a diverse group of individuals. Although the committee is not usually large and not all possible groups can be represented, this step can help to bring multiple perspectives to the selection process. With this in mind, the chair will select a committee that aligns with the expertise area being sought. Many institutions include membership from outside the department or student members. Perhaps because my institution is comprised predominantly of commuters, the committees I have served on with student members, including search and screen committees, usually work without meaningful input from the students. In fact, students are the least likely members to attend meetings. The situation at other institutions may be different, and students may actually participate in meaningful ways. Outside members, however, can contribute valuable fresh perspectives and also help make the department more visible to campus units and external constituents. Both types of committee members expand the potential for achieving diversity on the committee.

The Position Description

The first chore of the committee is to construct the position description. There may be more than one version of the description, depending on how the department wishes to advertise. Key elements of the description are identifying the department, institution, rank, qualifications (degree, experience), specialty area, and starting date of the position. There is also a statement of the position's expectations, including teaching load and level of instruction expected, research expectations, if any, and any other high-profile obligation that the appointee might be expected to assume. For example, there might be other position requirements such as a joint appointment in a campus center or institute or directing a specific undergraduate program. There will be statements about what to send as part of the application, how letters of reference will be handled, and where to send application materials. The description will also include a closing date or some statement indicating an open-ended search and the date that the committee will begin to review applications. In some cases there will be information about the institution and its setting and, of course, the mandatory statement regarding equal opportunity. These position descriptions must be approved by the campus affirmative action office.

Chapter 14 will discuss the position description again in the context of a subsequent mismatch of faculty interests and institutional expectation. If there are consequential commitments for the individual accepting the position, it seems reasonable to list these in the description. If the hire is expected to advise a significant contingent of undergraduate students or to develop distance education versions of their courses, it is in everyone's best interests to make this known up front. When such declarations are left unsaid, there could later be rigid resistance from the faculty member and frustration for the department and institution. More issues about disclosure and expectations for work beyond teaching and research will be discussed later.

Once the position description is complete and approved, it is ready for dissemination. The venues for this are usually part of the approval package from affirmative action. Typical outlets include scholarly journals and other higher education publications, a list of colleges and universities preparing individuals in the area of interest, disciplinary organizations, and reputable organizations with large readerships from underrepresented groups. There are organizations of this type that have been established expressly to meet the affirmative action requirements of colleges and universities, so it is wise to check that they are legitimately dedicated to generating candidates from the identified groups. Web site postings are also becoming more common.

Before leaving the dissemination aspect of the process, let us return to the title of the committee in charge. *Search* and *screen* are both action words. What has been described thus far and what typically follows is a process of passive advertisement and active screening of the applicants—typically little searching is done. If the department knows what it wants and where to find experts for this area at other institutions, there is nothing wrong with calling Professor X to ask if there are any doctoral students scheduled to complete their degrees or any postdoctoral colleagues who are about to enter the job market. If there are, send a description of the position and invite them to apply. Not everyone may support this idea. I once witnessed a situation where a faculty member was very disturbed that one of the finalists for a position was known to a member of the search committee and invited to apply. The reality is that if someone knows an excellent prospect or knows where candidates may be preparing, then this information should be tapped to create the strongest applicant pool possible. The advice here is to be *active* in the search component of the process.

The Silent Phase

Following the mailings, solicitations, publications, and position postings, the search now enters the silent phase. This is when the components of the applications are being received, logged in, and filed. These tasks are usually done by staff members, but the committee may do them in some institutions. In some searches, reference letters are solicited as part of the application. In others they may be solicited only for those applicants who make the short list (10 to 20). While this approach avoids the chores of letter writing for many of the references, it can slow the process because letters must be requested later, and it is often the writers who slow down the process. While the applications are arriving, another requirement of affirmative action comes into play. Each applicant is sent a form requesting personal information on gender, ethnicity, and other attributes to be completed and returned to the campus affirmative action office. Returning this form, however, is not mandatory in terms of keeping the applicant in the mix for consideration.

There are some deviations from these practices that concern obtaining references for candidates. Some search committees will call references to ask a series of scripted questions and record the responses. This can be done in lieu of or in addition to written letters. Some committees feel very strongly about contacting other individuals who may know the candidate. For example, a candidate may list some associates and a postdoctoral advisor but omit the doctoral mentor from the list of referees. There may be good reasons for this, but the committee may want to make the call anyway to verify that the real reason is not something of critical importance to the hiring institution. There exists some disagreement about the ethical and legal nature of this kind of information search.

Application Review

Once the deadline has passed or the date for initiation of application review has arrived, the committee can begin its review of completed applications. At this time, staff may send out reminders to applicants regarding missing documents. The first cut is typically made by determining whether the applicant meets the requirements for the position. Those without the appropriate degree, those not in the specialty area advertised, and those without the requisite experience can be eliminated immediately. From the remainder, the committee will shorten the list based on the important characteristics determined for the position. Variables may include teaching experience, specific research area and its potential for external funding, fit within the teaching and scholarly interests of the department, record of publication, strength of reference letters, and academic performance. The last is variable, but some institutions request graduate transcripts both to learn what didactic preparation the applicant has had and to assure that the applicant actually has earned the degree listed for the position. There have been notable examples of fraud in this aspect of applicant files. From this review, the committee arrives at a reduced list sometimes called the short list. If calls are to be made to references or others, this is the group that would be involved. The candidates themselves may also be called at this time to make certain they are still interested in pursuing the position and to tell them a few things about the institution and the position. There are times when candidates indicate low enthusiasm or notify the department that they have accepted another offer or are likely to accept another offer. Most departments will then seek input from the faculty at large for the purpose of paring the list further to a

ranked group of five to ten candidates. They will review the files
and the information gathered from calls by the committee to rank
the finalists. Depending on the practices and fiscal position of the
institution and department, several finalists will be invited for a
campus interview. The number can be a small as three and as large
as eight or ten.

Again, campus policy will require that this information be
shared with the affirmative action office, which asks for a list of candidates for the position and the rationale for the decision on each. It
is important to indicate the top candidates on this list who should
be invited for an interview as well as secondary candidates who
may be interviewed at a later date. Affirmative action will review
the forms received from applicants and may ask the department
to revisit those candidates who are from underrepresented groups.
Unless there are substantive justifications for not including them
in the interview group, the department will be asked to do so. The
approval process for interviews when there are issues with members of underrepresented groups among the candidates depends on
the verifiable objectivity of the decision-making process (rationale
for exclusion from the interview phase) and on how aggressively the
institution promotes diversity. In the case of the former, the chair
must make certain that decisions are objectively reached and that
appropriate criteria have been used to arrive at the list of finalists.
Further, the chair must establish an atmosphere for the process
where members of the faculty are sensitive to the academy's diversity goals and to the notion that it is important that all are valued as
participating members of the academy. In the end, the department
will have its interview list approved as submitted or as amended.

The Interview

This next step is most critical. The department must now decide
based on a visit of about two days for each candidate which one
will be invited to become a member of the department. The invest-

ment in terms of dollars and time is already substantial, but what may come of these short visits will add greater expense. It is crucial that the interview be structured to accomplish two major outcomes: 1) that the department learns as much as it needs to make the right decision, and 2) that the department and institution sell themselves so that all candidates really want the job. The latter is not simply a matter of the offer's tangible aspects but is often influenced by environmental issues such as the level of collegiality within the department and with individuals across campus.

Chairs need to be involved with the search committee in establishing the general parameters of what will be a packed interview schedule over about two days. Candidates will be asked to provide a seminar or colloquium, usually in the area of scholarship. At institutions where research and scholarship play a lesser role, the candidate may be asked to present an address on teaching philosophy or to teach a class. There are even instances where both a professional presentation and an instructionally related session are requested. Some caution in requiring both is necessary. While a research institution may want to send the message that teaching is also important, it can inadvertently send the message that it is not firmly committed to research or does not understand what it takes to develop a competitive research program. Even though this attitude is not intended, candidates from dedicated research institutions may not have encountered it before and their mentors often will steer them away. This clash of old and emerging cultures in higher education will be developed further in the next chapter. In any event, it may be best to schedule the professional presentation early in the visit to help the interviewee and to generate areas for discussion during subsequent meetings with faculty and others on the interview list.

The chair will play a key role during the interview process. For me, the best model is to meet with the candidate very early and again at the exit interview. At the first meeting the candidate is introduced to the campus and learns about the department and its students, the rationale for the way the department is structured, the type of degree programs it offers, what it is like to live in the area, and what roles the candidate will play as a member of the faculty. Any preliminary questions the candidate has can be answered at this point. The chair knows that additional questions will emerge as the candidate meets with others and can indicate that anything that arises can be addressed before the visit is over. At this point the chair should bow out of the process until the exit meeting. The astute candidate will have many questions on department operation that are really questions about the style, character, and philosophy of the chair. These questions cannot be raised and discussed while the chair is present. The exit interview can address new questions. Common ones are those associated with promotion and tenure and the faculty evaluation process. Unless the dean handles this issue, the nature of the offer, including salary, startup funding, and space, can be raised. During this meeting the chair should inquire as to the level of interest the candidate now has in the position. Timing is an important discussion topic at the meeting. When the department will complete its interviews and decide on a candidate and what other offers or possibilities the candidate may have are points for discussion.

In between the meetings with the chair, candidates will meet with faculty in the department and sometimes with students. Individual faculty meetings may have to give way to small group meetings due to time restrictions. Because one of the major goals here is to sell the candidate on the position, appointments with the dean and other administrators can be key. The willingness of these individuals to take time from their busy schedules to meet or have lunch with candidates expresses institutional-level interest in the candidate. Other meetings might be arranged with representatives from other schools where collaborations may be possible and external constituents (perhaps alumni) who can provide an external view of the department and can help with spousal placement if that is an issue. There should also be time for the candidate to see some area sites and tour the campus, events that usually happen with lunch and dinner. If they have not already been sent, candidates can be provided with department and institutional documents to provide additional information. Examples are annual reports, strategic plans, fringe benefit package, local cultural opportunities, department, school, and institutional faculty development programs, and school bulletins. Again, this is a recruiting effort and the department should put its best foot forward in this process, which, of course, must be done with complete honesty.

There are alternative scenarios for what follows. If three or four candidates have been interviewed, then the department will meet to determine how they rank. If eight or ten have interviewed or if it is standard practice, second interviews of the top two or three candidates may take place. These are more intense interviews and frequently involve higher administrators. There will be a stronger focus on the details of the offer and the parameters of the position. At some point a top candidate will emerge from the finalists. Again, institutional practice varies here. In some, faculty will rank the candidates and ask the dean for permission to make an offer to the top candidate. In others the dean may request an unranked list of three acceptable candidates. This happens more frequently with administrative hires, but deans can sometimes play direct roles in the selection process. In either or any other case, the affirmative action office becomes involved in the final approval. In some cases that office may preapprove an offer to any of the finalists ahead of time.

The Offer

There may be a number of campus practices impacting the actual extension of the offer. The practice in the School of Science at my institution is that, after getting the approvals of affirmative action and the dean for making the offer, the chair and dean will have a conversation on the nature of the offer. The elements of concern for the dean are salary and startup funding. Issues around teaching assignments and load, space, and other details are left to the chair. It is best to establish a range for the monetary elements of the offer so that the chair and dean do not have to reconfer as the negotiations proceed. The chair will have to develop a strategy for where to begin the negotiations. The first contact is by phone, and if the candidate is still interested in receiving an offer, the basic elements are laid out. Included are starting rank (including any years toward tenure if applicable), salary, space, startup funding, starting date, teaching expectations, and other special considerations (office computer, journal subscriptions, travel allowance, clerical or technical assistance, etc.). A date is set by which the candidate must respond, along with an invitation to contact the chair at any time with questions that may arise. Experienced chairs will say that time constraints are necessary to prevent tying up the position so long that, if it is declined, other candidates are no longer available. After the details of the position are negotiated to everyone's approval, the official offer is sent out from the dean or administration. Again, the letter may have to go through some form of administrative approval above the dean's level. This letter usually contains the basic parameters (rank, salary, etc.) of the position and a second letter from the chair contains the department-specific details of the offer. The search is closed when the candidate signs and returns the dean's offer.

There are some ethical issues regarding offers and whether they are legally binding and can be amended at a later date. Salary and rank are legally binding by signature, but other aspects of the offer are sometimes less clear. Chairs often have the authority to reallocate space, so promises made to newly recruited faculty members can be subject to alteration. There are cases when startup funding has been reset after the new faculty member has arrived. This funding is usually made available for the initial years to allow the faculty member to initiate research and seek independent funding. But when the faculty member is fortunate enough to land substantial external funding very early, some of the startup funding may be withdrawn with the justification that external funding is available to cover costs. Startup funding can be derived from institutional and school funds, department funds (only when there are large departments with heavy external funding), or a combination of these. It is extremely important for building trust and a collaborative environment that institutions and departments live up to the promises they have made in recruiting faculty.

Solidifying the Agreement

After the department successfully recruits a top candidate and that individual arrives and begins work, the next stage of the process begins. The department must remember that it has just attracted what it hopes is a top-rated new faculty member. Others may agree, and it must be understood that the new recruit still retains marketability. Unless the recruit took the position only because what was really desired was not available, the new faculty member is busy with and excited about his or her new role as a faculty member. But two situations can disenchant the new hire early and cause him or her to initiate a search for a new position. The first situation was discussed in the previous paragraph—that is, the institution was unable to deliver on its promises. While some items are in writing, institutions have outs based on budget constraints and previously unforeseen circumstances. The new faculty member may wonder that if the institution cannot be trusted now, what will it be like at promotion, tenure, and other career-critical milestones down the road?

The second issue of concern is social integration into the department and into the community. Factors at play include size and type of community compared to what the recruit is accustomed to, the level of collegiality in the department and across campus, and factors unique to new faculty members who are from underrepresented groups. Chairs can play a pivotal role by making certain the new faculty member touches base with others in the institution who might share common interests or with whom they may have similar past experiences. Advice on where to seek housing based on school systems, demographic makeup, religious centers, and other lifestyle issues may help make the new faculty member more comfortable in the new surroundings. Campus offices can usually help with these issues, especially those related to faculty members from underrepresented groups. There have been significant investments in the recruiting effort, and the institution does not want to lose out this late in the process because the final touches in acclimating the new faculty member have not been done.

Summary

Regardless of the type of full-time faculty hire that is requested and approved, the department will go through a prescribed series of activities it hopes will culminate in a new faculty member joining the unit. Chairs play important roles at several stages in the process. The first of these is a conversation with the dean seeking approval for a new or replacement line. This will involve data supporting the justification for the request. Chairs will also play a role in establishing the committee that will do most of the work. This committee should represent a cross-section of faculty, with individuals who are experts in the specialty area being sought, and perhaps external or student members.

The committee writes a position description, advertises the opening in appropriate venues, and collects and evaluates applications to create a short list of strong candidates for full faculty review. Once the interview list is determined, the chair again becomes a key individual in the process. It is the responsibility of all to help identify the best candidate for the position and to sell each candidate on the institution such that each one leaves hoping for an offer. As the highest representative of the department, the chair is a major information stop for each candidate and will be the primary information source regarding curricula, position expectations, internal resources, programs, and activities in place or in development. Working with the chair will be a critical area for would-be faculty members, and the chair should arange for meetings and meals for candidates with faculty members to allow these questions to be pursued.

Two additional points on the chair's role in faculty recruitment should be made. The first is that the chair, working with faculty and staff members, must be aware of requirements by the campus affirmative action office in this process. There will be policies requiring a series of approvals from that office for establishing the committee, constructing the position descriptions and ads, establishing the interview list, and making the final offer. Failure to follow these steps may result in delays and the loss of candidates. Second, the chair must follow through on the candidate's acceptance and make certain that all promises in the offer are met. New colleagues will expect to enter a welcoming environment and feel comfortable in knowing what is expected and what will be provided. Chairs must make certain that all bargains and promises are kept.

14

FACULTY CULTURE

It is always amusing to hear a dean, provost, or campus committee lament that faculty do not embrace what they have determined is the right path, the appropriate approach, or the most recent suggestion for change. Questions like "Why don't faculty members get it?" and "Why don't they understand how important this is?" are heard. Administrators seem mystified that faculty members do not always pay attention to what they and others outside the institution may believe are the most critical issues facing higher education. For example, "Why do faculty members show stronger allegiance to their disciplines than to their institutions?" "Why won't faculty members devote more time to distance education?" "Why is there such a resistance to or lack of excitement around assessment?" "Why are faculty members unwilling to teach extra sections of a freshman seminar?" "Why do faculty resist having regular conversations about the general education curriculum?" These are some of the questions heard from administrators. That such questions are ignored or unanswered by faculty members is not difficult for me to understand, but why those posing the questions cannot answer them is puzzling. In a nutshell, we get exactly the faculty we ask for during the hiring process and the type of faculty we select at the time of tenure. So why do we complain later?

This issue requires some analysis to understand more clearly our colleagues and their professional motivations. The process begins when permission for a new or replacement hire is granted by the administration. Departments then decide whether the hire will bring a new expertise or strengthen an existing area in the department. With that decision, a job advertisement or position vacancy notice will be written and sent through the institution for various approvals. The appointment level of the position, preparation criteria, area of expertise, expectations, delineation of teaching area, and teaching load are the core of the ad. Other elements may include information about the institution and department, the degree programs offered, and the potential for professional interactions within the institution and with external groups and organizations. Using as an example an ad from a science discipline position at a research intensive institution, the ad may include phrases such as "postdoctoral research experience required," "teach an undergraduate course in physical chemistry and develop a graduate course in the area of expertise," "produce a regular stream of peer-reviewed publications," "develop a nationally recognized, independent, and externally funded program in research" and "mentor and train undergraduate and graduate research students."

Assuming that all the steps outlined in Chapter 13 have been accomplished, a new member of the faculty is now on board. Referring back to the ad, the new faculty member understands clearly what the expectations are and immediately sets up a research facility using institutional startup funding. At the same time there is significant activity in preparing to teach existing courses or developing new ones. Sometime in the next year or two, after accumulating the required preliminary data, external grant proposals are submitted. While several agencies and foundations may be targeted, success is almost never achieved with the first volley. In the meantime, the assistant professor is recruiting research students and perhaps hiring technical help to aid in data collection. Peer-reviewed publication is essential to meeting the expectations of "productive" in the ad, and this becomes a strong focus. Between this and the constant efforts at fundraising, the new faculty member is expending a good deal of time, energy, and focus. Most of the rest is consumed with a satisfactory amount of service work.

A soon as the new faculty joins the department, the tenure process begins. Annual reviews and reappointment committee reviews will monitor progress and provide feedback as to what has been accomplished and what remains to be done in order to gain department endorsement for tenure. Scholarship is assessed, teaching is evaluated, and service is managed. The faculty member is also advised that external letters providing independent evaluations of scholarship and, perhaps, teaching will be required and that the faculty member should be thinking about peers who might be approached. Others will also likely give advice about what activities to forgo in order to maintain primary focus on what will really count. All along, the original expectations of the job description are reinforced and the faculty member responds with the appropriate focus.

Moving ahead to the point where tenure has just been achieved, some may say that the faculty member should now have time to focus more on other institutional issues. However, this is the time when the research team is growing and more students are being drawn to a successful research group. A second project has now been funded, and the faculty member has established productive collaborations with colleagues at other universities. These are the signs of success in this environment and what was originally intended for this faculty member. This expanded version of earlier effort is, after all, what will be required for the next promotion. This scenario will have different dimensions in other disciplines and at institutions where research is not such a primary focus. In the end, however, similar issues will arise. Faculty are sought and selected for a variety of faculty work–related reasons; these drivers are often not what others in the institution may have in mind in some situations.

We now return to the original scenario and to the issues raised by the questions administrators posed earlier. Why should the faculty member be expected to be interested in or willing to devote significant amounts of time to distance education, become engaged in developing objectives and measures for undergraduate student learning, or participate in regular conversations about renovating the general education curriculum? Why would the faculty member find added value in spending hours in meetings to align syllabi from courses around the region to facilitate student transfer or agree to take a responsible position in faculty governance? Faculty members recognize that they are part of larger groups and owe some allegiance to them and will make contributions to the common good. On the other hand, they have been trained and encouraged by the employing department and institution to prioritize so they can accomplish what the institution values and rewards and what drives their careers. The point here is not to question the value of these issues but to state that we have not screened applicants for these predispositions or interests and they were not used as primary selection criteria. To select a candidate for one set of criteria and then expect attention to be refocused to others will lead to exactly what we have today—a disconnect between what faculty value and what administration and others value, recognizing that the latter changes regularly. So with respect to faculty interest and what they regard as their professional aspirations and responsibilities, we get what we ask for and, thus we need to stop complaining so loudly that faculty won't do this, and that faculty don't see how important something has become.

Is the preceding scenario problematic or is it as it should be? It appears to present faculty and those who advise them as unicentric, selfish, and out of touch with the needs of students and the institution that employs them. But I have yet to encounter an academic administration that does not appreciate and highlight the superstar faculty member who publishes the transforming book and who makes the breakthrough discovery. I have also not encountered an administration that does not appreciate external dollars in support of faculty scholarship. In fact, they often boast about this aspect of the institutional portfolio. Of course, they want the other contributions, too. No one takes anything off the plate for faculty and many are happy to add to it. Gene Rice, senior fellow at the now defunct American Association for

Higher Education, has often spoken of the faculty full-plate phenomenon (Rice, Sorcinelli, & Austin, 2000). A related point is
that the model described—faculty members striving to become
recognized as disciplinary scholars as a condition for tenure—has
made American higher education the best in the world. So the
questions are, Should this model change or should it stay the same?
Is it appropriate for higher education in the 21st century? Will
different models emerge? Whatever the answers are, suffice it to
say that chairs will be caught between faculty expectations as supported by local and distant colleagues and institutional expectations that will add other types of work to faculty job descriptions.
Managing successful faculty careers while addressing institution-
building work will be the challenge.

   If one believes that the selection process largely dictates how
faculty will contribute to the university and what work they will
be comfortable with as components of their professional per-
sona, then how do we deal with this lack of alignment regarding
expectations? One place to look is at graduate education. There
are programs in place that introduce Ph.D. candidates to faculty
cultures and expectations at institutions unlike the ones where
they are earning their doctorates. Because few degree candidates
will be employed at research institutions, Preparing Future Faculty programs help them to understand that the nature of their
work will not mirror what they experience during doctoral preparation. However, there are problems with resistance to such programs, especially evident in disciplines where the Ph.D. student's
work drives the grant or contract objectives of the faculty member, and time away from research to teach at a local community
college jeopardizes the next funding round. Other approaches for
acculturating prospective faculty members are being developed
and constructed to avoid some of these tensions.

   Another area to consider in deciding how a department can
meet traditional and disciplinary-focused objectives while also
meeting the goals and mandates of accountability and the chang-

ing expectations of faculty lies in the notion of differential faculty expectations and the related issue of how the department will be staffed. The tension between disciplinary inquiry and discovery and institutional work, including accountability and the focus on student learning, will not depend on one faculty model that demands both to be accomplished in quality ways. Time and interest preclude this. The answer is not in less inquiry or research, because too many institutions base their reputations on the research profile and on the amount of external funding they are able to attract. How many administrators have stated that they are willing to forgo external funding for work on assessment, distance education, or undergraduate curriculum development? The problem is that nothing is taken off the table for faculty, but new responsibilities are continually added. If colleges and universities want everything, they must accept the fact that some faculty members will deliver some products and others will provide a different mix of contributions.

In Chapter 9, the concept of differential expectations for faculty work within the department was discussed as a way to meet the multiple needs of the present and future academic department. In addition, the assumption that each new line or replacement line will be a tenure-track line is likely to be increasingly erroneous. With other types of appointments, it will be possible to address the major department responsibilities by using different types of positions to focus on the divergent areas needing regular attention. Mapping out the mix of faculty and support personnel needed to meet the array of unit responsibilities anticipated will be one of the chair's most important functions.

Summary

There appears to be a growing divide between institutional and faculty expectations. On one end of this spectrum are the traditional descriptions of faculty positions to which candidates apply because what is described is what they are ready and able to tackle. Once on board, they are subject to reviews that reinforce these expectations as necessary precursors to tenure. Merit systems further support the cultural values of the unit and the career foci of the faculty member. The expectations governing this behavior are not surprising and follow the traditional lines in place for decades. While these values may vary in research institutions and those directed primarily to foster work in teaching, they all have strong disciplinary aspects and assume that the faculty member will do work that is recognized and favorably received by senior peers in the field.

On the other end of the spectrum are the institutions and their administrations. Here, there are pressures, unknown to or ignored by the faculty, that demand or encourage the institution to reinvent itself in a variety of ways. Part of this external pressure is manifested in the accountability movement. Other aspects present themselves through mandates from external organizations and groups to alter teaching assignments, emphasize undergraduate education, improve retention, renovate curricula, address grade inflation, and so on. Institutions respond with extensive programs and new goals in civic engagement as a way of demonstrating institutional value to external constituents. Although all faculty members expect to participate in institutional service, these new expectations are far removed from the occasional committee assignment they anticipated. In no way was this service element expected to be a detriment to the primary work in teaching or scholarship or a threat to a positive tenure decision.

Chairs are in the difficult position as the gatekeeper to the department, the home of those expected to do the work of the institution. Preserving the disciplinary-based expectations of the unit as described and promised in the position description and in the unit's tradition while responding to mandates for new faculty contributions falls to the chair. Chairs will have to prioritize and commit the department only to those activities where it can expect to have a major impact. Rather than set individual faculty expectations across this range of responsibilities, chairs may consider assessing the interests, experiences, and strengths of the faculty and differentially assign work.

15

GUIDING FACULTY CAREERS

Institutions generally do a good job providing feedback and support for probationary faculty as they proceed down the path to tenure. Probationary faculty are rightfully concerned about this process and most are uncomfortable to some degree about how numerous and how good their dossier entries in teaching, research, and service must be to meet the standard. Frequent feedback helps only to some degree, and it is likely that the uncertainty will continue despite the increased evaluation and written feedback that are provided. This period of considerable insecurity has been traditional in the academy and has become an acceptable right of passage.

Recently, many academic units, including professional schools, have enhanced the way probationary faculty are evaluated. This positive change has been prompted in part by successful appeals of decisions to deny tenure from internal committees and from negative decisions from the legal system. In addition, units now realize that the increased costs of recruiting faculty and investing in their early years as they establish themselves make it a good business practice to provide continuous evaluation to guide work and encourage productivity so that their "investment" succeeds. Annual reviews, usually with the chair, are now more common. In addition, many institutions follow a year-to-year reappointment system where a department faculty committee reviews the progress of probationary faculty each year and provides written feedback. The feedback includes areas where more focused effort is needed and identifies activities and products that need to appear before tenure. Other institutions use third-year reviews to accomplish a similar outcome. In some cases third-year reviews take place in addition to annual reappointment reviews. In systems with annual and reappointment reviews, faculty members receive at least two written progress reviews per year. This establishes a paper trail in case of legal proceedings and prevents the surprise negative decision at the end of the probationary period.

Because extensive systems are already in place and because of the guidance already afforded by both the annual and reappointment reviews, the focus of this chapter will not be on the probationary period review or steps the chair may take to prepare the case for tenure. Rather, the primary topic of this chapter is the chair's role in enhancing faculty success, with a focus on associate and full professors, because most departments have more tenured than probationary faculty. The faculty evaluation process (to be discussed in greater detail in Chapter 16) establishes goal setting as one of its most important developmental features. That process and other techniques available to the chair to maintain and restore faculty momentum will be presented. This process is most commonly referred to as faculty development—a somewhat uncomfortable term, and some faculty bristle at the suggestion that they need help in "developing." Indeed, most chairs will be able to say that members of their faculty are far more "developed" in some aspects of their work than the chair could ever hope to be. Nonetheless, some strategies may enhance outstanding careers even further and may be considered more guiding or facilitating than developing. Included in this discussion are strategies to help maintain the vitality of senior faculty, make the best possible use of the faculty cadre present, identify early signs of burnout, and help faculty who have been "stuck" to regain their former status as productive and respected department contributors.

The granting of tenure is based on two considerations. The first is that the faculty member has met a prescribed set of objectives that include a mix of contributions in teaching, scholarship, and service. At some institutions an area of excellence (terminology may vary) must be identified with the other areas also satisfactorily addressed, while at others, two areas of excellence are required. What constitutes excellence is determined either institutionally or within different campuses, schools, or departments. Thus part of the decision to grant tenure is based on a summative consideration. Tenure is also granted based on the promise that the excellent work already done will be extended and that the faculty member's reputation will continue to grow. The criteria for promotion to full rank usually reflect the expectation of further growth.

Looking beyond the tenure period (a seven-year span with the documentation for the determination accumulated by an early date in the sixth year—the predominant situation in American higher education), there is a long period of time to retirement. Newly tenured faculty members seem energized by clearing the hurdle of tenure and frequently have reached a point where they are beginning to receive some national attention for their work. Thus they usually maintain good momentum for several years. During this time, institutional support for faculty career enhancement as well as peer feedback are diminished and irregular. The only exception is the review associated with the move to full rank. The key time for intervening to ensure continued productivity is 10 to 15 years after tenure and may involve associate and full professor ranks. Questions to be addressed include: How does the faculty member remain motivated to maintain a high level of performance or even to generate a trajectory of improvement? What can the department or institution do to help? What steps are needed to allow senior faculty members the flexibility to alter their work focus over the course of a 30-year career? This question about changing the primary work area can result from individual choice, disciplinary changes, or changes in institutional direction and is a complex issue to deal with in academic cultures. The importance of an effective strategy to ensure continued senior faculty productivity cannot be overemphasized because such individuals represent the central workforce of the unit and the role models for those following.

An analysis of the demographics of higher education coupled with the expectations for significant change makes it even more important to keep senior faculty fully engaged in the work of the academy. A high percentage of the current faculty will be eligible to retire in the next decade at a time when their leadership will be required to prepare higher education for the future. The elimination of mandatory retirement also means that chairs need to make certain senior faculty members are still contributing at high levels. These factors, combined with the recent trend to replace tenure-track lines with full-time nontenure-track and adjunct positions, decrease the number of traditional faculty members who might be expected to participate in reshaping the profession.

Faculty Career Changes

Before discussing how a chair might work with faculty members to maintain career momentum, it may be instructive to examine some internal and external factors that could influence the 30- to 40-year faculty career.

The work of faculty members during the probationary period is marked by a strong focus on achievements that will gain tenure. During this time faculty enthusiasm and energy are at their highest levels, and even though there is always some mystery and concern about what is required for tenure, faculty retain a uniform focus. Some faculty members will maintain this strong focus for their entire careers. There are colleagues of mine who entered the profession as research faculty with an absolute commitment to do whatever it took to establish themselves as research players at the international level. They are now within a few years of retirement and are doing the best and most widely recognized work of their lives. One colleague who rose in the rank in research has now set aside other aspects of his responsibilities to again focus more on undergraduate teaching.

Other colleagues have seen their career paths move in different directions over the years. These new paths can be shaped by personal, disciplinary, or institutional changes. For example, there have been some significant changes in scientific areas where some disciplines have blossomed and expanded while others have fallen by the wayside in their interest to students and to external funding agencies. Consider nuclear physics as well as some other areas of physics that were booming several decades ago, driven by government grants and contracts. Physics has since had to reinvent itself by emphasizing biological and human health applications. For those faculty members in areas no longer in vogue, it was either change to another area of physics or change the nature of the institutional work. Faculty members hired years earlier with no expectations in research and graduate education and who lack preparation for the new work are placed in a difficult position. Finally, there are faculty who do not plan to do the same mix of work for their entire careers. These individuals are not necessarily bored, and they most certainly are not low-energy. They just become intrigued by the challenges of new work and new possibilities for accomplishment. This can mean switching from a research track to a teaching track that might emphasize, for example, working with at-risk students, working with honors students, or working with emerging technologies or pedagogies.

These examples show that the department chair cannot dispense the same prescription for keeping all faculty members motivated to further productivity. It also means that the chair cannot expect the same productivity across all areas of faculty responsibility. We know that faculty members are not uniformly productive, but this concept means that they are not proportionally engaged in teaching, scholarship, and service. Their talents are also not proportionately distributed and their interests will vary greatly. Since these factors can vary with career stage, the chair's challenge in invigorating the professional lives of faculty members is a substantial one.

Allowing for Differential Expectations

Not all faculty members are equipped or motivated to contribute equally across the areas of faculty responsibility, a concept that has been recognized formally for many years at some institutions. However, some institutions still strictly adhere to uniform expectations for all members of the faculty, an approach that yields winners and losers and results in emphasizing individual success at the expense of overall unit productivity. As resources become more scarce and increased productivity is demanded, this model will become more difficult to defend.

Recognizing the heterogeneity among members of the faculty has led to the concept of differential work assignments for faculty, allowing the department to capitalize on the individual strengths of each faculty member. If individuals are employed doing what they enjoy and do best, it would predict that unit productivity will be maximized. Also, consider the scenario where everyone has the same assignment and where a percentage of the faculty cannot succeed. This group will not be competitive with others and will suffer from poor morale. On the other hand, if the types of work required of the department are distributed according to interests and abilities, everyone has the sense of making a valuable contribution.

There are several models for assigning differential faculty loads. At some institutions faculty can select percentages of work effort among various areas of faculty responsibility. There may be maxima and minima associated with each—for example, teaching effort must be between 45% and 70%. Other models have been developed for institutions in states that have ranges for faculty work according to institutional type and mission. Other institutions negotiate the workload distribution individually. In all cases, the total workload for each faculty member would be

100%. The work assignment is accompanied by a flexible evaluation scheme that gives a matching evaluation or merit percent to each area of faculty work. Initially, there were some fears that individual election of work would lead to neglect of essential work. This has not occurred, but very small units may be vulnerable to such an imbalance. In such circumstances, the chair and the faculty need to be very intentional about their commitment to meet basic responsibilities.

A guiding principle that allows for differential workload assignments is the concept that the department as a unit will be assessed as to how it meets expectations in teaching, scholarship, and service. Three concerns for department chairs need to be considered. First, if differential loads are assigned because they best address the overall talent available for maximum productivity, then excellent contributions, regardless of the work assignment mix, must be recognized in the reward structure. The second point of concern for the chair is related to the notion of what it means to be a faculty member in higher education. I personally know faculty who, under the concept of differential workloads, would elect to be 100% research. While they may have immense talents in research, to totally eliminate their responsibilities in teaching and/or service would seem to violate the definition of the position they hold. Without expectations in basic responsibility areas, certain faculty will never interact with others to solve a problem or to take advantage of an opportunity because their work does not overlap. Thus "voids" should be avoided. Finally, care must be taken in encouraging faculty to frequently change their mix of work if they hope to be promoted to full rank. The assumption here is that probationary faculty are not involved because the compressed and high-pressure period prior to tenure is focused on the accomplishments dictated by unit culture and expectation. If promotion is in the plan, the faculty member and the chair must be cognizant of what level of excellence is required and which area of faculty work it should be applied to.

Facilitating Career Changes

Faculty members who define themselves early in their careers as striving to achieve excellence in their field of choice will not necessarily continue with that goal until they retire. They may be drawn to another field, they may realize they have become less competitive in their chosen field, or they may even develop "vertical ambition." A vigilant chair may recognize the signs indicating that a faculty member may be getting stale or may be spending more time doing uncharacteristic things. This type of behavior may be a subject of conversation during the annual review or even during some other less formal meeting. Using as guiding principles the notions that an interested and engaged faculty member will be a more productive faculty member and that a faculty member has the option to define the nature of his or her scholarly contributions, the chair should explore with the faculty member ways to facilitate professional development even if it means the old work will diminish as the new work emerges. Two examples from my experience as chair are relevant here.

The first is that of a colleague who joined the faculty a few years after I did, although he was older, having served several years as a high school teacher before returning to school for his doctorate. We will call him Ray. Ray was a behavioral ecologist studying the effects of the environment on insect behavior. He developed an interest in identifying how a certain insect hormone affected behavior. Any neuroscientist or cell biologist would predict that this research would be incredibly complex and involve interactions of many systems each communicating via a number of molecular pathways. Clearly, Ray was not trained to do this and was getting in over his head. However, he was a tenured associate professor and continued diligently to pursue this project. Ray was also intrigued by the potential of computers at a time prior to the availability of the personal computer. He constructed crude databases for recording his results, introduced the department faculty to computers, and soon became interested in creating computer-based ecology "field trips." The idea was to allow students to take a virtual field trip, collect data, analyze it, and develop conclusions. These exercises could be used to make scientific excursions to ecological settings when the weather was poor or to environments not available locally.

The chair recognized that Ray's computer work was groundbreaking and had great potential for visibility and scholarly productivity. The same could not be said for Ray's work in behavioral neurobiology. The chair was concerned that splitting his time between these two projects would result in Ray losing his competitive advantage in computer applications. During the conversation about developing a single scholarly focus, Ray divulged that he felt obliged to continue traditional lab work lest "he lose the respect of his colleagues." This was one of those moments when one realizes how the pressures of tradition can shape or distort careers and truncate creativity. Ray and the chair continued this conversation at later dates, and ultimately through support for and appropriate acknowledgement of the importance and scholarly nature of Ray's computer-based work, the transition was made and Ray went on to produce award-winning virtual field trips. Several years later he was promoted to full rank with the enthusiastic endorsement of the colleagues he feared would not respect him or his work.

The second example is that of a very productive faculty member who rose through the ranks rapidly. She maintained a well-funded, highly productive research program, provided graduate and undergraduate instruction, mentored undergraduate and graduate research students, and contributed significantly to institutional and professional service. This individual could not envision the remaining years of her career dominated by the same mix of submitting grant proposals, overseeing research, teaching classes, and conducting meetings. She approached the chair with an interest in becoming associate chair in order to gain administrative experience. With a carefully designed set of tasks she was able to accomplish some things the chair did not have time for and create new entries in her already impressive curriculum vitae. She has since gone on to head her own department and is now a vice president for research.

Common elements in each of these cases involve ways to adjust work expectations for faculty so they can pursue the things that attract and interest them. Accompanying this is support and encouragement along the way and a reward system that is flexible enough to allow equal merit for equal excellence.

Maintaining Senior Faculty Productivity

The term *senior* here refers to someone well past the tenure decision who has typically been promoted to associate professor. Although the timing varies across institutions, tenure usually begins at seven years of service. Assuming a traditional educational path, faculty may gain the first academic appointment at any time between their late 20s to mid 30s, depending on the discipline and whether post-doctoral appointments are required for hiring. Pushing beyond the tenure process, senior faculty are defined as those from 40–45 years of age and beyond. Examining a typical department of 20 or more faculty, several species of senior faculty can be identified. First, there are those who continued to move forward rapidly and were promoted to full rank less than 10 years post-tenure. Second, there are those who have yet to gain full rank but are working toward that goal and can be identified as having strong potential for achieving promotion. Finally, there are those at the associate professor rank who seem destined to remain at this level. These categories represent different challenges for the chair to ensure that productivity trajectories remain positive in some cases and are transformed from languishing to increasing in others.

The importance of maintaining senior faculty productivity has been thoroughly explored by Bland and Bergquist (1997) as well as by Lucas (1994). In the former, a series of internal and external factors were identified relative to senior faculty vitality. Lucas uses the results of surveys of senior faculty to define the factors that they feel are most critical to keeping them working productively. These are both excellent sources for information on what factors keep senior faculty members engaged and productive. However, one need only to look at the successful senior faculty in any department to identify some of these factors. Productive senior faculty members have an absolute and permanent commitment to their work. This strong intrinsic desire seems impervious to setbacks and rejections. When my institution was moving to a research focus, a colleague with such traits said we needed to have thick skin. This was at a time when most grant proposals were not funded and we had to continue to be productive in spite of resource restrictions. Even after having won those initial battles and achieving success, such individuals continuously seek to move to the next level.

Beyond internal motivation, there are other characteristics that define successful senior faculty members. Because of their strong disciplinary commitment, they are personally comfortable and confident with their status in their area of expertise. This is confirmed by the position they hold relative to other experts in the field. They know they are at the cutting edge. They also know the other players in the area and often collaborate with some of them. This networking further supports their professional status and provides opportunities to work with other leaders in the field to make even more valuable contributions. They now have an expanded scope of professional activities, usually multiple collaboration and more than one project. These general characteristics are seen in faculty whose major focal points are teaching or research. For research-focused faculty members in science and technology disciplines, this also means that two or three separate projects are active on site or in collaboration and that the research group has now expanded from perhaps five or six to twelve. If the projects are in bench research, each has its own external funding.

These are clearly very busy people. The notion that achieving tenure frees faculty members to focus on other aspects of faculty work would not be true in such cases. When tenure is granted for substantial scholarship in teaching or research, it is with the hope that the faculty member will continue to achieve in even greater ways. While changing focus is certainly permitted and is a benefit of tenure, many faculty members continue to build dossiers in the area for which tenure was granted. Regardless of the area of focus or whether it was the original area or resulted from a change of interest, time becomes an important factor for such individuals to continue to achieve in this more complex set of activities. Those faculty members who organize and compartmentalize their time with a strong primary focus are usually the ones to reach their goals early.

Another point concerns the decision on how a faculty member chooses the work that defines himself or herself from a professional perspective and how that may vary depending on career stage. Each faculty member must make this decision regardless of whether the expectations for tenure and further advancement are based on teaching or research parameters. For the probationary faculty member, the objective is to accumulate the accomplishments required to be in place five to six years from the date of appointment. The faculty member knows from conversations with the chair and feedback from faculty committees that certain things are expected. If the area of primary consideration is teaching, the faculty member must accumulate a set of accomplishments that may include, for example, some mix of good student satisfaction surveys, positive additions to student knowledge resulting from outcomes assessment measures, new course contributions that have attracted strong enrollments, professional presentations on teaching innovations, and positive peer reviews of teaching. If research is the primary consideration, then peer-reviewed publications in quality journals, published books, external funding, and speaking invitations are part of the accomplishments that must be in place. In either case the timeframe is set, but the work to be submitted (courses to develop, learning strategies to incorporate, aspects of research to focus on, journals to submit to, etc.) needs to be decided. The decision must consider risk, as the following example illustrates.

A faculty member defines an aspect of research that has a valuable outcome in terms of adding to the field and that is approachable with known techniques or variations thereof. The work would be attractive to funding agencies and should yield regular publishable results along the way. However, a second project is identified whose results will transform the entire field and be controversial because they will challenge the existing dogma and, therefore, the experts in the field. Obtaining funding and publishing the results will be difficult because grant proposals and manuscripts will be evaluated by these same experts. The former project seems ideal for the probationary faculty member because it promises the requisite productivity for tenure. The second, however, is very high risk. If the conventional scholarship in the area is not rapidly changed, the faculty member could wind up with nothing. The decision here is an interesting one and should involve the chair and department committees from the outset. Ask yourself how you would advise a faculty member facing this choice.

The previous scenario plays out much differently if the faculty member is senior. Here the tolerance for risk is much higher, and the faculty member already has status in the field that may permit a more open consideration of innovation by other experts in the field. The chair advice for this faculty member may be quite different. Successful senior faculty members value their autonomy and how it allows them to choose their work. Risk taking is a valued enterprise at many institutions and is a characteristic identified with active and successful senior faculty members.

The Chair's Perspective on Productive Senior Faculty

The department chair wants successful senior faculty members to continue contributing to the department and serving as role models for the more junior faculty. Taking into account the characteristics of engaged senior faculty, the chair must then create a unit environment that enables the desired continuation and growth. Networking can be supported by travel for the faculty member or by suggesting that a faculty member bring a collaborator or potential collaborator to campus. This can sometimes be done as an extension of the department's seminar or colloquia series. Time is another characteristic that can be addressed in a straightforward manner. Senior faculty are valuable to the department and institution and one should use their expertise and energy wisely. That is, when they are called upon for advice or participation, it should be for work that will not occupy endless hours of their time and is truly important. They will appreciate not only the selective nature of the chair's request, but will also be able to identify the work as worthy of their time. Excusing senior faculty from service for the betterment of the institution is not what is suggested here; rather, requesting their input on items of significant impact is the point.

The chair can also encourage, and even support, risky ventures for creative faculty, reinforcing the notion of autonomy. Support could come in the form of seed funding for a unique project or travel to a conference in an area of scholarship that stretches the faculty member's expertise. In teaching, this might take the form of attempting a new pedagogical approach in a large class. The department might fund a teaching assistant to help facilitate this work. While these experiments may occasionally fail, they do transmit a sense of trust and confidence from the chair to the faculty member. In many cases, these faculty members respond to challenges. Again, the pledge of support and the confidence act as an academic adrenaline for motivated faculty.

A good part of the faculty work environment is generated outside of the department, and although the chair can modulate internal department issues to some degree, what happens at the college or university level is largely outside of the chair's control. However, when the campus culture is not what it might be, there may be ways to shield productive faculty from its negative aspects by fostering a department-based institutional culture within a unit.

Productive faculty like to work in environments that are intellectually oriented, where faculty around them are content, where collegiality is the order of the day, and where faculty have real input into decision-making. If some of these elements are not present at the global level, they can be part of the department environment. It also helps if the institution has clear goals and everyone subscribes to them. This is sometimes not the case and my experience of more than 30 years at my institution provides a good example. The answer to the question "What kind of university are we?" has never been definitively answered. In fact, depending on the audience, campus administration and others have portrayed our mission in a variety of ways over the years. While this was disconcerting, our school and its departments have defined themselves in ways that are recognized by incoming faculty members and that have reinforced our expectations such that senior faculty remain steadfastly committed to our self-articulated goals.

It is important that faculty know they are doing the right things and doing them well. Rewarding excellent work is always a good way to get more of the same. However, reward can come in many preferred forms and the astute chair will know what types of things resonate with individual faculty. For the truly outstanding faculty member, there are special awards for which they can be nominated. Others prefer merit pay, often difficult to provide in recent years. Still others are much more interested in seeing written accolades in their annual reviews.

The Underperforming Senior Faculty Member

This category of faculty member may be an associate professor who is not on track for the final promotion or a full professor who has become stale. These members are not poor-performing, problematic faculty but those who are sometimes referred to as "stuck." The best way to combat this situation is through vigilance to recognize and address the early symptoms. There may be a drop-off in overall department participation, withdrawal from formerly stimulating and productive collaborations, or changes in the variety of activities. Goal setting can be used at such times to effectively prevent the situation from deteriorating further. Asking faculty to think about what formerly motivated them or new activities that might intrigue them can stimulate the formation of a plan. The chair should take the opportunity to buy in to the idea by providing encouragement and support. In addition, identifying changing interests or obstacles can be the subject of discussion at annual reviews or other informal venues that are compatible with the management style of the chair.

The fall-off in motivation and productivity is much easier to deal with early as opposed to several years down the road. A common cause for such situations is work overload. Some faculty cannot say no and actually seek certain types of work. There are times faculty overcommit and gain no satisfaction from what can be completed only to a level of mediocrity. Dealing with this situation includes goal setting with appropriate pledges of support, exploration of assignment changes (including release from overload) that may stimulate engagement, and possibly teaming the faculty member with someone inside or outside of the department to work on something new.

Poorly Performing and Difficult Faculty

These are different but related situations that most chairs face at one time or another. The interventions for poorly performing faculty are similar to those for underperforming faculty, but the task is tougher because the deterioration of performance is more severe and the faculty member may have lost self-esteem and accumulated resentment from the loss of status and self-worth that comes from extended lackluster performance. The chair may need to use more extensive strategies and allow more time to get such a career back on track. Change of assignment, released time to do something new, trips to a conference in consecutive years, seed funding for a project or an assistant are all strategies a chair may use to allow the plan for improvement a chance for success.

Difficult and cantankerous faculty members are very problematic because they are not quiet, low-performing colleagues. Rather, they frequently are aggressive and present obstacles to many aspects of the department's work. They can oppose all reform, insult colleagues, students, and administrators, express their opposition by making contacts with external groups and organizations, and can do any number of things that make department life unpleasant for everyone. In addition to egregious behavior, these faculty may also be poor performers. One of the key elements to maintaining faculty productivity is having a collegial, supportive environment of engaged scholars. Poorly performing faculty are not conducive to this environment, but openly hostile faculty members are toxic to an atmosphere that fosters excellent work.

Leaming (1998) and Lucas (1994) both discuss these difficult cases and offer some insight into how this behavior develops and what might be done to improve the way such individuals interact with the department and its constituents as well as to restore at least some of their value to the unit. In some cases the chair may be able to trace negative changes in the faculty member to personal issues. These can involve personal health or problems concerning family members. The weight of these issues can be overwhelming, and every other component of life suffers because of emotional upset. Personal health issues can include serious or terminal illness or can be mental in nature. In the latter case, family are also likely to have felt the impact of negative behavior. They may have some insight regarding its causes and can help formulate a plan to secure the appropriate intervention. There are also campus resources equipped to deal with issues requiring counseling.

Lucas (1994) conducted a survey of difficult, disconnected faculty to learn why they thought their behavior had changed for the worse. To summarize, the findings showed the overwhelming number felt they had become negative because they had not been treated fairly. Unfair treatment could be in the form of denied promotions, low merit increments, inappropriate teaching and service assignments, and the lack of perks others had received. While it is not uncommon for faculty to have views of themselves that may be disproportionately lofty and that they often know less than they should about the accomplishments of even their closest colleagues, there still needs to be frank discussion to stop them from festering to the point where faculty go to war or drop out. Another factor cited in the survey was the perceived lack of appreciation for the good work done before they stopped contributing. It is truly unfortunate that even a single career has been cut short due to failure to acknowledge a job well done. Another reason given was loss of influence or position. This has also been mentioned as a reason for resistance to change and some ways to disarm it are suggested in Chapter 22.

Reaching faculty who are actively engaged in obstructionism and other unpleasant behavior is a formidable challenge. Fortunately, I have not had to deal with faculty who actively oppose all initiatives or who act negatively to colleagues, students, and administration. I have, however, seen and heard of cases in other units and can only outline how those situations were handled. In many cases, totally unproductive and/or obstructionist faculty are marginalized if they do not respond to reasonable requests, opportunities, and investments in improvement. Sanctions such as withholding merit increments, loss of travel funds, and other discretionary perks generally available to faculty are common responses. When marginalized, the negative impact of these faculty on the department is diminished but their lack of productivity and the damage they can do in the classroom may continue. I recall a case when I was a very junior faculty member. A senior faculty member with administrative responsibility as graduate program director was removed because he was inattentive to the program requirements regarding paperwork, thus jeopardizing the degree process and making the program less attractive to potential students. The same individual was banned from teaching undergraduates a few years earlier, and ultimately the decision was made to remove him completely from the classroom. This left him with no responsibility aside from collecting his paycheck. However, it was decided that in the long run it was better to eat his salary than pay the consequences of his participation. Fortunately he was close to retirement at the time. These are the cases for which post-tenure review was envisioned.

Other approaches to bringing back a disconnected, poor-performing, and even negative faculty member into the department mainstream can be successful in some cases, and exhausting all possibilities is worthwhile because of the potential positive outcome for the department. Success here is like getting a new position without asking the dean for a new line and involves little cost considering the investment the institution already has in the faculty member. Getting to the root cause of the dropout is the first order of business. It is often easier for an external chair or a chair not associated with past department history with the problem to learn this background. While the present chair cannot negate the past experience and may not necessarily agree with the faculty member's position, just listening and expressing regret that things turned out to be disappointing can be cleansing and permit a new beginning. The chair may also seek to learn what the faculty member's initial objectives were upon entering the profession and what activities had been particularly successful. Perhaps there are some colleagues from the past with whom this individual successfully interacted. This information can help the chair to identify, or even create, assignments for which the faculty member is ideally suited based on past success. While this may be somewhat contrived, it sends the message that the chair has confidence in the faculty member and that the "new boss" has a task that requires special expertise. Former colleagues may also be asked to be a part of this mission if appropriate. Again, this will take time and effort on the part of the chair and success is not guaranteed, but the reward is great if success is even partially achieved.

A disconcerting observation made in the Lucas (1994) survey was that one in five dropouts were ex-deans or ex-chairs. This concerns me as it should chairs who are reading this and who one day will no longer be chair. I know of two experiences that provide sharp contrasts on how former deans and chairs perform after returning to the faculty. One would surmise that a person with administrative skills and experience in helping faculty develop their careers would be able to identify new career paths for himself or herself, but this is not always the case.

In the first experience, a former chair was asked by the dean to consider his appointment as chair over when he returned from his sabbatical. There were no problems that the faculty could identify, but the dean believed that the eight years already served were enough for any chair. The former chair returned two years later to find a new chair hired in an external search. He was still bitter about his removal and did just the minimum required, meeting his classes and participating in occasional service. About four years later, the replacement chair left and my appointment as chair began. At our first annual review (note: I had received eight reviews under his chairmanship), I asked what he would like to do during his remaining years on the faculty. My intention was to let him plan his work so that I could facilitate it in order to bring him back into the fold as a productive faculty member. His response was "I don't know; you tell me." This was quite surprising to hear from one whose responsibility was once to facilitate faculty productivity and help faculty who were stuck.

Other strategies for rekindling his interest in and commitment to department progress included appeals to his vast experience as an administrator and faculty member and how that might be used productively to benefit the unit. I suggested that he accept an appointment as chair of the curriculum committee to help us deal with issues concerning the increased demands for coursework within the major. He accepted the role but the committee rarely convened. At about the same time, an opportunity appeared to develop and implement a new fast-track graduate program at the master's level for the purpose of preparing students to apply to professional schools. The clientele would be those who were near misses in the preceding application round and those returning from other careers to update their credentials. This opportunity was assigned to the former chair because it was relatively simple to map out a two-semester sequence of courses from existing offerings, and it was something with high potential impact for which he could take full ownership. After a short period of time, he reported that it simply could not be done. The project then reverted to me as graduate program director, and a program of study was devised over the next two days. Did the idea really have potential? In 12 years, there have been more than 320 degree recipients and a professional school admission rate of more than 60%. The approaches used in this case—to provide a leadership assignment that reinforces the experiences and knowledge of the individual and provides a fast-turnaround creative opportunity to demonstrate value to the unit and reinforce self-value—failed. However, I believe they are valid approaches that will work more often than not. Unfortunately, this individual could neither overcome his disappointment nor adapt to another form of productive work.

The second example is quite different. My dean retired from his post at the mandatory retirement age for administrators and returned to my department as a faculty member. There have been no concerns about loss of power or influence, and he has been extremely active in promoting a center of excellence that he established several years ago. He wrote and submitted a major grant proposal, and during his first year back, completed a book in his area of expertise. The differences in the two cases are many but in the latter case, the individual was actively engaged in work that is scholarly and work that attracts the respect and acknowledgement of colleagues both local and beyond. In the former case, the deposed chair was concerned only with being chair and when that was removed, there was nothing on which to fall back. The lesson here to all chairs or other administrators who may return to the faculty is either maintain some elements of your former scholarship or establish a new line of scholarship related to your administrative position. This subject is discussed further in Chapters 3 and 24.

Resources and Strategies for Sustaining and Improving Faculty Productivity

Institutions routinely provide several types of resources that represent development opportunities for faculty, and chairs should be familiar with what is available. These resources should not be viewed as cures for weak performance but rather as resources available to all faculty members for the furthering of the overall objectives of the institution. Sabbatical leaves are available for retooling and expanding faculty expertise. There is usually a campus grants program to assist in opening new areas of inquiry or to sustain faculty work between grants. Travel grants are available to defray the costs of national and even international conference attendance. Other types of support for faculty members can be specialized grants, workshops, or consultant help for instructional improvement, the integration of technology into the classroom, the adoption of service learning options, and grant writing.

There are many items the chair can use to sustain excellent performance and to improve performance where it is lacking. Some suggestions given will be more difficult to employ in a department of less than five faculty members where flexibility with fiscal and faculty resources is more limited; however, most departments have budgets that may come in categories of expenditures or may be fully flexible. In any event, chairs, even in these days of fiscal challenge, have some discretion that allows them to make strategic investments to enhance a successful career or reinvigorate one that has lost momentum. Conference travel, technical skill workshop attendance, the opportunity to invite a well-known scholar to campus, or seed funding for a new idea may fall into this category. In the event that department funding does not permit this investment, a request that the dean become a partner in the enterprise should be considered.

Earlier discussion identified overload as a factor in diminished faculty performance. This and the repetitive nature of work assignments can contribute to what is referred to as burnout. The chair can usually find a way to change teaching assignments or even temporarily reduce load. (In circumstances where teaching loads are rigidly defined, this may require permission from upper administration.) Load reduction should not come at the expense of other faculty as it will cause resentment and can lead to a transfer of the overload to others. This sometimes happens during sabbaticals when the rest of the faculty pick up the load so one person can recharge. All gain is lost when those picking up the slack are overworked and diverted from their own activities. In all of these instances, the reduced load needs to be transferred to adjuncts or other temporary instructors, sections may be combined, or in some cases canceled. While these measures may be subject to criticism because they can be portrayed as adversely affecting students, the long-term benefits of restoring a permanent faculty member to a state of improved performance over the next several years make this temporary change justifiable.

Chairs can also use their contacts and experience to identify new opportunities for faculty members who desire a change in their professional focus. Transitions from research to teaching or administrative service can be facilitated by changes in service and instructional assignments within the department and suggestions for faculty appointments at the campus level. In cases where faculty members seek new challenges or where improved performance is indicated, chairs can sponsor experiments where risk is tolerated by a moratorium on the impact of negative consequences. A case in point is a faculty member who wishes to change classroom instruction from a traditional lecture format to group work and collaborative learning. National evidence shows that students do not always respond favorably to this approach and may rate faculty lower on satisfaction surveys. If such surveys are used heavily in faculty evaluation and merit rewards, the chair can choose to hold the faculty member "harmless" for negative evaluations for a period of time as a way to encourage experimentation and risk taking and to encourage faculty members to be bold in their attempts to improve performance.

Chairs can also arrange for special help for faculty. This may come in the form of arrangements for a struggling faculty member to work in research or to teach with another member of the faculty who is well established and successful. There may be some work tradeoffs for the mentor so that the time spent does not detract from productivity. There may also be cases where this approach is arranged with a mentor in another department if the struggling faculty member prefers to work on improvement away from the eyes of department colleagues. Similarly, interdisciplinary opportunities may arise from extra-departmental relationships that can be arranged for faculty members by their chairs.

Another resource available to enhance faculty work or facilitate improvement lies in the collective experiences of campus and external department chairs and heads. It is hard to imagine that any challenge a chair may confront in eliciting improvement, maintaining vitality, converting the detractor, and so on is a truly unique case never before faced by a department chair. So the suggestion here is to tap into that vast resource for advice and to discuss approaches to common problems. Some institutions have an informal chair group known as a community of chairs (see Chapters 7 and 23) where such cases can be discussed.

One final point of caution to the chair who actively invests in faculty improvement. It must be clear to faculty members that the department invests in all personnel to enhance performance and productivity. The development work of the chair cannot be seen to be targeted only at underperforming faculty members. Consider the first responses of the faculty at a large university where limited resources are diverted to low performers while high-performing faculty are left to their own devices when they wish to initiate an instructional innovation or conduct a set of experiments that may lead to a significant breakthrough. This advice is also applicable to campus-level offices devoted to developing faculty. The chair should endorse all good ideas that promote the goals and objectives of the individual, the unit, and the institution.

Summary

Academic departments are usually attentive to mentoring junior faculty through the probationary period prior to tenure. Chairs, along with senior faculty serving on promotion and tenure committees, play critical roles in reviewing and directing the work of their new colleagues. Once tenure has been achieved, there is generally less attention to faculty progress and some individuals may begin to show declines in interest and productivity. Because a large percentage of the department can be in this post-tenure category, it is very important that someone pay close attention to this group. For the most part, this responsibility falls to the chair.

Maintaining senior faculty vitality requires that chairs understand what factors are highly valued by this group. These individuals, productive associate professors working toward promotion and full professors, are well integrated into national peer groups and are considered leaders in their fields. They are often willing to take risks by assuming formidable challenges in order to make more than just routine contributions. They are busier than ever; they value their time. They also expect a collegial, focused, and intellectual environment. Within these characteristics lie the challenges for the chair. Promoting networking through travel and invitations to campus to external colleagues, investment in and encouragement for risk taking, protection of time diverted to routine functions, and the creation of a positive, supportive work environment are the chair's essential roles.

Beyond maintaining and enhancing the work of productive senior faculty members, chairs must also address those senior faculty whose performance has declined and those who are disenfranchised to the point where they present active opposition to department objectives. Keys to the former are recognizing, through the annual review process, when performance starts to slide or when faculty become engaged in new work. This may mean changing interests, in which case the chair can help direct and support a career transition where faculty members can focus on different areas. This may also mean changing the mix of faculty responsibilities within the traditional three areas. In the case of the problem faculty member, solutions may be difficult to find but worth the effort. Finding the root cause of the dropout is very important to devising corrective action. Chairs can use special assignments that recognize the expertise and experience of the individual in solving a problem, reintegration into the work with former colleagues, and selective developmental investment as possible approaches to returning the faculty member to a former high level of productivity and self-esteem.

16

FACULTY EVALUATION

One of the most sensitive and recurring responsibilities that a chair faces is conducting faculty evaluations. For most chairs, even those who have routinely conducted faculty reviews for many years, the review season is one of their toughest times and a major source of stress. Considering that most chairs believe that a healthy majority of their faculty members perform well, this says a lot about how difficult it is to confront and attempt to remediate poor performance or to deal with those whose self-assessment is inflated. For this reason and for the potential positive impact on the institution of the faculty development side of faculty evaluation, the evaluation process remains a major element of many chair development programs.

Because faculty evaluation has a major impact on faculty productivity and morale, it becomes very important to institutional well-being. The real challenge in conducting objective reviews results from the potential contradiction to chair roles that are strictly supportive in context. The chair's role as a mentor, a cheerleader, a facilitator, a confidant, or a champion with regard to faculty members and their careers can sometimes conflict when there is a poor review. In the faculty evaluation process over the course of my career, the probationary period (the time leading to promotion to full rank) and times when faculty performance was substandard were years when faculty evaluations were the most stressful. At such times, the chair must make certain that the elements necessary for a positive decision on faculty advancement are in place or that specific steps are followed to improve poor performance. While in such situations formative activities directing faculty to the necessary levels of performance do take place, the fact remains that a summative decision is ultimately made. In institutions where merit pay is the rule, an objective evaluation is made to set the increment for each member of the faculty. As any seasoned chair will relate, the decisions on merit pay, even when the incremental differential is minuscule, are long remembered by some faculty.

Before we discuss the faculty evaluation process, we should acknowledge that regular evaluation of all faculty members may not occur in all institutions or in some units within an institution. There are places where university bylaws stipulate that only faculty below the rank of full professor shall be reviewed on an annual basis, meaning that some faculty are not reviewed for two decades or more if they were fortunate to gain full rank early in their careers. In other places, the nature of the review itself is not specified and the process may take place in the chair's office with the chair reviewing whatever information he or she has collected. In fact, everyone probably knows of cases where reviews for merit pay are done in such a cloaked manner. In more recent times, prompted perhaps by criticisms leveled against the privileged life that tenure affords, most institutions are more prescribed in how reviews are done and more inclusive in who is reviewed. The most common mechanism is called the annual review. The process commences with faculty submitting written documentation of annual activities in a specific format for review by the chair. Subsequently, there is a written evaluation prepared by the chair and a face-to-face meeting between the faculty member and the chair. The order of these two meetings may vary, and the final document may go through more than one iteration.

Another point here is that others may play roles in the evaluation of faculty in certain cases. For our purposes, it is assumed that the chair is the one implementing the review process and the chair-centered model will be used throughout. It is recognized that in some units, special department committees may play some of the roles ascribed to chairs. Such faculty groups will be discussed further in the section on post-tenure review.

Chair Value in the Review Process

Although conducting faculty evaluations can be stressful, most are a pleasure and there are some real values to the chair in the process. After the annual accumulation of faculty accomplishments has been read, the ensuing conversation presents new information regarding the faculty member's activities, where particular obstacles have been overcome, where challenges remain, what they are struggling with, and what they have enjoyed doing. Accomplishments that were omitted from the written report are often brought to light. When the chair is a recent external hire or when the faculty member under evaluation is a senior individual, some relevant historical perspectives may emerge during the review process. This provides the chair with a long view of where this person has been and what path has been followed. The additional information shared during the one-on-one meeting can be extremely valuable to the chair in helping shape the work of the faculty member over the coming years.

A particularly important element of the annual review process is goal setting. When dealing with an accomplished professor who is performing at a high level, this is an easy process because such an individual will already have a set of goals for the next year that the chair can endorse on the spot. Setting goals with probationary faculty is more challenging because they are less experienced and want to know how much and how many of a variety of things will be necessary to gain tenure. The tight timeline for the tenure decisions at most institutions makes this a delicate period for chair mentoring. Goal setting to improve flagging performance can also be a tense encounter with denial and frustration frequently entering the discussion. Hard, valid data to support the case of poor performance needs to be available, and a plan for addressing the issues must be brokered at the meeting.

Another type of developmental opportunity may appear at the annual review. This concerns faculty careers and the transition they may undergo. While everyone knows faculty who are enthralled by their work in teaching and/or research and continue to vigorously and productively do that work until they retire, there are also faculty who decide that they want to change the nature of their work one or more times during a career. Conversations about such transitions can be initiated by the faculty member or the chair at annual reviews. Chairs may notice that a faculty member is losing interest in one area and gravitating to another. It is in the long-term best interest of all parties concerned to allow faculty to work in areas that are exciting to them and are likely to yield productive results. This conversation can then lead to the chair facilitating the transition through seed funding, workload adjustments, change of assignments, and directing the faculty member to opportunities inside and outside of the department.

Finally, the annual review provides an opportunity for the chair to indicate verbally and in writing that the individual has done a fine job. However, this does not take place often enough. For some faculty—and an attentive chair will soon learn which ones—what is said and written about them resulting from the evaluation process is more important than getting the extra 0.5% in salary increment.

Faculty Value in the Review Process

Some faculty will look forward to reviews or at least tolerate them. There are always some who will not anticipate them because they have not met the goals set the previous year. From an equitable, formative review, faculty can receive acknowledgement of excellent work and validation of goals and objectives set in consultation with the chair. Reviews can lead to the identification of new opportunities for the faculty through expressed interest that can be matched by ideas and potential connections from the chair. Aspirations may be expressed by the faculty member that can be realized through resources of various types available through the discretion, authority, or influence of the chair. Veteran chairs will be able to recall strategic investments that were made to initiate or bring to fruition an idea or piece of work accomplished by a faculty member. While such positive synergies can happen in other venues, the annual review is particularly conducive to these types of discussions because planning is a major item on the agenda. These developmental encounters serve in the long run to convey a genuine interest by the chair in faculty success and satisfaction.

Establishing Criteria for Evaluation

There are many different types of colleges and universities and many ways of categorizing them based on mission, size, complexity, and whether they are public or private. Within this global complexity there are likely to be differences in expectations within institutional subunits (colleges, schools, departments) in terms of what faculty are expected to accomplish. For our purposes, it is assumed that the model department will have faculty expectations in teaching, research and scholarly activity, and service. For those readers whose units may not have explicit expectations in scholarship, the focus for evaluation will be on the other two areas.

Regardless of institutional type or department values, one has to ask how many faculty members know the basis upon which they are evaluated. Although recent emphasis on annual reviews has helped with this problem, there are still many cases where merit increments are awarded at a time apart from the annual review and faculty are uncertain as to how the differentials were determined. While most faculty members would identify scholarly products and quantitative and qualitative aspects of teaching as elements that would be considered in merit awards, there is still a good deal of mystery around "what really counts" in such determinations. It seems logical that the criteria used to evaluate faculty during the annual review should constitute the criteria used in setting merit. The question is whether or not logic prevails in the way we conduct these reviews. It seems that one should mirror the other to motivate good effort and work from faculty members and to establish a sense of trust that what is acknowledged and encouraged is indeed what counts.

How does one construct a set of public criteria for faculty performance that enforces what the institution expects and the unit culture values? A safe and flexible place to begin this process is the institutional mission statement, a public, written statement where the institution defines its goals. This document will provide the general categories of faculty work, and departments will adapt them specifically to their work. Schools or other structural units may also be a part of the cascade of increasingly specific definitions of what is expected in the areas of faculty responsibility. These benchmarks for faculty performance would be reinforced, encouraged, and planned at the annual review and used as the basis for merit evaluations that include merit pay, bonuses, and special awards.

Next, the chair will help prepare a list of accomplishments under the faculty areas of responsibility. To maintain neutrality and avoid any chair bias, a preliminary list may be extracted from published lists compiled by experts in the field. Some of the better examples can be found in the works of Braskamp and Ory (1994) and Arreola (2000). While there clearly are differences in scholarly products across disciplines and in the types of the instruction provided by faculty, each unit will be able to translate their values into local language that all members of the unit can understand. The lists of noteworthy activities under the categories can be modest or extensive, and they all must understand that some discretion will be used by the chair when listings of accomplishments are presented or when contributions outside of the lists are evident. For example, a major committee assignment may be listed although the committee may not have met throughout the past year, or a valuable contribution in establishing an internship program with local government may appear with no algorithm in the faculty-developed schema to acknowledge this, simply because no one thought of the possibility. The important thing about this process is that faculty input leads to general faculty buy-in or, at least, awareness. Even if individual faculty fail to value certain components of the criteria, they at least know that most of their colleagues do, so there can be no claim of inequitable treatment against the chair. A desirable objective of this exercise is to create a set of criteria that allows all faculty members to identify what they do well so that all contributions are valued.

The process of establishing expectations for performance and reward can have an added benefit related to effecting change. Not only can traditional expectations be listed as valuable and meritorious work, but aspirational objectives can also be listed as a way to focus faculty energy and talent in new directions and achieve better outcomes. For departments aiming to achieve more visibility for their work in teaching, special consideration could be given to faculty who are invited and win competitive opportunities to present their work at external conferences. For departments wishing to build their research profile, submissions of external proposals may be a way to begin that process. If student learning outcomes assessment is a goal, successful programs to institute this type of assessment could be part of the evaluation criteria.

How Quantitative Should You Get?

After evaluation criteria within the areas of faculty responsibility are established, faculty will know what counts but they may not know how much each item is worth. This can be a very slippery slope to negotiate because faculty will want the highest value placed on their personal areas of interest and strength. Using the three standard areas of faculty responsibility (and some institutions may have more than three), the following questions might be asked: Does mentoring a doctoral student through a successful thesis defense count more or less than teaching an undergraduate class? Does landing a large multiyear grant have more value than publishing an article in a top-ranked journal? Ranking activities within classes can usually be accomplished, but assigning real point value to create a measuring differential will lead to endless debate. Similarly, comparing entries in terms of point value across the areas of responsibility will also invoke the age-old debate between faculty who have research programs and those who focus almost exclusively on teaching. These are but a few examples of the conflicts that may arise when absolute values are attached to specific accomplishments. A real-world example from an academic department at my institution will illustrate the problem. Colleagues who developed this schema will recognize themselves in this example, but their system is used with permission.

> Because a former department chair distributed merit increments inequitably, the department decided to protect itself from any future abuses by developing a detailed point scheme that future chairs were expected to use. A small portion of the raise pool was distributed on a percent basis determined by meeting very basic expectations in the three areas, but the major component of the pool was distributed according to the point scheme. The total number of points generated by faculty members was divided into the remaining pool and the value of each point was then determined for that year.
>
> There were 96 items on the list. Publications, for example, were accredited based on the journal in which they appeared, with three tiers of journals available. They were further subdivided by how many authors were listed and where the faculty member's name appeared in that order. There were over two dozen possible point values for a publication based on these variables. In the external funding area, the schema rewarded the dollars of direct funding with a point value per thousand and the number of indirect (overhead) dollars with a point value per thousand that was 10 times higher. This was in place because

indirect dollars reverted largely to the department budget and thus were of great community value.

The schema worked well until a new branch of work in the discipline emerged as the result of new hires. The issue of adding new journals to the publication tiers was accomplished, but the grant dollars ratings resulted in some severe distortions of merit assignment because the faculty in the new area were now eligible for funding from a source not available to most of the others. This source provided grants that were many times larger than typical department grants and that paid the maximum overhead rates. Because faculty with successful research agendas in this area had virtually no ceiling on the points they could earn, they were eligible for a majority of the pool. Teaching, on the other hand, was rewarded by how much we taught and how well it was taught (student surveys, etc.), but survey ratings were limited to scale; thus they were capped by the ceiling imposed by the rating scale. This situation had to remedied by dividing the pool by faculty area so one area could not dominate the distribution of salary resources.

Other problems that can arise with overly quantitative and public evaluation structures include faculty manipulating their own career objectives to earn points. While in the short run a few dollars may be gained in the salary base, the professional loss over time could be much greater. Such structures also limit chair discretion in awarding merit increments in cases where chairs are working developmentally with faculty to improve performance or to effect a change in career direction. Whereas the productivity as measured by the quantitative system may not warrant a significant increase, the effort clearly has potential and an interim award may be needed to maintain momentum. Finally, with the recent emphasis on interdisciplinary work and collaborations, a reward

structure that diminishes the contribution of multi-authored proposals, publications, and teaching seems counterproductive.

Even when all of these steps are followed and a set of evaluation criteria has been discussed and adopted, some faculty members will believe that they have not been fairly evaluated when it
comes to tangible reward because the merit increment was insufficient. Some faculty will ask what counts and will not be surprised
that the established criteria were used. Others will make a case
that their strong suits (which can actually change from year to
year) deserve more consideration. Finally, faculty are remarkably
unaware of the accomplishments of their colleagues, a crucial factor in merit consideration. It is, after all, a zero sum game when
you are provided X dollars for Y people in a merit system. While
faculty evaluation when performance is poor can be stressful, evaluation tied to merit increments produces stress for the chair even
from good to excellent faculty members because they measure not
only the size of the reward but also how it stacks up against that of
others in the department.

Evaluation Evidence in Teaching, Research, and Service

Although criteria lists may be somewhat arbitrary and uniquely
detailed according to unit values and culture, there are probably
some universal entries that will work for everyone. The key here
is to include multiple measures in each area. This way, different
work assignments and different strengths among faculty can be
recognized. In teaching, the number of traditional sections taught
would be one parameter. This would include lectures, laboratories,
recitations, seminars, clinical, studios, and the like. Undergraduate and graduate courses may be differentially valued. Individualized instruction might also be an element here. This would include
research sections (undergraduate, graduate), senior theses, honors
projects, and capstone experiences. These are quantitative measures, but the schema might also include qualitative consideration

such as scores on student satisfaction surveys, results of learning outcomes assessments, peer evaluations, and special awards and recognitions. Developmental activities in teaching might also be recognized. Included might be workshops and symposia attended, new pedagogies employed, new courses and programs developed, new learning materials generated, and new modes of delivery developed. In this example of measures for teaching, there are multiple ways to recognize faculty contributions. Not all faculty members will generate merit in all measures, but there are multiple alternatives available to everyone.

Research and scholarly activity has always been easier to measure but, again, the nature of the products vary by discipline and several variables are possible. The most frequently used measure of successful scholarship is publication. This means work published in peer-reviewed media such as journals, monographs, or books that break new ground and offer new insights into an area of inquiry, or software development. In other disciplines, performances and exhibitions are the scholarly products expected and prestige differential is determined by the local, regional, or national status of the event, the reputation of the venue, and the selectivity used to invite participants. In scientific, professional, and technical disciplines, external funding is one measure of the value of someone's research ideas. Because substantial amounts of funding are required to do research, gaining external benefactors is essential. Finally, visibility as a scholar is important and is reflected by presentations, colloquia, and other invitations to display and share discovery. Again, prestige in this area is a variable.

At this point it is appropriate to discuss scholarship in a more global sense. It is widely recognized that the traditional form of scholarship is discovery-based. However, it is now equally recognized that there are movements to expand the definition to include other forms of scholarship along the lines suggested by Boyer (1990). When the four forms of scholarship and others that have emerged from the more generic definitions of scholarship that have been promulgated are not fully implemented, the chair may be placed in a position where faculty have gained external funding or generated peer-reviewed publication in areas other than primary discovery. If these are deemed "worthy" contributions in the scholarship area, they should be weighted equal to those of the analogous contributions of traditional scholarship. This concept will be revisited when faculty guidance and differential faculty expectations are discussed.

The final traditional area of faculty responsibility is that of service. Service has many dimensions and arenas and can be one of the most difficult to evaluate because it is not always easy to determine contribution and impact. A chair usually has only a committee list without any knowledge of the work done or the effort and input provided by the faculty member. In some cases it may be difficult to determine if the group even met during the period under evaluation. If service is an evaluation area that is heavily weighted or if the faculty member presents service as a major focal point of the annual review or even promotion, the chair must investigate or ask for a summary of the faculty member's contribution from the organization leaders, committee chairs, or those who created the group and received its interim or final reports. This would apply only when the chair has no direct knowledge of the committee and its work.

Service typically has several levels, each with its own variables. Local or department service may involve committees and advising. For the former, one might assume that committee leadership would be a greater contribution than ordinary membership. A more substantial local contribution would be the director of undergraduate or graduate studies. At the next level is school or institutional service. Some of these group activities may have titles that sound more encompassing and important, such as "task force" or "council." Beyond the institutional level there may be statewide work involving multiple campuses. Advising was mentioned earlier and was also mentioned as an element of teaching. The placement here is a matter of unit or institutional culture. This contribution can vary by the number of students served as well as by survey results that can reflect the quality of work.

Other important types of service are rendered outside of the institution, such as community service. Because there is no local oversight of this work, it can be difficult to evaluate, so an evaluation from the external organization may be valuable. Common types of external assignments include service on boards related to faculty expertise, work with K–12, and organizing co-ops and internships with external constituents. There seems to be a split on the recognition of community service unrelated to the professional expertise of the faculty member. For example, working with the Boy Scouts or a service on behalf of a local religious group may or may not be a relevant listing on an annual report.

Another category of faculty service comes under the heading of professional service. In institutions where research is a major emphasis, many faculty will elect this form of service, which reflects the widely held belief that faculty identify first with their disciplines, secondarily with their departments, and finally with their institutions. Professional service can be significant and critical to the vitality of the discipline. It can include service on grant review panels, editorial boards, and juries, or as judges that set the standards for scholarship in the discipline, confer important awards, and distribute scarce funding. It can also come in the form of organizing professional meetings and as serving as officers or committee members in professional organizations. These forms of external service do not usually require confirmation because the service is by invitation or election and reflects the status of the faculty member as an expert in the field.

Before leaving examples of meritorious work for faculty, it is interesting to note a new criterion for review, review form entries, and guidelines for promotion dossiers. This new criterion has a number of titles, the most common of which are collegiality and citizenship. One might speculate that this new measure has appeared for reasons related to the lack of faculty affiliation to institutional goals, a reluctance to help improve the local environment, and the increased focus on individual work. While there are some good reasons why faculty should adopt these behaviors, this movement seeks to redirect faculty time and energy to the common good. A veteran chair will say that there is nothing more valuable in the department than a dependable member who steps up to help in a crisis and who will take on the tough assignment for the good of all. If this is not an explicit element in the evaluation paradigm, then it can be a discretionary factor when chairs tally merit for their faculty.

Evaluation Data for Chairs

How does the chair make certain that faculty members are queued to report the items prior to the annual review? Most institutions have annual review forms that each member of the faculty completes and submits to the chair. In some cases these forms address the important contributions identified by the faculty. If the form does not include this, the department should request permission to modify the form so that it does. If this is not possible, additional items can be solicited by an addendum to the annual review form. If the department has taken the time and trouble to set criteria for evaluation, then the faculty review forms should be consistent with the expectations.

Discussing the Contents
of the Annual Review Form

The annual review process involves a face-to-face meeting between the chair and each faculty member that takes place after the annual review form has been submitted and evaluated. This aspect of the review process can be one of the chair's most rewarding activities because it can be a time to endorse accomplishment and to encourage further excellence. It can also be a time to help remove obstacles to success and to provide alternative strategies for faculty progress. Goal setting in such cases is a natural extension of the positive atmosphere. It is fortunate that this is the case for most reviews conducted by chairs.

Equally important to the department, the individual, and the institution are those reviews that must confront faculty performance that does not meet expectations. Veteran chairs know how difficult this can be. Contentious interactions are always difficult, but those that involve colleagues, friends, and others with whom you share the unit environment have more permanent implications. These can be so difficult that some chairs avoid them by failing to address performance deficits and seek remedies. Addressing unsatisfactory performance can lead to a number of responses from the faculty member. Occasionally, poor performance is acknowledged and the faculty member pledges to improve or asks for assistance to effect positive change. More frequently, denial—either calm and calculated or animated and angry—may result. Armed with appropriate evidence the chair cannot allow or enable denial and must continue in a focused and even manner to insist that performance needs improvement. Making certain that there is an expectation for improvement is necessary for everyone's benefit. What should ultimately emerge from this meeting is a plan to address the deficiencies. The elements of such a plan will be discussed in Chapter 22.

The Written Report

Ultimately, a permanent, written evaluation is filed. Working from the model of faculty reporting their accomplishments using a form that reflects the faculty-defined categories of evidence and a face-to-face meeting with the chair that involves review of accomplishments, goal setting, plans for improvement where necessary, and accolades when earned, the chair must now construct a report that reflects both the evidence and the conversation.

In some models, the written report is prepared before the face-to-face meeting, and modifications may result from the ensuing conversation. As time passes and memory fades, this document becomes the actual record of the preceding events, so it must be accurately and clearly written. Most written reviews are not consulted in the future except to review progress made toward goals during the subsequent review. In these cases they become important for merit considerations for that year and as maps to guide faculty work in the coming year. In some cases, however, these reports can be critically important to the chair, the faculty member, and the institution.

Written faculty reviews are sometimes part of the documentation used in the decision to award tenure. The accomplishments of the faculty member are the major element in this decision, but the chair is also "reviewed" based on the annual assessment of the faculty member, the support offered by the chair, and the goals set in consultation with the chair. Similarly, promotion to full rank may also require a set of recent annual review reports. More common situations that require faculty review reports as part of the documentation are decisions of nonreappointment rendered during the probationary period or appeals of a negative decision on promotion or merit increase. These decisions have potential legal implications and thus precise documentation is essential to protect the institution and the chair from legal repercussions. The case must be objectively reported, identification of shortcomings in performance must be documented, expectations for improvement listed, and efforts to support improvement easily identifiable in the records of the yearly meetings.

The first thing to recognize in constructing the written report resulting from the annual review is that it will be read by several different individuals. In addition to the faculty member, the report will also be reviewed by the dean and possibly others in administration. It may also be reviewed by groups of peers during consideration for promotion, in appeals of decisions as just described, and during steps in some types of post-tenure review. Thus the review should be constructed so that those more distant from the details of the case receive a clear overall sense of earlier performance relative to the current year as well as an idea of where the case is going in the future. This is a general statement at this point because the particulars depend on whether the case is marked by excellence, satisfactory accomplishment, or problematic performance.

When the review document is likely to receive further consideration, providing an indication of the historical context of the case is warranted. This would be as true for cases that are moving forward to promotion (a continuation of the outstanding performance of the past) as it is for cases headed for nonreappointment (continued inability to improve performance). Other elements of history may be relevant for inclusion. For example, personal illness or other serious personal issues and career changes may be important for the new reader so that the evidence and performance evaluation can be best evaluated in the context of these conditions.

The report should contain the objective evidence related to the case. Included would be faculty-reported items, documentation or reference to same from others, results of evaluative surveys both mandatory and voluntary, and reports of direct observation by the chair. These entries constitute the substance of the review, and how they relate to past performance and whether they meet or exceed expectations will determine the bottom line of the review document.

Clarity and organization are required to ensure that the reader gains an accurate view of the faculty member's performance. It is helpful to review each area of faculty responsibility separately, delineating contributions in each area and how those contributions are evaluated. This can be accomplished by using appropriate modifiers to describe pieces of evidence. For example, just listing an item as a publication without distinguishing whether it is an internal publication or a peer-reviewed piece in a top-rated journal does not provide the reader with a true picture of the level of accomplishment. Likewise, just stating that funding was obtained for scholarship does not distinguish whether the funding was a modest amount from a university source or a major competitively won award from a recognized national source.

The section dedicated to goal setting should be written in specific language. If the goal was to submit a proposal for funding, then that should be explicitly stated. There can also be room for contingent statements or "possible" activities. For example, a goal might be written: "If my proposal is funded, I will initiate work on phase two of the archeological dig." A goal could state that the final chapter of a book might be completed by December but January is the more likely completion date. Assuming a calendar year review cycle, this would put the accomplishment into the next review period. These statements are allowable in most cases and demonstrate an engaged faculty member with back-up plans for continuing work and a long-range plan for continued productivity. However, such statements cannot be accepted in the evaluation if they are responses resulting from continued delays in productivity, such as if the book in question was due for submission two years ago and its completion has been set as a goal at more than one previous review. In cases where performance needs improvement and where the faculty member is in denial, the report may need to list expectations for addressing deficiencies that must be met. In other words, the chair sets goals that are in keeping with department and institutional expectations for faculty performance.

The report should also explicitly state what the department will do to foster faculty excellence, facilitate faculty career changes, and improve faculty performance. This is particularly important when a tenured faulty member is performing poorly and continuation of such performance will plague the department and the institution for years to come unless improvement is made. Assuming that the faculty member does not refuse to acknowledge poor performance and resist suggestions for improvement, the chair may be able to negotiate a plan that requires faculty effort and support from the department. Department support may include the investment of resources including funding for travel, help with establishing of new line of study, purchasing equipment to help in scholarship or teaching, and a variety of other interventions that may directly help or provide incentive for efforts to improvement. The tools available to the chair for such activities were discussed in Chapter 15.

Once the process of formulating the written reviews has been completed by the chair, it is a good idea to set them aside and review them a day or two later. So far, the process has been anywhere from routine to enjoyable for most faculty members, and the only changes that might be made are editorial. However, there will be cases where there are career implications, possible legal consequences, needs for improvement of performance, and those where the process has been contentious. The latter can be cases of poor performance where denial is predominant and those cases where the faculty member does not feel equitably treated, fully valued, or appropriately recognized and rewarded. Some face-to-face sessions can be less than civil and veteran chairs almost always have experienced raised voices, accusations of various sorts, and even threats. There are also cases where faculty members have refused to have the meeting or have abruptly stalked out of it. After such an event, the written summary report will almost assuredly evoke further emotion. The elements of initial contention will remain, and the written review may include some of the verbal exchange that occurred if it is considered an accurate reflection of what took place throughout the process. When one is constructing such written reviews, the one- or two-day set-aside provides a period to cool down and objectively consider the preceding events. This is the time to consider that the document will be read by more people than the chair and faculty member. How will this review be interpreted by subsequent readers? Framing the reactions of external individuals is key to directing any modifications that may take place at this point.

There are different opinions as to whether a draft of the report should be shared with the faculty member. If it is shared, the changes allowed should be limited to factual corrections, addition of omissions for either the record or the conversation, and editorial errors. In cases where poor performance is documented and the expectations for improvement are listed, the chair cannot allow negotiation of softer language or reduced expectations. If the faculty member is adamant that the review is unjustified or overly harsh, that individual likely has the option to file a response with the report. After contentious meetings, disgruntled faculty members have been known to refuse to sign the review. Signed or unsigned, the review moves on to become part of the permanent record. This is a confidential document and is available only to those authorized to review it. It also serves as the starting point to initiate the review process for the next year.

Faculty Evaluation and Post-Tenure Review

A special application of faculty evaluation that has become prominent in the last decade (see Chapter 1) is faculty evaluation associated with new policies on post-tenure review. These policies have resulted from external criticism that lifetime tenure allows faculty members to hold privileged positions unlike those held by most others in our society. The academy counters that the benefits of tenure preserve academic freedom. Although post-tenure review policies vary widely in their details, most can be defined as one of two species.

One type is referred to as triggered or initiated post-tenure review. As part of the annual review process, the chair must assess whether the faculty member's performance has been satisfactory or unsatisfactory. Defining this line is key to having an effective post-tenure review policy. Depending on the institution, one or two consecutive unsatisfactory reviews triggers a formal review where a committee determines whether the chair's judgment is correct. If it is, a development plan for correcting deficiencies is constituted whereby the faculty member must improve performance over a specified period of time or face sanctions up to and including dismissal. The plan is "developmental" in nature and as such would include institutional resources and some participation by the chair.

In the second type of post-tenure, periodic review, all faculty members are reviewed at a designated time interval, usually five years. This review is conducted by a committee comprised of faculty peers. Documentation includes the faculty member's curriculum vitae, a statement of accomplishments over the previous five years, and a plan for further work for the next five years. The annual review reports over the past five years are typically part of the record. Although the chair does not participate directly in this type of review, the annual reports will reflect not only the work of the faculty but also the chair's evaluations and efforts to foster improvement and enhanced productivity. While the vast majority of periodic review cases turn out to be laudatory in terms of evaluating the work of the faculty member, cases in which performance is deemed unsatisfactory and a development plan for improvement is indicated need to involve the chair.

Chair involvement in post-tenure review, especially in the initiated version, can be particularly delicate. The pressure associated with the annual review process is increased considerably when it involves an underperforming faculty member. The stakes are also considerably higher because that long-term outcome could be far worse than a negative written report and a low pay increment. There are always internal department issues that arise because the chair, a faculty supporter, facilitator, or encourager is now in the position to end someone's career. Other complicating factors include situations where chairs are junior in rank to some faculty members or where chairs may not hold tenure. Senior faculty subject to post-tenure review may well be empowered to serve on relevant committees that may affect the chair's future. While these types of power differentials can take place in evaluations and decisions apart from post-tenure review, they take on even more importance based on the potential consequences of the process.

Summary

Even after conducting faculty evaluations for many years, veteran chairs indicate that this responsibility represents one of their biggest challenges and is a major cause of stress. When one considers that most faculty are productive and receive positive reviews, the difficulty seems to be derived from reviews of faculty who are not performing up to expectations and from high-performing faculty who are dissatisfied with how their review translates into merit reward. Another stressor in the process is the dichotomy of the chair's role. Chairs are faculty facilitators, mentors, cheerleaders, developers, and advocates, but they must also render summative reviews that impact merit and advancement. The pressure created by the faculty evaluation process has recently been increased by post-tenure review policies that are based on the annual review process. Here, consequences for the poor performance by faculty senior to the chair may have career-threatening consequences.

Important steps in conducting equitable and effective reviews include defining the criteria on which faculty agree they should be evaluated. This inclusive list of achievements within teaching, scholarship, and service may vary among institutions and departments within institutions. The list should contain multiple measures within each area so that the many forms of faculty talent can be acknowledged. A priority system of the contributions may be negotiated with faculty. When annual accomplishments are reported, the form should call out the measures established to reinforce what the department values in the work of its faculty members. There will always be contributions that are not easily categorized and chairs must be ready to interpret where the best fit is and how they should be weighted.

The formal evaluation process includes a face-to-face meeting where accomplishments are reviewed and goals for the coming year are established. This meeting may or may not precede the preparation of a written evaluation by the chair depending on institutional practice. While some of these encounters are truly enjoyable as high-performing faculty members outline ambitious and exciting goals, others where performance is lacking can be problematic. Denial of deficiencies can be expected in some cases. Chairs must insist that performance be improved and set goals for improvement with faculty. Writing the final report or modifying an existing one based on the meeting is the final step and requires the signature of both parties. This document needs to be carefully prepared because it has implications for the faculty member and is a reflection of the support and direction provided by the chair.

17

FISCAL CONSTRAINTS
IN HIGHER EDUCATION

One of the major forces driving the changes that higher education is now undergoing and will continue to undergo is that of insufficient funding to continue the trajectory of the past. This concept has received much public attention at national and state levels and has been the subject of books and articles. The central concerns raised are that the cost of higher education continues to rise faster than other costs by a substantial margin and that middle-class families are being priced out of the market, even at state and local public institutions. Beyond that, there are grave concerns about the ability of first-generation students and that of many growing but underrepresented groups to access higher education and achieve a better life in the United States. Rising costs have not only priced some out of the market, they have also resulted in capped enrollments in some areas, thus reducing access for some.

The politics and overall economics of higher education cost escalation is an interesting one, but one that cannot be a major consideration in a book for academic department chairs. However, some discussion may be helpful for chairs in understanding this issue so that they can make suggestions for cost savings outside the department as well as develop internal department plans for reducing expenditures. For background, veteran chairs need only look back at their budget allocations over the past years. When I recently did this, I found that my budget has fluctuated within a 10%–20% range for more than a decade. In fact, the allocation in 2004 was less than 2% different (lower actually) than the one I worked with in 1994. During this period of time there was a net increase in state appropriation and significant increases in tuition at an institution where enrollment and external funding grew. So, where is the money?

The reader should remember two things as the discussion proceeds. The first is that I come from a large, complex institution that may have more extensive programs and responsibilities than smaller colleges. Second, I did say in the preface that I would not write exclusively from the perspective of a "company man," that is, as an extension of policy put forth by higher administration and even trustees and legislatures. This is not a call to anarchy by department chairs and other lower-level staff but rather a frank discussion of why costs have risen so dramatically and why we are criticized while at the same time our academic and research programs are threatened with foreclosure.

Costs

Putting aside unavoidable costs such as utilities, security, insurance, repairs, and basic institutional services (bursar, registrar, library, etc.), one must look to the primary source of college and university costs first to see what is happening there. People costs for an academic department far exceed all other costs combined. Using my institution as an example, it is interesting to note that there has been significant growth in personnel while the number of faculty has remained almost constant over a period of years. Who are these new employees? The vast majority fall into the category of professional staff. I can identify a few in the school, but not nearly enough to account for the large increases noted on the financial and staffing reports. The ones most visible are involved in the introduction and maintenance of technology. Beyond these few, most were hired to deal with compliance issues, serve special interests or groups, create new services, address accountability, or support campus-level initiatives. Some examples are listed below.

Any criticism of these programs, offices, and/or ideas may evoke potentially negative reactions from some readers, but they nonetheless need to be listed because they contribute to why higher education is facing a financial crossroads at this point. Thus, as an equal opportunity offender, I will proceed with some examples I have witnessed. Some new and expanding compliance issues deal with safety regulations, research compliance issues around human subjects, recombinant DNA, toxic and infectious agents, and conflict of interest. In addition, campuses frequently have significant infrastructure in place to deal with the Americans with Disabilities Act. A large campus will have staffed offices to deal with each of these. One inherently knows that regulations from all of these sources become more restrictive and expensive over time. Look back at campuses of 20 years ago, and some of these offices were present in more modest form while others did not exist at all. There are also a number of offices dealing with accountability. While offices dealing with assessment are prominent examples, one that particularly makes me wonder is our Office of Travel Management. This is the office that approves travel for faculty, staff, and students, the same individuals whose travel has already been approved and funded by a department chair. Now, consider that a department chair is allowed to sign off on a purchase order for a $100,000 instrument but needs the supervisory approval of the travel office to get a $1,500 trip reimbursed. These offices do provide the service of calculating the eligible per diem for the traveler, an activity that is apparently such a complex computation that a department chair could never be expected to get it right. Apparently there is some very important compliance issue behind this.

A look at our campuses today finds growing and extensive offices that provide funding and services related to faculty development, consultations on grant writing, teaching improvement, and technology utilization. Subsets of these offices include more specialized help for faculty from underrepresented groups, women, and other interests. The same can be observed on the student side. In addition, advising has now expanded to include career counseling, job placement, internship offices, and the like.

Other student-directed goods and services that have become more prominent include state-of-the-art recreational facilities, more elegant living quarters, and more attractive and menu-variable eating for on-campus students. One would expect that these are effective recruiting devices for students and assuring initiatives for their parents.

Finally, there are campus-level initiatives that require resources. These are commonly related to the educational mission, a variety of civic engagement activities, or other projects that propose to raise the local or national image of the institution. While these initiatives are typically the work of faculty, they can assume favored status by administration and, thus, are provided resources.

With the exception of the travel office, there is no intended criticism regarding the value of the programs and offices cited. At some level they all exist to protect the institution and its employees, provide access for students, create a more supportive environment for faculty, staff, or students, and demonstrate institutional leadership. All do, however, need fiscal and material resources and do not directly contribute to the primary products of higher education—teaching and scholarship. Many of these represent what we would call our institutional values—what we believe in and what we are willing to commit to. Colleges and universities frequently have special areas where they think they are leaders or where their historical traditions lie. Such areas may no longer be sought by students and may not be able to cover their costs but the institution remains committed to their continuation. However, during tough fiscal times that are predicted to be permanent, many will look very hard at maintaining some of these at current levels when productive and promising academic programs are threatened by a lack of resources and low faculty morale. Hence, there will be important conversations about investments in our values versus those in our teaching and research products. Significant reductions or institutional reconfiguration cannot be done exclusively on the backs of academic programs.

Finally, an additional increased cost comes with the recruitment of new faculty. Despite the restricted resources in higher education and the conversion of tenure-track lines to less expensive hires, the costs of recruiting tenure-track hires are escalating. Colleges and universities want to make quality hires and are willing to compete for the services of top-notch faculty. This competition is driving salaries higher far more quickly than salaries for current faculty are rising, resulting in serious salary compression where new faculty are offered salaries higher than those of satisfactorily performing faculty who have been in their positions for more than five years. Startup packages are also increasing, along with other costly perks such as reduced teaching loads.

Department Adjustments to Fiscal Pressure

For the purposes of clarity, it is assumed that the budget attributed to the department consists of all salary and fringe benefit costs for faculty and staff as well as all cash allotments available to purchase the goods and services needed by the unit. Included in the latter would be costs for adjunct faculty and teaching assistants/graders, supplies, phones, hourly wages, equipment, graduate student stipends and fees, travel, and copying. A budget reduction as small as 10% would be difficult to accommodate simply by reducing copy costs or restricting travel. The following are some measures available to the department chair to respond to budget reductions. Many of these are likely to require the permission of deans or other administrators.

The largest item in the budget is the one for faculty salaries and benefits. Most institutions have kept open faculty lines when they are vacated by retirement or resignation and use the base cash saved each year to shore up budgets. Other strategies include replacing tenure-track lines with less expensive, full-time hires (see Chapter 12). This saves some money but not as much as turning to other ways of meeting instructional responsibilities. Adjunct faculty typically work for lower wages and do not receive fringe benefits. The availability of qualified adjunct faculty may restrict this option for some institutions. Another way to cover the teaching responsibilities of a vacated line would include reducing the sections taught while raising the capacity of the remaining sections. Finally, there are the two options of simply reducing the number of sections offered, thereby restricting total enrollment, and of increasing the teaching loads of the remaining faculty. The former has the negative effects of disenfranchising students and possibly reducing unit or even institutional enrollment, thereby exacerbating the fiscal problems. The latter option can be sustained temporarily by appealing to the "team" or "community need" to serve its students. Over time, however, this will have severe effects on morale and will reduce department productivity in other areas.

More severe economic restrictions may require more draconian measures, including early retirement packages (short-term expense for long-term gain) or reductions in force for faculty or staff. Tenure makes faculty reduction more complex but possible depending on the nature of the financial exigency policy in existence at the institution. In some cases, programs may be eliminated. Such programs would likely be identified by a cost analysis indicating that they cost far more than they generate and by an academic analysis indicating that they are not likely to produce degrees that will be in high demand. Great care needs to be taken here because some fiscally untenable programs provide essential academic experiences for other more productive programs. Chairs will play a critical role in articulating the interrelationships among programs so that, if necessary, such reductions happen in ways that allow the institution to emerge stronger. Again, these are very significant changes, and chairs need to be involved in the decisions along with higher administrators and faculty members.

Reductions in expenditures that have lesser impacts, while not alone sufficient to address major cutbacks, can help to manage modest budget reductions. Some savings can be achieved in the areas of copying and travel. Class handouts can be a major source of copying charges, and other ways to provide these materials to students can save hundreds or even thousands of dollars each year. It is significant to note that the promise of technology reducing our costs (or increasing our time) does not always pan out. As an example, many faculty members in my department use Power-Point in their lectures and students want their own copies. Because some of the material is from copyrighted sources, faculty do not want to post them, so they duplicate them and provide them as handouts. This problem can be avoided by postings on course web sites restricted to the class, by posting on web-based course management systems, or by providing a copy in a binder that students can check out and copy on their own. The later is workable only with relatively small (no more than 50 students) classes. There are schools that are so cash-strapped that they will not allow copying of anything except exams. For classes with no copyrighted material, course packets can be assembled, copied, and bound for sale by institutional printing services or external entities, then sold in the bookstore. There are even courses where the course syllabus is included in these packets.

Other savings can be achieved by restricting travel, although in some disciplines this may have a negative impact on scholarship productivity and morale. Travel funding can be very important in disciplines where external funding is uncommon and at institutions that focus primarily on teaching yet expect faculty to be viable and up-to-date in their disciplines. The chair will need to carefully establish with faculty a mechanism that will reduce travel expenditures yet allow faculty to remain professionally engaged. Other aspects of professional development are also often the victims of budget reductions and must be planned for so that they do not disadvantage probationary faculty careers. Finally, some savings over the short term can be achieved by delaying equipment purchases or repairs and by substituting some assignments in disciplines with laboratories that require expensive equipment and materials.

Faculty Morale: The Big Risk
of Budget Reductions

Dealing with fiscal constraints can be successfully done most of the time if the problem is perceived to be temporary. The chair can usually rally faculty to rise to the challenge of a budget shortfall by indicating how far they have come, how solid the unit really is, and how talented and resourceful the faculty really are. The lasting power of faculty resolve is a function of the unity of faculty culture, the recent history of the department, and the prospects it and the institution have for full recovery. If these are not in place or if the fiscal outlook shows little hope for improvement, some faculty may demonstrate diminished morale and others may begin to test the waters elsewhere. Of course, those faculty who might actually land new positions elsewhere are the ones who have the most to offer. Other faculty members who would like to find new positions but are no longer competitive will have no choice but to stick it out. During these times, the chair will need to use all aspects of personal influence and creativity to maintain a positive outlook and keep the department on track.

How does the chair put a positive spin on a dire fiscal situation with little promise of changing for the better? One strategy is to direct the faculty focus to activities that are perceived as advancements for the unit. To be successful the chair will have to demonstrate full understanding and command of the fiscal situation and assure the faculty that the challenge can be met. In the meantime, despite fiscal austerity, the chair must emphasize that there are some things the unit can do to make real progress. These potential steps to improvement obviously will not include the acquisition of a new instrument, but they can involve low-cost activities to improve the curriculum, enhance student services, or establish new collaborations for faculty members. Examples might include developing a cadre of advanced undergraduates who might form peer advising groups for undergraduates or might serve as teaching assistants or recitation leaders in undergraduate courses. These possibilities may also save some resources if the activities they provide are routinely compensated ones. Undergraduate help may be garnered by developing an academic course for which credit can be given in lieu of pay, thus lowering costs. Another idea is to sponsor a career day for students where they can meet and interact with professionals who have degrees in the discipline or, even better, from the department. Such activities can gain favorable attention for the department and boost lagging morale. Finally, identifying new professional connections with nearby institutions or external organizations can distract faulty members from local problems by providing them with real possibilities for professional enrichment. It is vital that departments always move forward in some way—even when times are tough.

Summary

Virtually all institutions of higher education are feeling financially pinched. The impacts are relative to the standard of living of each. Public institutions are seeing flat or reduced state appropriations and limits on tuition hikes. Private institutions are seeing lower returns from their endowments and diminished contributions. At the same time, costs for all are on the rise. Costs are increasing due to compliance issues, accountability requirements, and a desire to provide the latest in technology and the most attractive accommodations in personal comfort. When looking at personnel costs, it is common to see flat or reduced faculty numbers but healthy increases in nonacademic hires. This trend has serious implications for the future because the new investments add little to the instructional and scholarly products of institutions.

Chairs will have to address diminished budgets while leading the department to bigger and better accomplishments. This is the "do more with less" phrase that is frequently heard. Departments have seen tenure-track lines exchanged for other full-time or adjunct appointments as cost-saving responses. Departments have also cut course sections while raising section capacity. Some sections are eliminated, especially those that do not meet minimum enrollment requirements, possibly slowing student progress to degree. More severe responses to budget reductions include early retirement programs for faculty and staff and program elimination.

Costs over which the chair has more direct control generally do not involve significant resources but may be able to help with mild reductions. The items are those of convenience and those that fall under the category of faculty development. Departments may restrict classroom copying to a syllabus and exams. Travel is a frequent target, although in some departments faculty members have travel funds available through grants and contracts. In disciplines where such external funding is uncommon, travel funding is more critical for maintaining scholarship. While such cutbacks can be tolerated over the short term, chairs must realize that faculty morale will be damaged if they persist. Chairs should consider promoting inexpensive activities for improvement that can be established as yearly department goals. Such initiatives can be successes that the unit can claim in the face of poor fiscal support. Appropriate acknowledgement of these activities can help boost morale.

18

STRATEGIC PLANNING

There are many opinions about the value of institutional, school, or department planning initiatives. Some will say that any five- to ten-year plan is never seen to completion and the final result is so different from the original conception that the time and effort involved are not justified. Others will counter that a plan should begin to evolve almost as soon as copies are made. Change is expected and each adjustment is then made based on documented circumstances so that the final and very different outcome years later does have a traceable lineage to the original concept. Beyond these diverging opinions, there are other values to developing a department plan. The fiscal restrictions and persistent calls for change facing higher education have made these values more important than ever.

The impetus for department planning may come from administration either as a routine expectation or because there has been a change in campus leadership. School- or campus-level change may be involved. Occasionally, state boards, legislatures, or trustees may request formal written plans for the institution and sometimes its schools. The request that departments develop plans is less frequent from such groups. Planning may also emanate from the department itself because the unit focus or aspects of the curriculum need updating, a significant number of faculty will be retiring, or there is new department leadership. Whatever the impetus, departments can use careful planning to gain momentum for change and to overcome known and anticipated resistance to change. It is critical that the chair recognize that resistance may come, not only from the faculty, but also from administration.

256

With this basic consideration in mind, the chair would approach this process to create a set of initiatives with the faculty that the dean and campus will view as aligning with plans that may exist at both institutional levels.

At the outset of the planning process, departments need to take stock of where they are currently. If the planning process is designed to be inclusive of all aspects of department responsibility, then a good deal of information must be pulled together. The next steps include deciding where you would like to be in program development, research productivity, civic engagement, and so on, the timeframe, and how the unit proposes to get there. That is, what resources, changes in focus, reallocations, suspension of past practices, types of faculty and staff, and the like will be needed to get the job done.

Within the details of department plans, faculty-generated ideas, and implementation, mechanisms for advancement would be described along with ways to address previous unit shortcomings and opportunities for innovations. Plans would also include obvious mechanisms to foster the enhancement of faculty visibility in the discipline while at the same time improving the environment and relevance of programming for students. Included might be new degrees or degree options, plans for interdisciplinary work, programming that is developed in collaboration with other units or external stakeholders, and plans for making the reinvented department attractive to potential students and a source of pride for present and former students. Major changes in the undergraduate or graduate curriculum or the development of a new or strengthened research agenda would be accompanied by an outline of faculty hires filling positions freed by attrition. Included with all elements of a five- to ten-year plan would be needed external resources and resource reallocations the department can accomplish. Of course, justifications will be required for new resources; the compelling nature of the plan will determine whether requests eclipse those that will come from other units.

Structural Elements of the Plan

Assembling the department plan into a cohesive document that will be favorably evaluated by the dean and upper administration is a key step in creating a viable strategic plan. The first step in the process is to determine whether the school and campus have their own strategic plans. In the absence of formal plans, schools and campuses will have mission statements. Campus-level mission statements are readily available via the Internet and comparing them across institutions will reveal that they share many ingredients in common. Each will likely promise to meet educational, social, economic, and/or cultural aspirations of the region and state, to be adaptable to changing need, and may promise to be at the forefront of discovery or creative activity (research universities). They may contain an explicit statement about a commitment to diversity of ideas, cultural inclusion, and ethnic representation. Many mission statements will also have unique features found less commonly. For example, one will make a promise to be collaborative while another may actively promote, and even expect, risk-taking. A third may be a pledge to be intentional about using technology to promote cost effectiveness and best practices. These concepts, the way they are structured, and the language used to express them are important elements in articulating the department plan.

Schools or colleges within larger universities will have plans or mission statements in keeping with the institutional versions, but at these levels, the generalizations of the institution's remarks become more specific and individual differences on how those promises will play out in individual units become evident. For example, how a school of education might serve its constituents and apply knowledge would differ from the way a school of engineering might express its intentions. The specificity increases still further when the overarching statements of the institution are interpreted within the context of an individual department. It seems that only the input of unit faculty can really articulate how the institution conveys its relevance and promise in a public way at the disciplinary level. In the planning process, departments should regard this as a real advantage and an opportunity to promote its future while remaining in line with institutional expectations.

Presenting the Plan

After the department has spent its time, energy, and insight examining its present condition, analyzing where the discipline is going, and setting an agenda for moving forward, the elements of the plan should be crafted within the framework of the school or college and institutional plans or mission statements. This is commonly referred to as mission alignment, a process that should result in the department's plan comfortably resting under the umbrellas of the hierarchical statements. There may be elements of the school's plan that may not be addressed by the department, and in most cases this can be justified by the inability to do everything within the confines of a single discipline or within the limited time span the plan includes. Since the plan is a living document, it will be able to respond to need as it appears.

Language is an important element of the plan. Everyone is familiar with the "new" and constantly emerging language or jargon of higher education. Perhaps some in the business can remember when "assessment" or "civic engagement" first appeared in our documents or in spoken language. There are other universal terms and programs we now use, such as "best practices" and "service-learning," as well as institution-specific terms describing their cultures. These often appear in mission statements and plans and, where appropriate, departments should use the recognized language to identify elements of their plan that reinforce institutional values, again demonstrating the concept of alignment. For example, if the institution promotes risk-taking, bold, new moves into unique academic programming might be presented as a commitment to the risk-taking ideals of the institution.

As an example of using carefully crafted plans to gain support and resources for change, an academic department lost a faculty member who was solely responsible for coursework in a required element of the discipline. The dean, who was quite familiar with the discipline, did not believe that this element of the discipline should be required of students and thus felt the vacancy might be better filled with a faculty hire from another area. Using the opportunity afforded by a school retreat to evaluate department five-year plans, the department prepared a document that mirrored the structure of the school plan prepared by the dean. The school plan indicated a commitment to collaboration and interdisciplinary programming, to serving external need, to serving other campus units, to engaging the community in mutually beneficial ways, and to promoting interdisciplinary research. Using these basic elements, the department made the case that one department in the school and another in a related school required the course in question, which supported interdisciplinary ventures and collaborative work. Further, without the hire, a program affiliated with a governmental agency would be jeopardized as well as an expectation of the K–12 system for teacher education. In addition, a community-based research project within the school would be weakened and the potential for interdisciplinary research funding would be diminished. The presentation of the case using the school plan was compelling and the desired hire was approved.

Summary

Strategic planning seems to depend on institutional culture; some use this as a tool to guide their activities while others seem to make things up as they go. Regardless of institutional culture or the predispositions of campus leadership, academic departments can use the planning process in several advantageous ways. Planning requires that the department continuously recognize its present situation relative to its future aspirations. The process looks at where you are, where you want to be over time, delineates a path to get there, and identifies what resources will be required. The plan is a dynamic, evolving guide, and must be adaptable to changes encountered along the way.

When constructing a department plan according to the steps just outlined, chairs should consider crafting the document using the guidelines provided by institutional missions and goals statements. In larger institutions there may be college or school statements that also need to be considered in this process. Presenting the plan in this way ensures alignment with institutional values, a key factor in gaining school and institutional endorsement of department plans and critical if new resources are required. The language used can help place the department's plan under the larger campus umbrella of plans. Thus, if the institution promises to encourage collaboration, promote risk-taking, or value civic engagement, then these key concepts should be appropriately highlighted in the document.

19

THE CHAIR AS CAMPUS ENTREPRENEUR

The concept of a department chair as entrepreneur has been discussed in surveys and books that describe chair responsibilities or the desired characteristics for chairs. What this conceptually means in the context of normal chair work is undefined, but the dictionary defines *entrepreneur* as "one willing to take risks in order to generate profit." With that general description as a starting point, expansion of the concept allows us to consider what a chair does to fulfill the role of entrepreneur. Chapter 20 will expand chair entrepreneurial work further to include work with constituents external to the institution.

Campus-Level Activities

A survey of any campus will identify department chairs who are rarely involved in interschool or campus-level work. Rather, they manage the department's affairs and attend to their personal disciplinary activities. While they may be quite effective within this limited scope of activity, they will not be able to bring the department future opportunities that may facilitate real progress. Successful chairs, however, are aware of campus-level opportunities and selectively participate, and even initiate, innovations where the department can gain advantage. Selectivity is a key ingredient that department chairs use in driving the nature of campus-level work. Time is limited and the projects selected must have the potential to benefit the department and propel the institution forward. The benefits have many forms, such as enhancing enrollment and opportunities for new resources both internal and external, or gaining political capital that may be useful at a later date. Involvement can also enable chairs to shape an initiative in such a way that it does not damage the unit. Finally, the visibility gained from certain campus initiatives can be used to department and institution advantage. The department chair must be able to envision some return on the investment of time, energy, and expertise in choosing where and how to engage in campus-level projects. Some examples may be instructive for ascertaining value in campus activities.

General Education

The general education reform movement provides a good example. The campus committee charged with leading such a project may consider ideas that could place the department at a disadvantage in terms of eliminating courses that the department teaches or suggesting courses that the department would have to develop and offer. In one case department enrollments may fall while in the other enrollments may soar. If budgeting and faculty lines are linked to enrollment, the implications for the department are considerable. Alternatively, a department such as accounting may not be involved in any of the discussions, making chair contribution less critical unless the proposed curricular changes negatively impact the progress of accounting majors. Beyond impact on department budgets, faculty lines, and teaching assignments, some suggestions for general education reform may create problems for students' ability to complete their degrees on time. In this case, chair awareness is essential so the appropriate information can be conveyed to those structuring the requirement before its finalization.

Interdisciplinary Programming

Another area to consider for campus-level chair work is what might fall under the umbrella of interdisciplinary initiatives. There are examples of such ventures in virtually every aspect of department and faculty work. Moving to a culture of interdisciplinary work is now regarded as one of our greatest challenges and is one of the most intriguing opportunities for institutions of higher education. However, the barriers to this movement are considerable, and those who can overcome them in a timely fashion will be at significant advantage.

We frequently hear that employers are critical of our graduates because they have not mastered the requisite knowledge and skills or because the mix of their experiences lacks relevancy to the needs of the employment world. Many of these shortcomings can be traced to traditional degrees that have not changed in their structure or basic content for decades. Many of the needs in the employment sector require skill sets that are the amalgamation of several degree programs that graduates rarely have. This shortcoming requires extensive employer retraining of newly minted graduates. Formulating new interdisciplinary degrees can have a significant positive impact in solving this problem and at the same time will help to improve our relationship with those we are supposed to be serving. There are however, several structural/fiscal and cultural obstacles to overcome, and chairs of academic departments will have to be major players in sorting through these and facilitating change.

Obstacles to interdisciplinary arrangements. One institutionally based cultural obstacle, and one that also applies to establishing general education requirements, is when faculty think only they know what is essential in the curriculum. Institutions of higher education are unique, sheltered environments and tend to construct the experiences, content, and attitudes of students based on that limited view of the world. Our students should "know this, be able to do that, and have an appreciation for the following" is how this attitude plays out. This is difficult to say as a member of that culture, but the world we academics envision is not a perfectly accurate reflection of the real world. This accounts for much of the disconnect between the education we impart and the education that end users—employers—expect. This can be easily exemplified by mixing the terms *education,* the primary product of our institutions, and *training,* an expected outcome in some employment settings. The latter term can raise strong, negative responses in some sectors of university culture. We do not invite external input into the conversation when we articulate what general education should look like or what a major in a given discipline should have mastered. For example, we claim to emphasize communication skills, but the skills that higher education seeks to develop in students are not the particular skills that external end users need and expect to find. That is, they may place far more emphasis on grammatical and structural correctness than is demanded in many of our courses. Similarly, the critical thinking skills we so emphatically promote cannot even be uniformly defined or disciplinarily exemplified within the academy, never mind to outsiders. We need more voices at the table if what we produce is going to be regarded as relevant and worthy of greater investment.

Another obstacle to interdisciplinary programming involves the notion of ownership. Degree programs belong to departments, which keep tallies of the degrees they award and collect a set of alumni who affiliate with the department and become future donors. Interdisciplinary programs have no defined owners because they belong to two or more units, and in some cases, participants may even be from different schools on campus.

Shared ownership is a difficult concept for some. Interdisciplinary degree programs are comprised of existing courses from participating units and perhaps new courses, some of which may be team-taught across departments. Just describing this set of possibilities magnifies points of contention. There are examples of attempts to construct interdisciplinary programs between two units where each requires its own core curriculum, thus rendering the interdisciplinary effort as nothing more than a double major. When ancillary requirements are added to the general education requirements, the degree becomes so packed with requirements that no elective or exploratory experiences are possible for undergraduates. In addition, no rational student would find the degree attractive. The cultural problem to overcome here is that traditional beliefs about what a student must know in the major have to be translated to the new degree. Sometimes violation of prerequisite listing may be necessary. In some cases, prerequisites are necessary for student success while in others they reflect tradition and afford convenience in planning for the delivery of the curriculum. These need to be examined and some modifications of courses may be necessary to allow the new programs to succeed. Developing new courses, especially those that are cross-disciplinary, is a challenge that involves unit cultures, differential content expectations, faculty workloads, and faculty time. Chairs will play essential roles in facilitating solutions to these issues.

Finally, there are some obstacles to interdisciplinary programming that are structural or fiscal in nature. While the chairs of the units involved cannot solve most of these directly, they can at least show where the problems are and push for solutions with their deans and other campus administrators. Again, the issues of ownership and of any budgetary variable that rewards degrees conferred can come into play. Faculty workload issues may develop, especially if the partnering units have different teaching loads. Parceling the "credit" or financial return for team-taught courses and providing fiscal support for new courses that belong to neither department are also issues that require satisfactory resolution.

Graduate-Level Programs

The examples described thus far involve undergraduate programs, but similar concerns regarding quality and relevance have been expressed by our end users about graduate training. In general, improving graduate programs in emerging areas of science and technology can be addressed in existing graduate programs where the curriculum is not uniformly mandated but rather constructed according to the interests or research needs of the individual studies. Graduate programs in other discipline areas can accommodate cross-disciplinary experiences by requiring a minor in another area. These programs are criticized because they assume all graduates will take faculty positions in institutions similar to the one in which they did their graduate work. However, it happens that many take faculty positions in institutions where research is not a primary emphasis and in industrial and government settings. Graduates who become faculty have little or no teaching experience and have not been exposed to alternative faculty cultures and the full range of faculty expectations. For those entering work in government and industry, the ideas of teamwork and nonownership of the products of the professional work, as well as the likelihood of moving from project to project, are cultural practices that come as a shock. The issues around preparing for academic careers in a variety of institutions are being addressed by a national program called Preparing Future Faculty. As discussed in Chapter 14, there is some resistance to this program because of the time away from the research or dissertation project that some programs require. Likewise, there are internship programs in industry and government that provide experiences in the new culture for those students who aspire to such positions. These programs also face some of the time-away-from-task criticisms noted previously when students take time to teach and experience alternative faculty cultures.

Interdisciplinary Scholarship

The idea of promoting interdisciplinary collaboration to solve complex problems is becoming more prominent, not only in science and technology, but also in the humanities and social sciences. It is widely accepted that many of the questions we seek to answer require multifaceted approaches that employ the skills and techniques not typically found in a single individual. Evidence of higher education embracing cross-discipline work in scholarship and programming is seen in the emergence of interdisciplinary centers and institutes on our campuses, as well as in institutional mission statements. While some may have only research as their objective, others also have developed complementary graduate programs with some in-house faculty to augment those participating from several units on campus.

The advantages of department participation in such ventures are many. The chair should personally make the first overtures for inclusion or even originate the idea to consider formalizing collaboration through the formation of recognizable campus structures that bring visibility to the concept. Others from the department may eventually become involved to relieve the chair and participate in working out the details. The chair, however, will have to become involved to negotiate issues surrounding resources, faculty time, and agreements to share proceeds, and to identify appropriate faculty participants.

Some examples of interdisciplinary programs, institutes, and centers might provide ideas where potential department and institutional benefits can be identified. Imagine a center for bioethics that would combine faculty from the schools of liberal arts, science, dentistry, law, and medicine. All of the units have something to gain and something to give in such a venture. Ethics is now an essential component in many graduate programs residing in professional schools, and a strong potential for a graduate program in this area exists. Further, external funding opportunities are available for studies in this area, and applicants that are part of a center or institute for bioethical studies would have an advantage because the institution has identified itself, through the formation of the center or institute, as having made a highly visible commitment to ethics as an area of focus. There are sufficient emerging and predicted issues resulting from advances in the life sciences areas to keep any unit like this busy for decades. The prospect of increased opportunities to secure funding can also be a stimulus for faculty involvement, and success can be attributed on department annual reports and other media that report on department activities.

Other interdisciplinary examples might include a center for philanthropy that brings together faculty from economics, law, philosophy, and religious studies to examine patterns and motivations for individual, corporate, and foundation philanthropy. The work of such a center would impact many aspects of American life such as religious organizations, nonprofits, philanthropic trusts, and other recipients of voluntary giving such as colleges and universities.

Another emerging concept for a center is one that seeks to unravel the factors that allow certain organisms to regenerate components lost to accident or diseases. Such centers might be called "centers for regeneration" or some iteration of this concept. This process has long intrigued science, but only recently have the molecular tools required to define this process became available. The collaborating players here would ideally come from medicine, molecular biology, developmental biology, and biomedical engineering. The toolboxes used by these disciplines are quite different, but together they bring a powerful set of approaches to a complex problem. These are all problems with strong human health implications and include limb regeneration, spinal cord injury repair, degenerative processes reversal, and wound healing. Some approaches would involve using stem cells, an area of considerable ethical and political controversy. Innovative structures like these centers are attractive to funding agencies and can sometimes attract state government investments to promote startup companies as well as private industry investors that may have an interest in developing devices or medicinal products to promote the types of repair required. Some federal support programs are specifically designed to promote collaboration among academe, government, and industry. Grants and contracts are also attractive incentives for faculty participation and provide opportunities to tap new sources of external support.

Each of these examples, whether involving academic program development, research opportunities, or both, offers the potential for department improvement, raises the visibility of the department, or opens new sources for funding. They also promote faculty achievement and success. There will be many possibilities, and the chair must select those with the most promise and decide how much personal versus delegated time must be put into each venture. There are two areas of caution for chairs. One is the possibility that faculty may feel that the chair is spending too much time promoting the work of units outside the department or school. Thus the chair must be very public about bringing new opportunities in teaching, research, and professional visibility to department faculty. When faculty benefit personally from the preliminary work the chair has done, much of the criticism subsides. Results should be made public through regular reports on progress and how the initiative positively impacts the department. The other area of caution is that working across campus can bring the chair information and insight not available to others in the school, including the dean. Depending on the personalities involved, this advantage may not be appreciated. The dean should be kept up to date as the venture develops and the benefits to the school should be reinforced at every opportunity. Special functions commemorating milestones in the progress of the initiative should include invitations to deans of all schools from which faculty participants are drawn.

Summary

Chairs who confine their work on behalf of the department to intradepartmental topics will not be in a position to bring campus opportunities to the unit or its faculty. Beyond losing these concrete advantages of a campus-level presence, there will be political losses to the unit due to its lack of presence in discussions and initiatives that have the backing of higher administration. There are many ways for a chair to generate directly or indirectly through faculty participation a productive and positive department image on campus.

Chair work at the campus level can identify areas where the department may become a partner in a new interdisciplinary program or become a component of a new campus institute or center. Partnerships of this type bring visibility to the department that can extend beyond campus, generate new income streams through increased student enrollment, and make the unit eligible for external funding. Further, such endeavors can create new opportunities for faculty members to expand their scholarly work, engage in new collaborations, and obtain funding. In addition, chair work at the campus level provides an early opportunity to learn of new policies and plans that may have a positive or negative impact on department operations. Input at these early stages can effectively leverage change to protect or ensure the department's position. At the least, the department will have a longer timeline in which to make adjustments for the change.

Chairs who have a substantial campus presence must be wary of two things. First, they must avoid the perception by department faculty members and deans that they are working more for campus than they are for their own units. This can be avoided by regularly involving faculty members in these projects and in reporting the benefits for the department and its faculty of this work. The second concern is that chair work on campus can give the chair information not known to anyone else in the school, and because deans do not like surprises, chairs should routinely report on activities that are outside the norm and involve interactions with other units.

20

THE CHAIR AS EXTERNAL ENTREPRENEUR

In Chapter 19, chair efforts to create new value for the department and new campus opportunities through strategic involvement and creative collaboration were discussed. In this chapter, the concept of chair as entrepreneur will be expanded to include partnerships and alliances with external constituents. Partnerships of this type are not as immediately evident as those found on campus. Thus chairs must respond to all inquiries and suggestions that emerge from external sources and be prepared with creative answers to problems and needs that exist externally. Potential audiences may include but are not limited to business and industry, K–12 public education, civic and arts organizations, government agencies, and nonprofit enterprises. It is important to realize at the outset that success in this area will present challenges because the partnerships require the melding of distinct organizational cultures.

Many states have suffered financial shortfalls due to more than just a cyclical downturn in local and national economies, and for some, the fiscal challenge will be permanent unless their economies are rejuvenated. This is especially prevalent in states that have traditionally depended on the manufacturing jobs now going overseas. Individuals from this sector are not prepared, from an educational perspective, to assume the jobs of a knowledge-based economy. Further, public K–12 systems are lagging in preparing young people for the new economy. Together, these situations seem to predict a gloomy future, yet in these dark clouds lie some opportunities. These opportunities have the potential of allowing higher education to demonstrate its public value and restore the trust it has lost.

Working With Private
or Government Organizations

Institutions could work more closely with external constituents developing academic and other programs in ways that improve the local economy and that help local educational organizations in better preparing the workers of the future for higher education. This is a tall order for any institution, and the type of work that requires the expertise of the disciplinary practitioner, not the provost or the president. Hence, academic departments through the enterprising groundwork that likely will come from department chairs, will be at the forefront of this type of work. From at least one perspective, this type of work is the substance of civic engagement. Others may disagree, but it seems that efforts in civic engagement should be beneficial to both sides and needs to encompass far more than volunteering and providing external experiences for students.

The notion of approaching external stakeholders and asking what types of academic programs would serve their needs and provide the kinds of experiences they desire in employees is largely unheard of in much of higher education. We have always trusted our own intuition as to what a student really needs to know for a college degree. After all, we are the self-anointed experts. While this attitude does not exist in professional programs where education and training is monitored and accredited by external agencies, it does exist in the arts and sciences, and because programs in these areas are the very core of many academic institutions, this becomes a serious issue. It is proposed that we invite those we are supposed to be serving, the same people who contribute much of the tax revenue that flows into our budgets, to the table to see if we can form partnerships for meeting institutional and constituent need. At the same time, such relationships can enhance our external relevance, polish our tarnished image, and improve our financial situation.

In deciding which constituents in the external environment to approach as potential partners and the types of new programming and activities that might be appropriate, the chair will first have to envision how the department might productively interact. This will depend on the cadre of available faculty in terms of their interests and suitability for working with nonacademic colleagues. The chair would be in the best position to make this assessment and should be able to identify potential participants. Once confirmed with the identified department members, the chair can initiate contact. Identifying external partners may not always be obvious, but where the department, school, or institution has external advisory boards, they may help facilitate this process. Arranging for an invitation to a function attended by board members may allow for a planned but spontaneous discussion. In raising the future direction of the organization, agency, or industry, a question about appropriate preparation of new employees or retraining of incumbent employees may be raised. From there the discussion may lead to identification of academic courses currently available, graduate or certificate programs that may be possible, or even new programs that might be jointly developed and offered.

Entering into joint program development with nonacademic partners can be daunting. Higher education has its values as expressed by what all students must master, what courses are required in general education and in the major, and what degree holders must accomplish. An employer may be far less interested in such values and focused rather on whether an employee can operate a such-and-such and analyze the data produced, can work effectively in a certain environment, or can negotiate a contract with several competing parties. At first, it appears both sides are hopelessly apart and the cultural difference is too severe. However, the dialogue should be kept alive by counterproposals explaining institutional values and why certain things that are important to academics should also be important to external employers and their employees. At the same time, academics, in this case the negotiating chair, should listen to the values and expectations of the external partner. Each iteration of the back-and-forth process may bring the sides closer together until an acceptable formulation is crafted. The value of this exercise goes far beyond the negotiated product; it also serves to help each side understand the other's cultures and perspectives. If nothing else, this builds trust.

Some of the elements of a newly negotiated program may identify courses and other experiences that the institution does not offer or does not have the expertise to offer. This is where the term *partnership* really needs to take on new meaning. If the course/experience is one that requires an external perspective (industrial, government, etc.), then perhaps a member(s) of the external organization may be interested in teaching or providing the experience as a part of the program. This would mean hiring an adjunct faculty member to deliver this part of the new program or arranging for student internships in the external organization. If more than one element of the program requires special expertise not represented among department faculty or if regular instructional assignments make the new work impossible for the department to assume, the partnership expertise would be an alternative strategy. The obvious benefits to the department would include the opportunity to advertise new degree programs with specific employment possibilities and the increased revenues that would accrue to the institution as the result of a new tuition revenue stream.

Such an arrangement has some hidden benefits. Criticism leveled against higher education regarding the relevance of its educational programming and the skills of its graduates would usually come from constituents similar to the partners in the current enterprise. But when they are part of the design and delivery of an educational program, they cannot level such criticisms without assuming some of the responsibility. If criticisms are made, then both parties would work behind the scenes to make improvements. In addition to converting critics into partners, another benefit is the goodwill generated when the institution is seen as working to address a societal need by developing new programs that economically benefit the local region and perhaps the entire state. This community-focused effort will not be lost on the state legislature, especially if the external agency provides strong support for institutional budget requests by indicating how important such programs are to their economic health. Finally, external organizations, especially private companies and industry, may provide resources for these programs in the form of waiving salaries for adjunct faculty who work for them, providing new or used equipment, providing support for staff necessary to deliver the program, or as fiscal resources made available through their community relations program or directly from some of their operating units.

An example of a successful external partnership is represented by the development of biotechnology degree programs in Indianapolis. A major life sciences industry approached the school of science at the local public university with a request for a biotechnology degree program to create a uniformly prepared stream of new employees in areas of biotechnology product development that were undergoing increased regulatory scrutiny by government agencies. The initial model proposed by industry was a two-year terminal degree program. Although such programs were not recognized as within the mission of the public university, rather than decline the university countered with a full four-year degree based on basic science courses routinely offered by the school. The continuing dialogue led to a two-year degree that would fully articulate to a four-year degree. Other local biotechnology industrial concerns joined the partnership, and the degree programs served as a model for the development of a two-year program at the emerging community college. The state government joined the effort by funding a grant for retraining the incumbent workforce in biotechnology. Soon thereafter, funding from local government allowed young people exiting foster care to enroll. A government-related organization representing displaced workers also joined the growing enterprise with funding for their clientele. Institutional program funding was obtained from internal reallocation, private organizations, federal government programs, industry community investment programs, and the state workforce development department. In addition, industry has provided instrumentation and expertise in space renovation, and will contribute employees to the instructional teams that will provide the industry-specific components of the program. The program has developed an extremely high public profile, including cabinet-level recognition from Washington, D.C., as well as support from the mayor and the governor.

Working With Public K–12 Education

Another external partnership that has significant potential for positive impact on higher education is one with the public K–12 system. In many areas the public school system has been identified as being deficient in providing the desired number of graduates who are ready for college or work. This jeopardizes the college-educated pipeline and the ability to staff increasingly sophisticated jobs with a high school graduate. While the level of deficiency varies widely, it is probably fair to say that there is room for improvement everywhere. Working with K-12 school systems has been a regular activity for schools of education. Their interactions, however, are focused around teacher certification issues rather than content issues. These two aspects of teacher education have long been points of tension contrasting the how versus the what of the educational process. Without exploring this area of controversy, we still need to learn more about why so many students fail college-level courses that they had already "successfully" taken in high school and why they are so unprepared for the next step they will face as freshmen.

The type of partnership suggested here attempts to address the root causes of some of these problems. While the academy's civic engagement with K–12 can involve hosting school field trips to campus, faculty appearances before selected high school classes, faculty mentoring high school projects, and faculty judging events or projects completed by high school students, these activities have not really improved student performance or eased the transition from grade 12 to the freshman year of college. The answers to these problems are not readily apparent and will be different for the various basic disciplines common to high school and college/ university curricula.

A project that has attempted to identify and correct these transitionary disconnects can be found in Indianapolis. A private endowment and a consortium of local school districts funded this project, which sought to map what is taught in high school to what is expected at the local public university. The subjects involved primarily the basic sciences (biology, chemistry, and physics) and mathematics. In some cases, it was found the curricula were aligned, but in biology there was little connection between what high school teachers taught and what the university curriculum expected. This situation developed because the secondary school teacher education at some college institutions did not require a major in the subject to be taught. Instead, classes outside of those endorsed by professionals in the field were accepted. The tendency is for instructors to teach what they know and are comfortable with rather than material they are uncertain about or have never been exposed to. In biology, many high school teachers were focusing on descriptive aspects of the subject such as anatomical structures and classes of organisms; however, the discipline has become increasingly cellular and molecular in seeking to identify mechanism of function. University biology programs with a descriptive emphasis are still offered, but most will include courses in cell biology, genetics, and molecular biology as curriculum essentials. Another factor in the disconnect comes from parental pressure to offer "advanced" biology in high school. This results in new courses geared toward parental aspirations for their children related to professional careers. Thus we have human anatomy and human physiology courses appearing in high schools, but few biology degree programs at the college level include such courses.

These observations led to the development of high school teacher workshops by university faculty to address the lack of coverage in the identified areas. Under the project, high school teachers would also be able to submit proposals for the development of new instructional modules to upgrade the curriculum. The long-term impact of this project on the college performance in biology of high school students who have experienced the new curriculum has yet to be determined.

The valuable message of this type of partnership is that the university is seen as working toward the public good by improving instruction in the public schools. The project has the potential of securing funding from local and state sources as well as from federal programs. For a program in sciences like the one outlined here, there are grant programs available at the National Science Foundation. The university benefits from a better prepared local student population and a supportive high school administrative structure that is likely to recommend the local university to its students during their college search.

The point here is that academic departments must be more active in program and project development and in partnerships with external organizations. These types of activities will require new ways of thinking relative to standard academic cultures. Department chairs will be the lead individuals—either by doing this work personally or by carefully selecting appropriate faculty to work in these areas. To be successful, chairs will need to translate opportunities into attractive packages that will resonate with the professional interests of the faculty. Risking the time and energy for this enterprise has the potential to reap profits in individual and unit productivity, visibility, and relevance.

Summary

In the future, chair work will have to include more interaction with external constituents. Whether or not all aspects of these interactions will fall under the umbrella of civic engagement depends on the definition of this relatively new concept in higher education.

Such ventures present new challenges for chairs. While there are different campus cultures that must be accommodated in campus-level work, the cultural divide involved in working with external organizations can be even more pronounced.

External interactions may be initiated with either academic programming or collaboration for solving problems as the intended outcome. The former may have many outcomes, including new degree programs, internship or service-learning opportunities, professional contracts, and collaborative teaching with industrial, business, educational, or government partners. In leading such initiatives for their departments, chairs should understand that major programming initiatives, such as new degrees, are usually difficult to begin. The key for both sides is to keep the dialogue going by taking obstacles into account and providing explanations as well as alternatives. This brings the two sides closer together and provides an opportunity to articulate values and justifications for their positions.

To promote such endeavors at the department level, chairs will have to bring new opportunities for professional development and personal productivity to faculty. This applies to both innovative programming and partnerships centered on research and scholarship. Successful partnerships with external groups can generate new income streams for the unit through increased student interests and enrollments, direct contributions of equipment, program support and instructional expertise, external funding eligibility, and advocacy to government agencies for appropriation support. Well-conceived projects should be eligible for many types of external support in the form of new revenue and other resources. In addition, this work has good potential to raise the unit's visibility and alleviate the negative perception that some of the public now has of our colleges and universities.

21

PREPARING TO LEAD CHANGE

Whether you are a continuing chair, a newly appointed chair, or someone considering becoming a chair, you will be expected to lead and implement a change agenda. In fact, the environment within and without the institution will make the need for change evident without anyone explicitly directing a specified blueprint for it. Chapter 1 presented the changing nature of chair work. These are times when a variety of forces are pressuring higher education to alter many of its longstanding modes of operation. While the prospect for major change may seem daunting, especially as the pace at which it is mandated accelerates, it can provide opportunities that may lead to satisfying outcomes and gain recognition for you as an administrator. Without the challenges that leading change offers, the position of department chair can be mundane and routine.

A chair should acknowledge that change is difficult for most people. Before recalling past department efforts to change when faculty resistance made the attempt difficult or even impossible, one must realize that resistance to change is not a phenomenon restricted to faculty. In examining the hierarchy of higher education and the peripheral stakeholders in that enterprise, there are many ways that resistance can thwart positive change. In public institutions, there are policies, rules, and expectations that may originate from the legislature, trustees, president, provost, and dean. While many of these have a legal basis and others are routine, some are arbitrary and could be obstacles to success at the department level. For example, the micromanaging dean may not allow flexible categories of expenditures from department budgets and this may inhibit program implementation and growth, faculty development, or acquisition of major instrumentation. At another level, because the legislature is a political body, mandates on tuition and fee structures enacted to "protect" taxpayers may handicap a new training program that is creating positive economic development outcomes for the local region. Resistance is not exclusively a faculty characteristic—chairs, on rare occasion and only with absolute justification, are also guilty of resistance.

A second element of the change process to which a chair must pay early attention is whether the suggested or requested alteration is actually beneficial in an overall sense. Some institutional reconfigurations, budgeting decisions, programming reductions, and so on, may negatively impact individual units while at the same time positively improve the college. What must be initially understood is the impetus for the change—what problem does it solve or what advantage does it create—before it is embraced. If the goal is acceptable but its department-level impact is threatening, then opposition without alternative pathways to solve the problem or realize gain is not helpful. Academic department chairs must assess the change agenda and construct a response outlining how the unit can advance the agenda, indicating where the agenda may inhibit or enhance department contributions to institutional goals, and suggest alternative routes to some elements of the change agenda.

An example of a mandated change that emerged from the trustees of a public research university in response to citizen complaints that faculty did not work (i.e., teach) enough hours, was a new section-based teaching load requirement of three sections per semester for all faculty. This presented many dilemmas for various campus units. What was a section? Freshman English is a section but so is a laboratory in science, a recitation in communications studies, a studio drawing course in art, and a clinical experience in nursing. How were they in any way equal? In addition, some campus schools were research intensive where teaching loads had significant impact on recruiting research-motivated faculty and on the research productivity of faculty. Chairs responded with workload definitions for their units, gained section credit for individualized instruction (research students), allowed for approved release, and suggested that the model be applied to the unit rather than individual faculty. Thus the problem of workload definition and assuring the public that faculty time is spent in significant but different ways was achieved without disrupting institutional productivity, diminishing faculty morale, or terminating valid institutional goals. The approach to a seemingly impossible dictum was transformed into something quite manageable through maintaining the dialogue and continuing to redefine the issue.

The final general principle related to change is that the scope of the change is not proportionally related to the resistance response that it may provoke. For example, a faculty member may not be upset with a new program that will diminish department majors (after all, her classes will be smaller and easier to teach) but may react when the new order of department notepads are yellow and not the accustomed white. Even changes that appear to be advantageous to everyone can sometimes be met with skepticism or even resistance simply because it upsets the status quo. This phenomenon is widely recognized in many organizations, including higher education, where the propensity to resist is better tolerated than in other settings.

The Authority of the Chair

What can a chair call upon to leverage change when the initiative will not be uniformly considered as desirable in outcome or process? Chairs must realize that they have two sources of power to bring to the table. The first is positional power, that is, the power of the office of chair. Some institutions define the extent of chair authority while others have no written position description, and the chair's discretion in making changes results from unit tradition. It is interesting to note that chair authority within an institution can vary according to department tradition and culture. At one extreme, chairs are appointed to do routine management functions and carry out decisions made by faculty committees. At the other end of the spectrum, chairs can exercise unilateral decision for faculty hires, implement changes in the curriculum, and make tenure recommendations, but the use of such authority, even if permitted by institutional policy, is discouraged because it alienates faculty and abrogates the concept of shared governance.

The second type of power available to the chair is personal power. If you are a chair or should be appointed one, it is presumably because the faculty and administration have confidence that you will be thoughtful and effective in your leadership. You should be regarded as someone who has gathered the appropriate information for developing a plan to deal with whatever issue is facing the department. Your personal influence with individual faculty members and the faculty as a whole should gain you a fair hearing on your change agenda. Clearly, this is the only real power that a chair should exercise except in the most extreme situations.

Laying the Groundwork for Change

There are many possible change-related initiatives that a chair may have to bring to the faculty. They will all raise questions, if not opposition, from some members of the faculty. Some, and there are many more, examples are systematic improvement in teaching, developing a research agenda, elevating expectations for faculty performance, changing disciplinary focus, and developing graduate programs. Even if changes similar to those on this list have already been accomplished in your current unit, it does not take too much imagination to see that each of these might raise some consternation among faculty. Examining each one will show that some faculty will feel singled out for criticism, ill-prepared for different work, unable to work at a higher level, left out of future planning, or disenfranchised about their work focus. In bringing about change in areas like these, very careful planning that takes into account the strengths and interests of the individual faculty will be critical to making the transformation work.

Knowledge of the department and its faculty is a necessary precursor to the change process. This is where a veteran or internal chair is at great advantage. A newly appointed external chair will need to become acquainted with the existing culture and individual faculty personalities. A joke among faculty in my school is that when a new administrator is appointed from the outside, a line of faculty (faculty and chairs if it is a new dean) will form at the door on his or her first day on the job. The agenda, of course, is to let the new person know "how it really is" and how faculty have been undervalued and underrewarded over the years. It will take the new external appointment some extra time to sort through this situation.

Implementation of a change agenda where the key individuals or groups are deans and other administrators and those from other units is a very different proposition. Positional power either does not exist or has less relevancy, and personal power can be less persuasive. The following sections may be helpful in developing ways to approach such individuals and groups. However, the tools available to overcome resistance of this type will be more limited.

Framing Sensitive Issues

There is no single path to smooth success in the change process, and there are many places where things can go awry. There are, however, some measures that may be taken to predict where resistance may occur and thus help to formulate a contingency plan ahead of time. Higher education has some unique characteristics that set it apart from other organizations. However, fostering change and dealing with the resistance it induces have common threads in a variety of organizations. Thus we can learn much from those outside of higher education.

From the world of business comes the concept of framing (Bolman & Deal, 2003). Organizations need to periodically change their approach in order to remain on the leading edge. In the business world, there are many examples of organizations that develop innovative manufacturing or management programs that make them frontrunners with significant advantage over the competition. But success may cause the leadership to preserve what gave them the advantage. They realize too late that others have been adapting and transforming, and soon the former leader is outpaced. Constant vigilance for promising new directions and flexibility in instituting alternative practices are lessons to learn from this example.

While acknowledging that there are many ways to enhance success, they all involve some alteration of the status quo and so are subject to possible failure from resistance. These changes can be a major challenge to organizational leadership. The greatest impact is sometimes garnered through truly creative ideas that involve risk. The willingness to engage in high-risk innovation can be the most difficult to ingrain because it poses major threats to the status quo and to the comfort levels of many in the organization. The power of framing allows leaders to systematically analyze the impact of the creative change on several levels of the organization and its people. If at least some of these can be identified prior to the change effort, then the new idea can be presented in such a way as to diminish fears and gain supporters, thus enhancing the chances of adoption.

Framing allows the change agent to view the problem from several perspectives or frames. Each frame presents a different focus because each emphasizes a different set of attributes. Looking at the same problem from these multiple perspectives can elucidate possible solutions and identify potential points of resistance. The challenge in this approach is to identify what frames are best matched to the problem.

The structural frame takes into account the hierarchy of the organization. It identifies the vertical relationships among individuals, such as reporting lines. Thus it recognizes dean-to-chair-to-faculty relationships. It also looks at horizontal relationships, including those among faculty in the department and faculty across schools. Another component of the structural frame is the set of policies and procedures that govern who does what work and how that work is accomplished. In other words, this is the infamous bureaucracy of our profession. It may include academic procedures, written (and unwritten) policies, legal restrictions or the university's interpretation of same, and those responsible for implementation or oversight. When considering change that may impact the lines of responsibility, institutional policy, and interpretation of local or federal statutes, an examination of the proposal (framing) will identify places where conflict is likely to emerge and places where some preliminary work of negotiation or policy restructuring will be needed.

An example from my campus involved a massive effort to redefine our general education curriculum. The initiative came from the schools of liberal arts and science, the two largest undergraduate enrolling schools on campus. The hope was that the other undergraduate schools would ultimately adopt the curriculum as well. A joint committee from the schools worked diligently and proposed a new curriculum. Within a very short period of time, department chairs from several departments in both schools met with the committee to say they would oppose the curriculum because the number of required credit hours would, when added to the requirements of the majors, exceed the credit hours required for the degree, thus mandating another semester of work for most students. The structural frame violated here was the degree requirements for majors in the various departments and how the new curriculum impacted them.

The human resource frame is perhaps the most critical one at the department level. This framing exercise involves constructing an inventory of the values, skills, requirements, and attitudes of the faculty and staff who will be affected by the new agenda.

A chair well acquainted with the department faculty will be aware of each individual's potential for or tolerance of change. This information may be learned from past responses to change or from an examination of the individual's professional history. Those who take risks, embrace new challenges, or alter their career paths are more likely to be comfortable with change. Many of the examples of change listed earlier (improving teaching, developing a new disciplinary focus, raising performance standards, moving to graduate education) will have profound consequences on a subset of the faculty. Will they be singled out for poor performance? Will they be left out? Will they be unable to improve? Are they prepared for advanced-level work? These will be real fears for some. With the analysis from this frame in mind, the question is whether there are ways to introduce these changes without disenfranchising some of the faculty. In other words, can the blueprint for change be formulated so that everyone has a place in the new world order?

In the examples just cited, the framing process will have revealed that some faculty have limitations in terms of knowledge and skills. The primary consideration in dealing with these deficiencies is whether the individuals have the potential for adaptation or retraining. Are they willing to refocus their work to other productive areas? Are they willing to take a course or attend a workshop in instructional design or the use of technology? The chair can make these things happen by identifying the issues and offering, sometimes privately and at off-campus settings, the resources for retooling, improving effectiveness, or sharpening skills that have been dormant. These preemptive moves can alleviate some of the anxiety that comes with significant change.

The third frame to consider when engaging in the process of change is the political frame. This lens examines the power structures that will be challenged by the new agenda and permits the change agent to select the appropriate timing and venue for introducing the concept and provides an opportunity to grease the wheels. Here, the opposition is identified and allies have been

prearranged. Much of this behind-the-scenes work requires negotiation, compromise, and consensus building. There may be times
when the preparation can smooth the path to change and there
may be occasions when the battle must be won publicly.

The final frame to consider when planning for change is the
symbolic frame. This one is more difficult to address because it
deals with institutional rituals, ceremonies, and traditions. Higher
education has many rituals, including honors day ceremonies;
commencement; student, faculty, and staff awards; and initia-
tions and convocations marking the start of a new academic year.
Rituals may also include the addresses from administrators and
reports from campus or individual schools. Together these events
and activities represent unit and institutional culture—replacing
one with a new ceremony or eliminating one to accommodate
an important and potentially effective initiative may be met with
resistance. The symbolic frame may help to avoid such failures by
identifying ways to include the change agenda within the existing
tradition or by creating a new ceremony that is patterned after
what is in keeping with the campus or department culture.

Examining the impact of the proposed change through some
subset of these four frames allows the change agent to anticipate
the sources of support and resistance, permits the opportunity for
prenegotiation with key players, avoids the unnecessary introduction of irrelevant reasons to oppose the initiative, and allays fears
of those impacted by the change. All of these will not come into
play in every instance, and it is the change agent's task to identify
which frames are relevant and important for each.

Summary

A regular item on the chair's agenda is, and will continue to be,
providing leadership in change. Tolerance to change varies with
each individual but it should be recognized that most individuals
will resist some initiatives, and some will resist nearly everything

that presents an alteration of the status quo. Chairs can be effective change agents using their personal power to convince others and only resort to the overt use of their positional power in rare instances. In leading change, chairs need to be familiar with the tolerance for change among faculty as well as with the department's and institution's history of embracing change.

Chairs will be able to plan change more effectively if they engage in the process of framing the issue at hand. That is, assessing how the change process may impact other aspects of department and institutional cultures can help define the best ways to approach the change agenda. Evaluating the impact of change on structural elements such as institutional policy, degree requirements, and the hierarchical reporting lines on campus is a primary consideration, as is ascertaining how change might impact members of the department. The latter would be influenced by tolerance for change and the perceived or real gain or loss at the individual level. The political frame takes into account gain or loss of power or influence that may result from the planned change. The symbolic frame considers how that change may effect the ceremonial traditions of the unit or institution. Chairs can spend much time examining all of these parameters, and in some cases they will have to guess about some outcomes. Following this process does not guarantee successful change, but it can help predict many points of resistance so they can be avoided or dealt with early in the process.

22

UNDERSTANDING AND OVERCOMING RESISTANCE TO CHANGE

Resistance to change happens in all organizations, although the details of the underlying reasons may have distinct features. The forms of resistance vary somewhat between business and higher education and the major patterns have been reviewed in the literature of each (Bolman & Deal, 2003; Kotter & Schlesinger, 1979). One does not need to be an administrator to recognize some of these when they appear at department meetings whenever change in some aspect of faculty work or university operation is the subject of discussion. Some forms of resistance have obvious or potential remedies, while others require more work by the chair. In this chapter, the types of resistance will be examined followed by some strategies to overcome them. A second aspect of resistance that was introduced in Chapter 21, and one that never seems to be mentioned explicitly is resistance encountered when dealing with upper administration. The reasons for resistance from this sector overlap with those to be discussed for department-level change.

Types of Resistance

Both business and higher education recognize self-interest, or what Leaming (1998) refers to as vested interest in the status quo, as a driver in resistance. This type of resistance emerges when individuals perceive the change as a threat to their position, status, productivity, or some other element of their professional lives. The following are some of the many examples of this type of response.

You are considering a second hire in a subdiscipline of your department. Some faculty would welcome a colleague closer to their own interests because it may foster collaborations in research, create the potential for team teaching, and permit expansion of the curriculum in that area. Other faculty may see the new hire as a threat to their uniqueness, as a competitor for graduate students, or someone who may force them to modify their courses. Another source of resistance may result from establishing a graduate program with a new committee assigned to generate a curriculum and approve new courses. The standing curriculum committee that had routinely held this responsibility would now have to share decision-making on curricular matters with the new group. Further, on the personal level, the committee chair may feel that his or her authority on curriculum matters has been diminished.

A second recognized cause of resistance is a misunderstanding about why change is proposed or a lack of trust in the justification for change. This type of resistance commonly occurs when the source of the initiative is upper administration or outside groups such as trustees. Upper administration is seen as out of touch with faculty and department issues or as responding to external constituents who really do not understand what we do and how well we do it. Faculty would consider trustees in the same light. When this type of resistance is encountered regarding an issue with direct department-level impact, it often means that the proper framework for change has not been constructed.

Although it can be related to some forms of self-interest, fear can be a potent cause of resistance. Fear can take many forms depending on the issue and the individual. Leaming (1998) identifies these as individual causes of resistance, but they can be considered the many faces of fear. Business uses the phrase *low tolerance to change* to describe fear in its various manifestations (Kotter & Schlesinger, 1979). One type of fear concerns losing value or becoming obsolete. A senior analytical chemist at a teaching-oriented institution may be daunted by the new hire who has had firsthand experience working with all the latest instruments that the veteran faculty member has only read about. Using technology presents another real fear for some. While those who routinely use technology in a basic research area would not be daunted by analytical or other complex devices, someone focusing solely on instruction who is expected to employ digital technology in teaching may feel overwhelmed by the sophistication of what is available and not even try the most fundamental options. An interesting one I have encountered is the fear of more responsibility—change may mean more service or mentoring responsibilities. I once had a faculty member say he was reluctant to seek promotion because it might entail additional responsibilities associated with committee service restricted to those of full rank.

Fear can also have its roots in basic personality traits. Some people have a very low capacity for risk-taking. Faculty can become very regimented and any minor disruption, never mind transformational change, can be unsettling for them. Another type of fear is associated with having to admit that the traditional way of doing things was somehow flawed—admitting this may make some feel that their personal status has been compromised.

A form of resistance that is particularly difficult to overcome is the type where the data and justification for change are acknowledged and assessed, but the conclusion about what to do conflicts. In this case, the cost/benefit ratio is calculated using different values, with the conclusion that it is better to keep things as they are. There are times when suggestions for change may do more harm than good or involve a disproportionate effort as opposed to keeping everything as is. Everyone does this type of assessment, but here individual values are assigned differently, leading to an alternative bottom line.

A final form of resistance, one that does not appear in most literature, is one that I have learned to recognize. It is more a delaying mechanism than a resistance mechanism, though it can develop into the latter. Individuals who are consumed with process and less concerned with products and timeliness express this type. For them, the debate about the change is what matters, resulting in a seemingly endless set of meetings with old territory rehashed several times. Part of this attitude comes from the desire to be heard and to have input and the desire to have full faculty approval. While elements of this behavior can be laudatory, in practice it can unduly delay important initiatives.

Overcoming Resistance

The following strategies will not be effective in every instance where resistance is encountered. The strategy to use must match the resistance to be overcome, and some issues will require the combination of several approaches. Getting it right can be difficult. Thus chairs need to be thick-skinned and persistent in their efforts to effect positive change. They must also accept the fact that they will not win every case.

The first step in instituting a change agenda is what I termed laying the groundwork for change in Chapter 21. You will be introducing something that may raise controversy. You already know something about each of the players and the history of the department in terms of how it has reacted to past efforts to alter aspects of its work. With this information you should be able to predict the source(s) of resistance and the explanations that will be put forward to attempt to justify the status quo. Expect to be correct in your assessments about half of the time. Laying the groundwork will include some elements of the strategies discussed next.

Perhaps because I am from a scientific discipline, I believe that appropriate data (collected and analyzed from well-designed experiments or studies) is very compelling to others. These data may be derived from department sources and may include trends and comparative data from other institutions and departments. For example, a decrease in department majors over a five-year period may signal a need to reinvigorate the undergraduate curriculum. When this information is combined with a documented revitalization of the curriculum accompanied by a surge of new enrollments at a peer institution, it may be persuasive enough to stimulate reform. Institutional data may also be helpful in demonstrating how the department compares to other units operating in similar environments. Segments of this type of information may be released over a period of time to ensure assimilation and avoid information overload and a sense of crisis. First providing the change agenda to a faculty committee, then letting that group report to the faculty at large may give the impression of a more global basis for concern and support a call to action.

Data can be compelling, but they must be disseminated in ways that make certain the message is heard. Faculty and administrators are busy people who may read a piece of information and immediately put it out of mind because it is not of interest to them at that moment. The subject of communication has been addressed several times, and the change agenda is a place where a consistent message delivered in a variety of ways is often what is required. There are now many ways to deliver information to our constituents and the advice is to use them. Some that I routinely use are ad hoc memoranda titled "Announcements." Occasionally, an email version is used. Data items listed as "Announcements" or "Reports" published as part of the department meeting agenda offer a hard copy version that everyone holds simultaneously at a gathering. As an item on the agenda, the chair points out the data and offers some insights as to what they may mean and how faculty might want to respond. If the data are compelling, resistance due to the lack of appropriate information about the need for change should be diminished. Good news and the positive results of department innovations can be reported in the same way so faculty are not always confronted with data about shortcomings and what should be done better or differently.

Another strategy for overcoming resistance is to seek participation in solving the problem. If the issue is seen as one that is important to the unit but the response presented is not acceptable, a group of faculty might be assigned to develop alternatives. An example mentioned earlier used a faculty committee to deliver the message. Of course, the chair would know ahead of time how a particular group might receive the request and choose a messenger accordingly. The chair must not be totally invested in his or her solution, but must be open to other approaches; the desired outcome is to find a solution that leads to improvement. Remember that your faculty colleagues are in the profession because they are bright and creative—assigning them the responsibility to find an acceptable solution to a difficult problem can overcome resistance and create advocates for change.

Some individuals oppose change out of fear and that fear can emanate from several sources. Change may be limited, as in hiring a second faculty member in British literature, or more systemic, as in altering the work expectations of faculty by moving more heavily into research and graduate programming or changing the unit's disciplinary focus. These changes may be perceived as threats to individuals or groups of faculty. The chair can privately and publicly reassure the original faculty member in British literature that there will be a continuing need for his or her services by suggesting an expansion of the curriculum in that area or a new team-taught course involving both faculty members.

Other changes are more systemic and will require careful planning by the chair. It is important that everyone find a comfortable place in the unit structure that emerges. In initiatives where faculty work expectations change—for example, when graduate programming is introduced, thereby increasing the research emphasis—the chair must be supportive in identifying important roles for all faculty. In such cases, there will be veteran faculty who have worked for years in other areas of faculty responsibility and for whom the prospects of becoming competitive in research or directing graduate students are quite intimidating. This is especially true in the scientific and technological fields which change rapidly and where state-of-the-art expertise plus recent productivity are required to be competitive for the substantial funding necessary to support this work. There are further implications regarding the reward structure, the potential for promotion, and the "value" in which certain faculty will be held in the department that also must be addressed.

In Chapter 16, faculty evaluation was discussed and one of the suggestions offered was that faculty be evaluated under models that allow for differentiated roles in the department. This process allows for emphasizing particular talents for competitiveness in the reward structure and gives everyone the opportunity to work to a 100% effort level. This application is particularly useful in situations where there are changing expectations for faculty work. Faculty who will not, and perhaps should not, be working in research and graduate programming would continue to make a contribution to the department through more focused work in undergraduate instruction and service. Other qualified faculty would be active in research and graduate research, instruction, and mentoring. This is a concept that has been applied at Kansas State University, Millikin College, the University of Maryland System, and others. The function of the chair is to see that all department responsibilities are met within the expectations of differential faculty workload expectations.

Distributing work according to faculty strengths and interests is one aspect of dealing with resistance; constructing an environment where all contributions are respected and rewarded is another. Identifying acceptable workloads for all faculty members will not achieve the desired consensus unless excellent work, regardless of the mix of teaching, research, and service, is proportionately recognized. Recognition may come in several forms, the most obvious of which is merit reward, if the system permits it. Because improvement and increased productivity of some kind should be the objectives of our change agenda, reward should not be granted simply because someone accepts a specialized workload but because the work done is of high quality and at a scholarly level. Other ways to recognize good work are through nominations for awards in teaching, research, advising, community service, and so on. Finally, the good work of faculty across all areas can be listed in the normal communication to faculty (memos, agendas, emails) and in department annual reports. These types of recognition let everyone know that all good work is valued and help faculty to appreciate the importance and significance of each other's contributions.

There will be change initiatives when the resistance encountered will be impenetrable using the strategies thus far described. In such situations, the chair may need to negotiate with an individual to gain either support or at least to blunt active opposition. Something of value is offered in return, such as assignment-based or resource-based work. The former may be a changed teaching assignment, released time, or appointment to a committee (or removal from a committee), while the latter may be support for a summer project, technical or clerical support, or conference travel. Chairs must be careful using this strategy so faculty do not expect personal contractual arrangements for every step forward. Even more care needs to be exercised when partial or "reshaped" information or threats are used to defuse opposition. While one can imagine situations where the change initiative is so compelling and the opposition so absurd that even these extreme measures would justify the end, the chair is best advised to try every possible approach to change—some more than once—before resorting to them. Using extreme measures will make the next excursion into change even more difficult due to loss of chair credibility in the eyes of some.

Before leaving the topic of overcoming resistance to change, there is another side to the process that has not been discussed thus far. It has been assumed that the chair brings the agenda to the faculty and that the chair alone must generate the data and make the case for the initiative. However, there are approaches to bring both internal and external advocacy to the discussion, and such individuals can be convincing allies in gaining acceptance.

Informal interactions with faculty were discussed in Chapters 8 and 9. These informal conversations that take place at the mailbox, in the coffee room, in the hallway, or as add-ons to other conversations can be opportunities to raise items for change. These issues can be raised along with some of the anticipated objections to show that the chair has thought this through. Some ways to defuse the objections can be addressed as well as any concerns the individual faculty member may have. These can be discussed candidly in impromptu one-on-ones, giving the chair some insight about individual support and points of opposition. The personal power of the chair comes into play on such occasions. When this type of internal advocacy is successful, the chair can take a back seat in the meeting at which the change agenda is brought to the table and discussed. When other faculty members raise points of objection, it is often the internal advocate, another faculty member, who counters the point because that issue has already been discussed and resolved. Other faculty sense support from within the ranks and will be more open-minded in their consideration.

There are times when the stakes for change are so great or when the timing is just right that external advocates for change can be employed. For external advocates to be effective in suggesting or endorsing change in department operation, they must be credible to both faculty and administration. (The importance of credibility as a chair characteristic was discussed in Chapter 2.) The external program review process is sometimes used by institutions as part of their assessment programs, which was discussed in detail in Chapter 5. If such a review is planned in anticipation of a major change initiative or if the timing of the initiative and the review are aligned, then the issue at hand can be raised with the team and their input and suggestions obtained. Departments often feel that administration uses such reviews to reinforce criticisms made against the department and force their agenda on the department. However, departments should be proactive in directing review teams to address their weaknesses, evaluate the validity of their plans, and determine whether their aspirations are reasonable and their resources sufficient to achieve improvement and advancement. The recommendations of an external review team will be taken seriously only if the team is comprised of individuals who are recognized by the faculty as credible within the discipline and as representing institutions they respect. Typically, departments have some input into team selection and should choose representatives from successful departments at peer institutions that have achieved greater success (i.e., the institution is perceived as more advanced or has a superior reputation) than that of the unit under review. This approach can be effective in countering both faculty and administrative resistance.

Clearly, a full program review is not going to take place to support every new initiative. There are more modest versions that can be helpful in crafting plans for change. Experts (chairs or senior faculty) from institutions of recognized success may be hired as consultants to help plan change and to allay fears among faculty. Often there are disciplinary organizations with professional staff or part-time associates who are university faculty or administrators that will visit campuses to present data on national trends and provide examples of successful innovations elsewhere. Such individuals might be invited to present ideas on change as part of a campus seminar or colloquium series. The topic would address, at least in part, the planned initiative, its merits, challenges, and potential. The consultant may also be asked to stay an extra day to meet with groups of faculty and administrators to discuss the initiative as an experienced but neutral party whose only interest is in seeing the department move forward. The status of the individual can catch faculty attention, but it will be lost if the chair does not move the conversation ahead very briskly to consolidate the gain made. There are some costs involved, but if the unit needs some major shifts in the way it does business, this approach may be worth the resources expended.

Initiating the Change Agenda

One way to ease into plans for change is by piloting the initiative. This approach appeals particularly to faculty in units that are "experimental" in nature. Although it may not work in every initiative, it can be used to produce data in cases where miniaturizing the proposed program can be accomplished. If this is to be a real experiment, then the protocol used and analysis that follows must be valid. An example might be the assessment of student learning. A faculty member, assuming that at least a few support the process, will use student performance data as a baseline, design an intervention or new learning experience to address areas of weakness, and then measure student performance using the same instrument. Sharing the data and divulging the time required to complete the experiment may convert other faculty. Thus the practice may spread to other parts of the curriculum.

Another way to ease into the new agenda is for the chair to be the first to demonstrate buy-in. Take as an example raising the research expectations in a science department. The reality of such a venture is that external funding sources to support this work will be essential for long-term success. Departments that have not traditionally sought such funding usually have underdeveloped research programs often limited to areas in the discipline that are investigated by descriptive rather than analytical approaches. This type of work has very limited potential for funding, thus keeping the department in a steady state of mediocrity. If the chair, however, can find the time among his or her other duties to submit a proposal for external funding, it sets a challenge that others may take up. It is important to remember that not everyone has to join the parade and that individual faculty can embrace change in their own time.

Celebrating and Capitalizing on Successes as They Emerge

As the department moves forward in its new venture, there will likely be continuing detractors and skeptics. However, if the initiative is well planned, successes will emerge that the chair will need to report regularly, both to reward those responsible and to convince those not yet engaged. The strategies here include some that were listed earlier—written announcements to faculty, verbal announcements as part of faculty meeting agendas, email messages, newsletters to alumni, and communications with the dean.

In the assessment of student learning example, progress can have other beneficial effects. Successful strategies in assessing student learning and in developing new approaches in instruction to improve learning are experimental outcomes that can be presented at conferences and are appropriate for publication in professional journals. There are newly emerging paper and electronic journals devoted to the scholarship of teaching and learning and for which this type of work would be appropriate. There are also opportunities for internal and external support for this type of work that help fund the extending of the initial work and seed the ideas of others who are drawn to the visibility and accomplishments of the pioneering faculty. This type of personal visibility and professional recognition can provide momentum in support of change.

In the second example, when faculty seek external grants to support high-profile research in scientific areas, initial success in receiving funding can energize others to write successful proposals. The funding granted allows for more financial independence and supports training students in up-to-date techniques and instrumentation. This type of success leads to traditional professional accomplishments, such as presentations and publications, and can catch the attention of other faculty within the institution as well as those at other institutions, resulting in an extension of the scholarship through collaborations. These successes in the change agenda would make appropriate entries for the annual report that upper administration and other units on campus would read. In addition, such highlights would make attractive entries in alumni newsletters to inform former students that the department is not standing still but is actively working to improve instruction and advance the discipline. Chairs should be particularly vigilant to publicize department successes in general, with special emphasis on those that position the department for success in the future.

Summary

Framing issues can help the chair anticipate resistance and either plan routes around it or deal with problems before launching the new initiative. Types of department-level resistance can be driven by individual self-interest, a lack of understanding of the issue at hand, an alternative conclusion regarding the need for change based on a different set of values, and fear. The latter can take many forms resulting from loss of influence, perceived inability to be successful under new conditions, or having a low tolerance for any type of change.

Chairs will have to employ different strategies to deal with resistance. One that can be effective is using data to back the claim that change is warranted. Examples may be diminished enrollments in programs or courses or lagging graduate applications. Most faculty members will respond to accurate data obtained in appropriate studies. The timing and mode of data dissemination can be critical to its full assimilation by faculty members whose primary foci may be on other matters. Some types of fear can be overcome by assurances that all affected individuals will have a place of respect and value in the new world order that emerges. Regular reporting of the successes achieved by the change process can help to allay fear and erode resistance. Chairs can also anticipate resistance and preempt it by discussing aspects with selected faculty ahead of time so that they become voices of support. Another approach is to delegate a committee to the problem and ask it to recommend a solution. All of these approaches are made more effective by careful framing.

Change is difficult in all organizations, and success is rarely achieved with every initiative. It is likely everyone has seen a perfectly reasonable and even highly necessary suggestion for change fail because of a lack of forethought about how and when to initiate the process, who might object, and what arguments might be posed in opposition. Chairs must realize that resistance will not come exclusively from faculty members; upper administration can also be an obstacle to positive change. Here the chair's toolbox to overcome resistance is more limited.

23

CHAIR SELECTION
AND DEVELOPMENT

The way new department chairs are selected varies widely according to institutional practice, atmosphere in the department, and the financial resources available to attract an individual to the position. The search may be restricted to internal candidates or may be external with allowances for internal applicants. Although I can cite no actual data, I expect that most chair vacancies are filled internally. What happens once a chair is hired in terms of training for the position is also variable, but the emphasis on the importance of this position in recent years has led to more systematic efforts at providing chairs with opportunities to develop the skills required for leading today's academic department.

Selecting Chairs

Prospective chairs can be either active or passive in pursuit of an academic chair position. An actively engaged individual sees the chair post as a promotion and a progressive step upward in academic administration. Such a faculty member will identify opportunities to gain administrative experience as evidence of preparation for chair work. These experiences include appointments as graduate program directors, associate chairs, associate deans, and "chairs" of subdisciplinary sections of large departments. Some experience in campus-level administrative work can also add to the portfolio. The active potential chair will scan job advertisements regularly and seek positions across the country.

The passive chair aspirant may not realize that he or she is even interested in such a position until it becomes available. Ideas about becoming chair may only occur when the current chair does something that is not well received and the individual concludes that he or she could have better handled the situation. The passive applicant will usually seek the chair position only in his or her home department and will begin to think about it only when the retirement or removal of the current occupant is imminent. An even more passive applicant may consider the position only upon the urging of fellow faculty members or the dean.

Department Chair Searches

Department chair searches take two basic forms in U.S. colleges and universities—external and internal. The external search is characterized by national advertisements and a budget to pay for these and invitations to several candidates for campus visits. Such searches are common in research-intensive universities, professional schools, departments where there has been a history of discord and faculty power struggles, and departments with no viable internal candidates. For research institutions and some professional schools, the objective of an external hire is to bring in an individual from a more prestigious institution or one with a top reputation in the field, thereby raising visibility and signaling that expectations will increase. The department with long-term internal problems uses an outside search when it is realized that there is no one in the internal pool who can bring all sides together. It is felt that the external hire with no affiliation to any existing group has the best chance to reunite the department. The external search does not preclude internal candidates; however, faculty believe that external hires have more leverage to extract additional resources from administration than do internal candidates. This opinion is also prevalent when higher administrative positions are vacant. If this is a strongly prevalent attitude, highly qualified and very knowledgeable internal candidates may be overlooked.

The internal search is a more common practice. The advantage here is that the candidates are already familiar with the institution and the faculty in the department. This familiarity can save a great deal of time during the early stages of the appointment because the chair may not be besieged with individuals who have been "undervalued" and "inequitably treated," and who expect the chair will recognize and rectify the errors of the past. An external appointment will have to investigate these issues carefully by talking to many people to sort them out. There is also some comfort for faculty members and deans in hiring from inside—while all may not prefer the internal candidate, knowing the demeanor, behavior, and philosophy of the new chair at least removes some of the fear of the unknown.

Internal appointments. There are two kinds of internally appointed chairs. At some institutions the chair position is a rotating one where one faculty member steps up for a specified term, with three years being the most common. There may be limits on the number of consecutive terms, generally varying from one to three. The candidate may be required to have tenure or be of a certain rank. If the chair is nontenured or of rank below full professor, he or she is at some disadvantage in terms of effecting change and dealing with senior colleagues. In some instances, especially in small departments, the choices may be few and a faculty member may take the position reluctantly and out of a sense of duty to the unit and institution. While such decisions are to be praised at one level, one might question whether such an individual is prepared to make the tough calls in times where change and the challenge of leadership are necessary to the department's well-being.

Internal chairs can also be selected as the result of a typical search, limited to internal candidates, conducted by a committee, and characterized by a regular interview process. The resulting appointments are set for a specified period of time but are usually renewable. Applicants are frequently individuals who want the job, which can be good or bad depending on the applicant and the motivation for applying.

Whether the search is external or internal, it offers the opportunity to select an individual who desires to assume the responsibilities of the position and who has faculty and administrative support to make changes leading to improvement. Higher education does not move quickly, and many projects will take more than three years to implement, making a rotating chair reluctant to initiate major change efforts. Change is also painful to some, and temporary chairs may be hesitant to make faculty members or others uncomfortable since their term will end and someone else, possible an aggrieved faculty member, will take over the helm.

Chair Preparation

As implied in several places in this book and backed by surveys and ad hoc conversations with chairs, one of the greatest needs in higher education is training and orientation for new chairs. Experiences as a faculty member and those associated with the work of committees, councils, and task forces and appointments as a special program (e.g., director of the honors program) or office (e.g., Office of Teaching Excellence) administrator, are not of themselves adequate preparation for the roles and responsibilities that will face the department chair in the early 21st century. A survey of department chairs conducted by Susan Barr of Virginia Military Institute indicated that one of things chairs felt they needed was an official description of the position (Barr, Lees, & Brown, 2000). This would be hard to imagine in most organizations, but how many readers of this chapter who are chairs have a description of their responsibilities and a delineation of the extent of their authority? Where such documentation does exist, most chairs would be surprised to learn that their responsibilities are considerable and that their authority is far greater than they may ever exercise. How many chairs would unilaterally appoint a new faculty member and institute a new curriculum without the approval of the faculty? These things do happen in institutional cultures that are not limited to professional schools.

Because chair training and preparation have been recognized as crucial to success, these activities are more prominent in higher education. Institutions are providing workshops and other programs to help prepare chairs for their work. These may be management function orientations offered by the dean's office designed to notify the chair of administrative deadlines, demonstrate formats for reporting of various types, and provide instruction on how to complete appointments forms and similar items. While these workshops help the chair to complete paperwork accurately and on time, they offer little support to the chair in the difficult areas that often lead to sleepless nights. In addition, sometimes sessions for chairs on budgeting are offered. These may explain how the budget works, how expenditure categories are established, and how resources can be moved within categories.

Other institutional programs for chair preparation may include sessions offered by faculty development offices. These sessions cover more than management issues and provide some ways to deal with more difficult chair encounters such as faculty evaluation, setting standards, and responding to requests when resources are limited. Case studies are frequently used to help chairs think about issues they will face. Such sessions are helpful but lack the actual perspective of chairs on campus because they are the product of professionals who are not chairs. As a direct appeal to veteran chairs who may be reading this, I suggest that you team with faculty development professionals to craft chair development opportunities for your new colleagues. The faculty development personnel can address available programs that support faculty and department work on campus and communicate the nuts and bolts of institutional policy and procedure. Successful chairs with years of experience can provide examples and insights into the real challenges of the positions and can relate their attempts, both successful and unsuccessful, to effect change, deal with problematic faculty, address complaints, resolve issues with legal implications, and deal with the dean. Having colleagues from campus conduct or at least participate contributes the campus viewpoint on common problems. This is often missing at external sessions that may deal with the same topics.

Continued Chair Development

Preparation for a faculty career in higher education involves a minimum of 8 and often more than 12 years of education and training. A new chair may be fortunate to have two or three half-day management orientations and perhaps a workshop or two as preparation for the role. Six months later, faculty reviews are due and the new chair relies on the advice provided by a few workshop examples and his or her personal experience of being reviewed. At the same time there may be some student complaints regarding an adjunct faculty member, the resignation of a faculty member who teaches a key course in the curriculum, and a major instrument failure near the end of the fiscal year. All of these challenges have been faced by other chairs, but it is hard to imagine that the initial chair preparation training will be sufficient to make these comfortable times for the new chair.

In the same way that faculty members expand their horizons using new teaching approaches and keeping current with the latest advances in disciplinary scholarship, chairs will also need to constantly hone their administrative skills. The faculty model is reading what others have developed or learned, attending conferences on the topic where the latest findings are shared, and in networking with others working in the same area. Present and would-be chairs reading this book are now engaged in the first of these activities. There are many valuable print resources for department chairs, some of which are cited in this book. There are also other publications that provide timely advice and suggest ways of dealing with vexing issues facing chairs. Beyond chair-specific publications, there are higher education publications that deal at a more global level with issues that chairs may ultimately encounter.

There are also conferences and national workshops designed for department chairs. Many have long, successful histories and offer sessions by recognized experts or veteran chairs. The advantages of these sessions are that they get chairs away from campus, they allow chairs to see how things are done at institutions that operate differently, and they provide new perspectives on campus cultures. It seems that no matter how difficult a certain policy, attitude, or individual might be in your life as chair, there will be at least one person at such a conference who will have a tale of greater woe.

As a final resource for continuing chair development I suggest, once again, campus colleagues or perhaps chairs at other institutions who may have become close acquaintances. Chapters 7 and 15 discussed forming a community of chairs as a venue for discussing challenging issues. This is a nonthreatening environment and one where considerable wisdom is shared. Less formal structures are possible that sometimes include chairs who may have been active in new-chair training sessions and are typically available for consultation.

Summary

Chair positions are filled by searches restricted to internal candidates or wider searches that solicit applications from individuals in other institutions. The internal search is the more common one. Reasons for turning to a more expensive external search might be to raise the profile of the department and standards for performance by bringing in someone from a more prestigious institution, to address chronic and serious intradepartmental discord, or because no acceptable internal candidates can be found. Justifications for internal searches are that candidates will be familiar with the faculty and administration and will have experience working in the institutional environment.

Once appointed, chairs are thrust into the position without any formal preparation. This situation has been recognized as a serious weakness in higher education, and the last decade has seen an increase in institutional attempts to offer chair orientation and training. These programs may be comprised of half-day events focusing on management items such as deadlines, paperwork requirements, and administrative policies. There also may be sessions on budgeting for the novice chair. Beyond these efforts, there may be workshops provided by faculty development personnel that address some of the personal challenges chairs face. While these can be helpful, they need to have the active involvement of veteran chairs who can offer firsthand experiences and strategies for new chairs.

Beyond the initial activities, there is not much follow-up or in-service training for chairs. Colleges and universities are advised to provide chairs with literature (books, newsletters, journals) that deals with chair issues and chair development opportunities through attendance at chair conferences and workshops and higher education conferences where issues related to chair work may be discussed. Chairs may also consider consulting with campus chair colleagues on a regular basis.

24

Exiting the Chair Position

Whether you are thinking about seeking a position as chair, have recently been appointed chair, or have been serving as chair for some time, it is likely that you will not remain in that position until retirement. In fact, you may have already planned to spend only a defined period as chair and have plans to move on thereafter. This may be true whether you were appointed for a nonrenewable term or whether you would be eligible for reappointment for an undetermined number of terms. We can all point to examples of sitting chairs who continue to extend the period they plan to serve, but still, most leave the position and spend some period of time doing something else before retiring.

This chapter serves as a reminder to all would-be or present chairs that it is never too early to plan for some aspects of your exit from the chair position. There are several elements of this planning, and some of those depend on what you see yourself doing after you leave the position. The overall plan involves readying the department for your departure and preparing yourself to do new work. But before we discuss your future beyond the chair, it may be appropriate to consider succession. Although some institutions launch wide-scale external searches, they do allow for and frequently encourage internal candidates, while other institutions restrict chair searches to internal candidates. If an internal chair is likely to be appointed, it is incumbent on the sitting chair to groom a successor so that a prepared and experienced individual will be able to step in and keep the department moving forward.

Selecting and Grooming Chair Successors

Chapter 2 presented the desired characteristics for chairs according to both deans and faculty. Although all the attributes listed are
not likely to be found in any one individual, there are some basic
characteristics that can be identified and developed in department
faculty members. Aside from intelligence, expected of all our colleagues based on their degree level and professional accomplishments, common sense and a calm, controlled demeanor are also
essential. An effective leader must be able to make the case logi-
cally and forcefully without overt emotion.

Another essential characteristic to seek among colleagues who
could be potential chairs is what might be termed the *we perspective*.
Faculty members are trained to be independent scholars. In spite
of the recent emphasis on teamwork and collaboration, the culture
of individual accomplishment is alive and well in higher education. Faculty members may work with others in teaching and may
have several collaborative ventures in their scholarship. However,
when it is time for promotion and tenure, faculty are asked to document their contributions to such partnerships and to provide statements of support for these delineations from their collaborators. In
fact, one has only to read some recent faculty position announcements where the successful candidate is expected to develop an
" . . . independent, externally funded line of research . . ." to see that
expectations for a significant level of individuality will continue into
the future. Chairs should not ignore the institutional pressures for
individual accomplishment when advising their faculty on reaching their career objectives. However, chairs should try to identify
faculty members who display a sense of the whole and are willing
to balance their professional life by contributing to the common
good. This manifests itself through willingness to contribute to
department- and campus-level projects. The ideal individual is one
who is selective and works on meaningful and important issues so
that sufficient time remains for individual contributions in teach-

ing, scholarship, and professional service. This is an essential quality needed by a potential chair because his or her own personal performance will be evaluated by how the unit performs.

Finally, the potential chair must have an interest in administration or at least be willing to consider such a transition. There are some faculty members who plan to move up the ladder from the outset of their academic career and are easily identifiable. There are others who decide to seek administrative positions after several years in rank. While most institutions require or prefer full-rank chairs, associate professors are also considered at some institutions, a practice more common in small departments and new departments where there are few eligible candidates. In departments where there are no "declared" administrators, chairs might explore this possibility with selected faculty during annual reviews or even during casual conversations. Two types of faculty are appropriate for these conversations. First, there is the highly successful individual who contributes equally among all responsibilities and is so organized and focused that the work of the chair could be accomplished without compromising disciplinary interests. The second type of potential chair is the mid-career professor or associate professor whose career progress seems at a plateau but who remains engaged and hardworking. Such an individual may be increasingly involved in "we work" through student mentoring programs, new programs, and affiliations with campus initiatives. Conversations with either type of individual may be launched with a question such as "What would you like to be doing in five years?" This provides a segue into exploring the idea of an administrative appointment in the future.

Chapter 7 discussed the associate chair model, where a faculty member is appointed by the chair to complete some routine tasks of department administration, and it is one that interfaces with the concept of chair succession. Likewise, the approach just described of identifying a faculty member with an interest in administrative work requires the chair to enter into a mentoring relationship with the individual so he or she may gain administrative experience.

Practical and relevant examples of administrative roles that a chair might assign to an apprentice chair could include scheduling classes, making teaching assignments, and hiring adjunct instructors. These activities have political sensitivities regarding when faculty prefer to teach versus when peak student demand for classes exists, who will teach the large freshman class versus who will teach the small graduate seminar, and the risks associated with outsiders entrusted with the education of students. Experienced chairs will have negotiated scheduling and assignment issues and will know ways to approach key individuals to make things run smoothly. Because the potential chair must be able to work successfully within the same environment, these experiences will allow for a more seamless transition later.

While the faculty and the dean will be involved in the ultimate selection of the new chair, a carefully selected and appropriately mentored associate chair will have an advantage, especially in departments where chairs are internally selected. Apprentice chairs who have effectively completed routine assignments and who have made distinct contributions to department improvement are likely to have gained the confidence of the faculty and the dean in addition to demonstrating some leadership qualities.

Preparing for Your Next Role

Your next step may be a return to faculty life or a move to another administrative post. Before discussing the destination of the move, a few words on the impetus for the transition are appropriate.

Term of Service

The term or number of terms for a chair appointment may be set by institutional or school policy. Thus the incoming chair may be able to anticipate when the transition out of the position will occur ahead of time, which is especially true for rotating chair positions. An incoming chair may specify a time period for service at the outset of the appointment period, but this can and typically does change over time. On occasion, a chair will make a conscious decision to step down based on a growing interest in pursuing something else, a desire for a less stressful life, ambition to move up, or a difficult working relationship. In addition to the policy and personal limits to serving as chair, there are externally determined reasons that define the term of chair service.

While the vast majority of chair appointments are made with strong faculty and administrative support in the hope that the tenure of the new chair will be good for the department and institution, this does not always happen. Chairs make tough decisions that impact the lives of others. As one might imagine, some decisions are correct, some are justified, and some are just plain bad. Even when the tough decisions are not unreasonable, they can be poorly received by those affected and result in disgruntlement. A colleague and I have identified the process of generating such outcomes as collecting negatives. Some faculty members think that the chair's job is to support their good work by providing them with whatever resources they request. While chairs may agree with this at some level, reality sometimes results in needing to decline some requests for reasons of policy or resource priorities and restrictions. Some faculty will remember such events for years but forget the times when support was provided. When reminded of such times, they may feel that such support was deserved and justified. Once the accumulation of negatives reaches a certain level with a subset of faculty members, support for the chair begins to erode. The interesting thing about this phenomenon is that a group of detractors may form who have no uniform complaint. In fact, they may not even support each other's issues, but nonetheless they represent a coalition of sorts. There could also be disagreements with the dean or other administrators over policy, budgets, or position allocations that may result in poor working relationships. Chairs can usually sense these declining conditions and must either adopt new strategies to improve them or make plans to move on. Failure to do so will usually lead to worsening conditions and a search for a new chair.

Returning to the Faculty

Much of the preparation for this type of change is related to the number of years spent as chair, the number of years before retirement, and the nature of the institution in terms of its expectations for faculty performance. Returning to the traditional faculty role after a three-year stint as a rotating chair at a small liberal arts college with a strong emphasis in undergraduate teaching is quite different from the same transition after 12 years as chair at a fast-growing research university. In the first case, the chair probably was granted one or two sections of release from a typical four- to six-section annual load. Upon returning to the faculty, the teaching load would be expanded but could be done without adding all new preparations so that the teaching hours are substitutes for what had been administrative hours. Because there is no major expectation in scholarship and the time spent in administration is relatively short, there would be no major crisis in terms of reviving a dormant program to one of productivity over the short term. The three-year administrative assignment is also short enough in this case to prevent a major decay in knowledge and skills in areas of faculty responsibility.

The second case of the 12-year chair in a rapidly evolving institution with a research agenda is quite different. It might look like the following:

> The institution and department have undergone much growth and change in this period. The research expectation has grown considerably, and the chair has been a major participant in planning and implementing measures that have resulted in this progress. She, however, has not been able to maintain a high-profile, individual program of research during this period of institution building. As a part of these

changes, the chair has hired many new research-active faculty members and overseen a large instructional program
where graduate assistants and adjuncts have participated
with tenure-track faculty in teaching. Because of the nature
of the institutional change and the size of the operation, the
departing chair has not taught classes for eight years. Pedagogy has changed dramatically and technology is now an
essential part of the instructional process.

This scenario poses some personal challenges to the departing
chair. If the discipline is a scientific, technological, or professional
one, not having his or her own independently funded research
program will place the chair returning to the faculty at a distinct
disadvantage in becoming fully competitive in the new milieu.
Careful preparation for a return to the faculty is critical in extreme
cases such as this.

Chairs who assume positions at institutions that are pushing a
rapid change agenda need to pay close attention to how they may
fit into the landscape they are creating. Established institutions
with high scholarship expectations are generally in a state of near
equilibrium; they are mostly the same as they were 10 years ago
and as they will be 10 years from now. If the department is in one of
the rapidly changing disciplines noted earlier, the chair would have
been selected based largely on having a top-notch research program
and would have negotiated a personal package to keep that agenda
active during the term of service. Along with external funding, this
package would allow the chair to employ senior research associates
to keep the program vibrant and productive. In such a situation the
transition back to faculty ranks is less complex.

For those who have established new environments and expectations for significant change while serving as long-term chairs,
other strategies and support mechanisms are needed. The chair
may seek to keep an active scholarship program viable through
collaboration, which is done ideally from the outset but can be

reestablished later. (This process was described in greater detail in Chapter 3.) Such strategies can help the busy chair stay in touch with some elements of the relevant literature and can demonstrate some rudiments of productivity that can be expanded when the administrative assignment comes to an end. On the teaching side, the chair might begin giving lectures in courses or co-teaching courses in the semesters prior to returning to the faculty. This helps to reacquaint him or her with the material and the prevailing student culture. The final and most important point here is that the chair should seek a transition leave or in-house (or external) sabbatical leave for the purposes of retooling, a common practice at many institutions. While some may criticize this as committing resources to a situation where there will be no short-term product, it is justified in many ways. First, faculty members who take chair positions give up much to do this work. Even when the chair's salary is attractive, there are time restrictions on disciplinary productivity that result from the burden of administrative responsibility. Second, chairs were likely to have been resourceful and successful faculty and can resume that role. Thus the leave concept is an investment in the future potential of the individual. Finally, a leave allows the returning chair to develop a focus outside the department routine, to essentially "dry out" from the administrative role.

This concept of chair disengagement is one that deserves further exploration. The basic elements also apply to deans and other administrators who step out of their positions but remain at the institution in some other capacity. These individuals are accustomed to calling the shots, making the decisions, and solving problems, and these tendencies may continue after the title has been passed. This may not always be a matter of control but could be a sense of responsibility to make certain everything is done correctly and that problems are addressed. This type of commitment can be especially difficult to deal with if the new chair is dismantling department structure and replacing it with elements that define the new regime. The sabbatical leave can alleviate these difficulties by providing time away for the former administrator during the transition.

The former chair is likely to be the most knowledgeable individual on the faculty regarding institutional practices, policies, and politics. However, it is best if the returning chair remains low key. Participation in faculty governance and on faculty committees should be negotiated with the dean and the new chair during the early transitionary phase. However, it is appropriate for the retired chair to be available for consultation with the new chair at his or her discretion. When the chair has voluntarily stepped down to resume a faculty career this can work particularly well. There may be faculty members who were strong supporters and still feel an allegiance to the former chair, but they must transfer that support to the new chair.

Moving Over or Moving Up

Chairs on the administrative career path will seek new positions after a requisite period of time. Moves can include positions as chairs or heads at other more prestigious institutions or positions as deans. The latter may include the home institution, but the timing must be right for such an internal move. Chairs also may seek other types of administrative positions such as center or institute directorships, positions in faculty development offices, associate deanships, and positions in the private sector. If moving up is the intention, then chairs must establish and document a record of accomplishment that would make the application stand out. Especially important are experiences in critical areas and evidence of successful leadership.

If a chair is moving to a similar position elsewhere or to the position of dean, full rank will be required in the vast majority of cases. Administratively ambitious chairs should also pay close attention to the emerging issues in higher education so as to be able to discuss them during the interview. Aspirants for high administrative posts clearly need to have more than a local management view of higher education.

Conversations with colleagues searching for deanships and discussions with organizations that help institutions develop applicant pools for administrative positions can reveal common questions asked during the interview process. Other areas of institutional focus can be obtained from the position description and gleaned from institutional mission statements and other pronouncements. Included are questions about experience managing large budgets and budget reductions, items that will remain on the agenda for several years to come. Another area of discussion is one of leading change while not disenfranchising many at the institution for whom change will be or has been difficult. Valued change successes can be in the areas of the establishment of innovative degree programs including interdisciplinary degrees, interdisciplinary centers and institutes, collaborative ventures with industry, business or government, programs for student recruitment and retention, and strategies to raise funds from private foundations and federal sources and from alumni and other friends of the unit or institution. Success in developing approaches for diversifying the student body and the faculty will also be of considerable interest. While the chair personally would not be involved in all elements of these activities, good things that happen during his or her term can be attributed to successful leadership. Demonstrating success or presenting solid ideas to address many of these issues will be necessary to elicit an offer for a higher administrative post.

The mistake most chairs make, even those with administrative aspirations, is in failing to document their successes in ways that make them leap from the curriculum vitae. While these accomplishments can be included in the letter of application, they also need to be prominent in documents such as the vitae that may be used by search organizations to identify administrative candidates. Documentation is essential here and one way to keep track of relevant accomplishments is to develop an administrative portfolio (Seldin & Higgerson, 2002). While this method has other uses (including internal reviews), it provides a way to list leadership work as it happens so that it can be easily retrieved for other purposes.

Summary

Most current and potential chairs will move to another position unless they retain the chair position until retirement. Exiting the chair position may be predicted by institutional policy limiting chair terms, the personal plan of the chair, or by faculty or administrative discontent with performance. In any case, the chair needs to prepare both the department and himself or herself for the transition.

Because most institutions appoint chairs from within the department, the current chair has the responsibility of preparing a potential successor. There are no guarantees that the selected individual will be offered the position, but the chair can at least provide the opportunities and experiences that will allow a faculty member to determine if administrative work is a viable career. Chairs may also choose to bring the potential successor into some of the decision-making processes that are part of the routine work of the chair.

The chair must also be personally prepared either to return to the faculty or to seek another, usually higher, administrative post. For the former, the chair may plan well ahead of the transition to reestablish or strengthen the scholarship agenda and catch up on the recent advances in instructional pedagogy. The longer the time in the position of chair, the more challenging these efforts will be. Restarting or ramping up scholarship can be facilitated by collaborative work to provide a start point for meeting the productivity expectations for faculty members. Team teaching can be a way to catch up with the changing student culture, employ new pedagogies, and integrate technology into the classroom. For a move to other positions, the leadership work done as chair will become the major item of interest to the selection committees. Rather than personal accomplishments, contributions to department productivity and efforts at institution building will be key items to emphasize in the curriculum vitae and in letters of application.

25

THE BENEFITS OF SERVING
AS CHAIR

This book has examined the many and growing responsibilities of academic department chairs along with the new challenges expected in the future as higher education experiences some significant alterations. Challenging old issues remain, perhaps in even more prominent ways. One that comes to mind is conducting reviews of faculty colleagues who are not meeting job expectations and require help in improving performance. It is not defining the protocol for facilitating improvement that is vexing for chairs but rather the personal interplay with the faculty member who is in denial about the evaluation that keeps chairs awake at night and makes them wonder whether the job is really worth it. There are other challenges, but the toughest ones involve dealing with people under difficult circumstances. They can be irate parents, disruptive students, or deans whose behavior is unpredictable. Before concluding, I would like to return to some of the thoughts each one of us had when we sought or agreed to take the position and to some of the reasons why many of us have stayed in the chair position for years.

Compensation

Let's begin with tangible items. The position of chair usually comes with a salary increment that varies depending on the institution. The most beneficial version is a permanent increase in the base salary. The amount offered can be considerable and is influenced by whether an external search identified the new chair, the previous salary of the appointee, and the general salary profile of the department. Usually, the new chair would expect to receive a salary above, at, or at least near the top salary in the department. Certainly it would be in the top 20%–25%. Some members of the faculty may not support this level of compensation, but most recognize that the job is not easy and feel that chairs should receive solid compensation for the responsibilities they bear and the headaches they endure. After all, many know how difficult they and their colleagues can be!

Aside from base salary increases, there are other ways to reward those who take on the position of chair. Some do not seem adequate, which may result in few individuals choosing to step forward in these challenging times. Other compensation models include a temporary administrative supplement that is withdrawn as soon as the chair steps down. The drawbacks here are the significant downward adjustment in lifestyle that results when the term is over and the fact that the supplement does not usually enhance the retirement account. Other models provide one or two extra months of pay for those in systems where faculty members are on 10-month contracts. It seems that conversion to 12 months makes sense since chair work is year round and, although summer may be slower in some aspects of the job, there are personal issues around individual scholarship and teaching left unattended during the academic year that must be addressed during this time. Remember, when chairs return to the faculty they will be expected to be productive teachers and researchers just like the rest of the faculty, so allowing them to stay active and current in these areas while serving as chair is essential. I favor 12-month contracts at a good relative salary level for academic administrators whose contributions may be among the most important made at the institution.

Workload

Another benefit usually afforded the new chair is a reduction in teaching load. At smaller institutions that focus on teaching, this may be a reduction of one course per year or per semester to allow for administrative duties. At research institutions it could very well mean that chairs would be excused from teaching altogether. In other situations, deans leave this decision to the chair expecting only that the unit's teaching obligations will continue to be met in a quality fashion. I realize that a few readers may not consider this to be a benefit. I had a colleague chair from a large liberal arts department who chose to return to the faculty after a single three-year term as chair because he did not like the reduction in teaching he was forced to endure to meet his administrative responsibilities. He calculated how many sections he would be able to teach in his remaining years to retirement and decided that it was simply not enough so returned to his full teaching load as a member of the faculty.

Influence

Some benefits of serving as department chair are more subtle than paychecks and workloads. One is the issue of power—the appointment to chair will immediately result in a gain of power or status. The members of the faculty have elected or recommended or accepted you as their chair and the dean has made the decision that you can do the job. The majority of these individuals give you the opportunity to prove yourself and most will be willing to work with you at the outset to determine and implement your agenda. You have gained a level of respect and influence, and you hold a position with a distinct role while still retaining faculty status. You are now both professor and chair.

The term *power* does not quite fit academic culture. Chairs who exercise their authority in an autocratic or arbitrary fashion usually do not last in most institutional cultures. Perhaps a chair should be described as a person of significant and recognized influence. This conveys the idea that what a chair says or suggests should be taken very seriously. Put in this way, the chair has the opportunity to champion new approaches, effect changes in faculty direction, promote curriculum reform, and do other things that may lead to positive outcomes. While the same suggestion from another faculty member might be dismissed or countered before the entire idea is presented, the chair can usually expect a civil audience that allows for the full articulation of the concept. This power of expression is an important aspect of chair leadership.

Impact

The potential for impact is another attractive benefit of serving as department chair. Most faculty members, even the top performers, have limited impact on the department and even less on the institution. Imagine an English department of 35 faculty members at a major public university. In rating faculty performance, the third-rated faculty member demonstrated excellent classroom performance, served on major campus and professional organization committees, made three invited presentations, and published the fourth volume of what will be a major seven-volume anthology. While this is an exemplary record, there were two others whose record was judged at least marginally superior and those whose work was rated just short of that of number three. The published volume may gain peer recognition and perhaps will be mentioned by the dean at a school-wide convocation, but next year there will a new example of faculty excellence to take center stage. It is usually difficult to have significant and lasting impact when doing the traditional work of faculty. Because of the types of contributions they can effect (increasing graduate program enrollments by 25%, instituting a new curriculum, doubling external funding or gifts, etc.), chairs can have considerable and long-lasting impact.

Realizing that they can have more impact probably prompts some faculty members to seek administrative posts. In fact, thinking back to the early 1990s when the chair of my department announced he would be stepping down, I made the decision to throw my hat into the ring. At that time my department was entering into a new incentive-based budgeting system and was anxious to reach its potential in research. I believed I could have more impact on achieving this goal by pulling from the top than by pushing from the bottom. The opportunity to put some strategies into place to meet student demand while enhancing department resources to make a real research thrust certainly seemed to have more impact potential than if I just forged ahead with my own research agenda. And I was correct in this assessment—the department's research profile improved far more than I could have contributed as an individual.

There are other examples where chair creativity and leadership can have a far-reaching impact. Forging an innovative academic program can bring recognition from other units on campus and attract the attention of higher administration. Furthermore, such endeavors would be worth sharing as regional or national models at appropriate conferences. This type of recognition naturally extends to the institution and department. In addition, the chair under whose leadership the program was developed and successfully implemented now has a major accomplishment that should take a prominent place on the curriculum vitae.

Personal Growth and Improvement

Serving as chair will add new personal skills and enhance personal characteristics. Some of this will come in the form of exciting new opportunities and some will come as the result of the experience gained in dealing with difficult situations and interactions. Many individuals function within what might be called their personal comfort zones, but moving from a faculty position to chair means that some individuals will have to leave their comfort zone and adapt to activities that are not part of faculty life. For example, a chair may have to negotiate collaborative ventures with chairs of a professional school or engage in budget negotiations with the dean who is also dealing with more experienced chairs from other departments. Also, faculty members are comfortable speaking publicly to peers about their professional work but they are not usually comfortable speaking to a wider audience about the many nuances of the department or to external groups about the more generic aspects of the department and institution. Even more daunting for some is speaking to the media. Some faculty have no problem with this while the majority become speechless. Chairs cannot avoid most of these situations and so must be prepared to expand their comfort zones. Once this is accomplished, many opportunities for continued personal growth and improvement will result.

Returning to the learning experience idea as a way of rationalizing particularly difficult situations, one can take valuable information from these encounters or let them become debilitating. If one can learn from a situation, then the next experience may be approached in a different manner or, at least, the really unpleasant part can be anticipated and possibly avoided. An example may be a faculty review where there are some tough issues to discuss with a volatile faculty member who is in denial regarding the quality of performance or the value of contribution. Situations such as these can be approached in more than one way, and chairs can learn what works and what does not work so adjustments can be made in preparation for the next conversation. A chair will not always have the right answer for a particular problem or situation. Experience dealing with such challenges, and conversations with others who face similar issues in their departments, can help build a repertoire of possible solutions and prepare one for what can be derogatory and even threatening responses. As a good thing associated with serving as chair, personal growth can result from difficult encounters and the experienced gained will be useful in future work relationships.

Expanded Campus Opportunities

Another benefit of serving as chair is the opportunity to learn more about many things relevant to institutional operation and decision-making. The chair appointment automatically comes with membership to some new committees. Faculty members are accustomed to learning about budget news, new institutional policy, enrollments, and building plans from chairs who have received the information at meetings with deans. Chairs learn this information sooner and also hear more about how local decisions have been made and the alternative approaches that have been considered. If this added information is not considered confidential, chairs will have to decide whether the added insight should be passed on to faculty. For example, the dean in consultation with chairs may discuss whether salary increments are justified during a year of severe budget restrictions. Alternatives might be to forgo increments, provide cash bonuses instead of base increases, provide increments only to faculty members performing in the top 25%, or provide a small overall increment. Whatever the final choice, one can imagine that the other possibilities will cause much discussion among faculty who think they would be better off under some other alternative or are upset that a certain possibility was even considered.

Chairs represent the department or the school on high-profile committees. Before questioning why this would be a good thing, recognizing that most chairs and faculty members do not "need" a new committee assignment, consider that such assignments can lead to new connections on campus and extend the chair's knowledge of how other units work. For example, the chair of anthropology in the School of Arts and Humanities is asked to serve on the search committee for a new chair of chemistry in the School of Science. On this committee, the chair will learn what credentials a top chemist needs by reading the applications and listening to the evaluations of those closer to chemistry. The chair will also learn what is important to colleagues in science in terms of faculty qualities. Finally, the anthropology chair may learn that a member of the committee from chemistry specializes in elemental analysis of organic-based materials, an area that would be of interest to the forensic anthropologists in the department.

Helping Others to Reach Their Potential

A major benefit of serving as chair is imbedded in some of the most difficult work chairs do. This is the opportunity to help faculty members reach their potential as educators and scholars. Some of this work is related to evaluation, but this does not mean always correcting deficiencies. In most cases, it is a matter of polishing what is already good work. So why would a chair want to do this type of work? The easy answer is that the better the faculty perform, the better the department will look to others. The more complex underlying answer is related to why most of us are in the profession—we are teachers dedicated to our discipline who want to help others perform at their full potential.

The notion of teaching here is quite broad and includes guiding, facilitating, enabling, and fostering. Experts in higher education will say that the most important individual in the life of a new faculty member is the department chair. The chair most likely played a major role in recruiting the new faculty member and was the university contact throughout the negotiations. The chair helps the faculty member to get a good start with teaching assignments and other activities related to preparing work areas and gathering materials. This coaching role for chairs continues beyond the tenure decision throughout the career of the faculty member. A chair who understands this role will be effective, not only with probationary faculty members, but also in expanding and improving the work of senior faculty members who wish to continue with their traditional work or those who wish to make career transitions. In all of these examples, the chair is seeking to implement ways to enhance the effectiveness and productivity of faculty and to provide a supportive environment that will encourage and reward continued accomplishment. Success in these endeavors will lead to a better department.

The aspiring department chair will give up much to do this work in the 21st century. There will be sacrifices of personal scholarship and teaching, and perhaps some personal investments in terms of time at the office or in traveling to accomplish department business. The rewards, however, can be great. Once the transition from me-my-mine to we-us-ours is made, the concept of finding ways to enhance the work of many becomes the objective. This includes looking at what the unit needs to do as a collective and deploying and supporting the faculty and staff in ways that address unit mission and ensure quality. This overall approach must be melded with a consideration for the individual goals of faculty members. This requires individual work, frequent feedback, the offering of alternatives, selective investment, personal assurances, and respect for all types of contributions.

Summary

After the many chapters outlining traditional and emerging responsibilities for chairs, challenges in dealing with faculty members and other administrators, and negotiating the minefield of effecting change, one may wonder why a sane, rational person would consider becoming a department chair. The challenge element will attract some; using the position as a steppingstone to higher posts in academe will attract others.

For those without higher aspirations, there are many positive elements to doing this work. On the plus side there is usually an upward salary adjustment involved and chairs are generally excused from some teaching to provide time for administrative work. Chairs will have opportunities to influence change and foster unit improvement. These efforts have the potential for impact beyond what might be accomplished by a faculty member. The types of changes in novel programming, faculty productivity, collaborative models, fundraising, and the like that may be part of chair initiatives will be of interest to others in higher education, thus providing opportunities for sharing and the development of a personal scholarship associated with department leadership.

Serving as department chair will require the individual to grow as a person. This personal growth may come about because of the difficult encounters that may take place, the innovative new work that is envisioned, and the new relationships that must be forged. One aspect of personal growth is that as chair the individual becomes privy to more information than is directly available to faculty members. Access to expanded information allows the chair to act outside the realm of normal faculty work, ultimately creating new environments where a chair can learn to perform effectively. Another area of personal growth and one of particular satisfaction is the work associated with successfully guiding faculty members to productive careers.

BIBLIOGRAPHY

Arreola, R. A. (2000). *Developing a comprehensive faculty evaluation system: A handbook for college faculty and administrators on designing and operating a comprehensive faculty evaluation system* (2nd ed.). Bolton, MA: Anker.

Barr, S. H., Lees, N. D., & Brown, B. E. (2000, Fall). Preparing chairs for expanded roles in post-tenure review: New perspectives for chairs. *The Department Chair, 11*(2), 9–10.

Bland, C. J., & Bergquist, W. H. (1997). *The vitality of senior faculty members: Snow on the roof—Fire in the furnace* (ASHE-ERIC Higher Education Report, 25[7]). Washington, DC: George Washington University, Graduate School of Education and Human Development.

Bolman, L. G., & Deal, T. E. (2003). *Reframing organizations: Artistry, choice, and leadership* (3rd ed.). San Francisco, CA: Jossey-Bass.

Boyer, E. L. (1990). *Scholarship reconsidered: Priorities of the professoriate.* Princeton, NJ: Carnegie Foundation for the Advancement of Teaching.

Braskamp, L. A., & Ory, J. C. (1994). *Assessing faculty work: Enhancing individual and institutional performance.* San Francisco, CA: Jossey-Bass.

The future of the American faculty: An interview with Martin J. Finkelstein and Jack H. Schuster. (2004, March/April). *Change, 36*(2), 26–35.

Hecht, I. W. D., Higgerson, M. L., Gmelch, W. H., & Tucker, A. (1999). *The department chair as academic leader.* Phoenix, AZ: ACE/Oryx Press.

Kotter, J. P., & Schlesinger, L. A. (1979). Choosing strategies for change. *Harvard Business Review, 57*(2), 106–114.

Leaming, D. R. (1998). *Academic leadership: A practical guide to chairing the department.* Bolton, MA: Anker.

Lucas, A. F. (1994). *Strengthening department leadership: A team-building guide for chairs in colleges and universities.* San Francisco, CA: Jossey-Bass.

Mallard, K. S. (1999, Fall). Management by walking around and the department chair. *The Department Chair, 10*(2), 13.

Muraskin, L., Lee, J., with Wilner, A., & Swail, W. S. (2004). *Raising the graduation rates of low-income college students.* Washington, DC: The Pell Institute for the Study of Opportunity in Higher Education.

Rice, R. E., Sorcinelli, M. D., & Austin, A. F. (2000). *Heeding new voices: Academic careers for a new generation* (New Pathways Working Paper Series No. 7). Washington, DC: American Association for Higher Education.

Seldin, P., & Higgerson, M. L. (2002). *The administrative portfolio: A practical guide to improved performance and personnel decisions.* Bolton, MA: Anker.

Tucker, A. (1992). *Chairing the academic department: Leadership among peers* (3rd ed.). Phoenix, AZ: ACE/Oryx Press.

Upcraft, M. L., Gardner, J. N., Barefoot, B. O., & Associates. (2005). *Challenging and supporting the first-year student: A handbook for improving the first year of college.* San Francisco, CA: Jossey-Bass.

Wergin, J. F. (2003). *Departments that work: Building and sustaining cultures of excellence in academic programs.* Bolton, MA: Anker.

Zimbler, L. J. (2001). *Background characteristics, work activities, and compensation of faculty and instructional staff in postsecondary institutions: Fall 1998* (NCES 2001–152). Washington, DC: U.S. Department of Education, National Center for Educational Statistics.

INDEX